Günter Grass's *Der Butt*

Sexual Politics and the Male Myth of History

Günter Grass's
Der Butt

Sexual Politics and the Male Myth of History

Edited by

PHILIP BRADY, TIMOTHY McFARLAND,
JOHN J. WHITE

Clarendon Press · Oxford

1990

Oxford University Press, Walton Street, Oxford OX2 6DP

Oxford New York Toronto
Delhi Bombay Calcutta Madras Karachi
Petaling Jaya Singapore Hong Kong Tokyo
Nairobi Dar es Salaam Cape Town
Melbourne Auckland
and associated companies in
Berlin Ibadan

Oxford is a trade mark of Oxford University Press

Published in the United States
by Oxford University Press, New York

British Library Cataloguing in Publication Data
Gunter Grass's Der Butt: sexual politics and the male myth
of history.
1. Fiction in German. Grass, Gunter, 1927–
I. Brady, Philip II. McFarland, Timothy III. White, John
J. (John James), 1940–
833.914
ISBN 0–19–815860–2

Library of Congress Cataloging in Publication Data
Data available

Typeset by
Latimer Trend & Company Ltd, Plymouth
Printed in Great Britain by
Bookcraft (Bath) Ltd.
Midsomer Norton, Avon

Contents

Acknowledgements

The editors would like to thank Luchterhand Verlag, Darmstadt and Neuwied, for permission to quote from *Der Butt* and Galerie Maria Rama, Berlin, for permission to reproduce the etching which appears on the jacket.

References

The German and English editions of *Der Butt* referred to in the text are listed in the Bibliography. Also included in parentheses in the body of the text are all references to other works by Grass, to interviews with him, and to secondary literature on *Der Butt* and related topics. Everything referred to in this way is listed in the Bibliography. All other references are in the footnotes.

Introduction

In Günter Grass's latest and—it has been rumoured—final novel, *Die Rättin*, a group of women sail the Baltic in a boat named *Die Neue Ilsebill*. They reach the point where, in the seventies, the titular flounder of *Der Butt* had been caught, and the woman at the helm, reminded of the fish's futile hopes and promises, 'lauter Hoffnungen und wunderhübsche Versprechungen' (65), angrily pretends to call him up once more from the sea. He—not surprisingly—does not respond. The women's anger against the flounder, 'yesterday's rubbish'—'Mist von gestern' (65)—in the judgement of one of them, is, however, ultimately futile, as indeed is their anger against the male sex. From their boat they witness the mushroom clouds and the flash of the nuclear cataclysm that destroys them and the world and leaves Gdańsk to the rats. In other words, *Die Rättin*, taking up in 1986 where *Der Butt* had left off in 1977, closes the open ends of the earlier novel, cuts short the expansive confrontation between men and women, and proves finally and unambiguously illusory the prospect held out by the flounder in his own closing speech: 'Das Feminal . . . sollte nicht nur urteilen, sondern auch begreifen, daß fortan den Frauen Macht zufallen wird. Sie werden nicht mehr wortlos am Rande stehen müssen. Die Geschichte will weiblich geprägt werden. Zeitenwende!' (530/521).

It is worth noting how much of *Der Butt* is subverted by the later novel, not in order to make of the two works two halves of one whole, the one demolishing the hopes raised by the other, but in order to suggest that the familiar enmeshing of one work within another that is characteristic of Grass can provide a broader context for a single work, in this case *Der Butt*, without blurring its outlines. Thus, the historical density, the crowded canvas of *Der Butt* emerges all the more sharply when set against the loss of history and the depopulation of *Die Rättin*; thus too, the domestic close-ups which interlock with all the history have no place in a Gdańsk populated only by rats. In short, *Der Butt*, when set alongside the grim finalities of *Die Rättin*, seems like a luxuriant, eleventh-hour recapitulation, a revelling in confrontations and overlapping identities at a time when there were still issues and identities to play around with.

Hindsight can, of course, offer no more than indirect approaches to *Der Butt*. Nevertheless, the richness of such a work is underscored by Grass's later elaborations of a number of its themes. The novel's seventeenth-century poets, impotent in the face of war and plague, reassemble for a more discursive encounter in *Das Treffen in Telgte* of 1979. The narrator's pangs of conscience again confront other people's pangs of hunger in *Kopfgeburten oder Die Deutschen sterben aus* (1980), whilst Calcutta, the scene of that confrontation in *Der Butt*, has become the setting and the central theme of Grass's most recent work, the autobiographical diary-plus-poem *Zunge zeigen* (1988). But, if *Der Butt* supplies a variety of themes which are taken up in Grass's later work, it also reveals many striking continuities with what preceded it: Grass's flounder is another species to be added to that growing fictional menagerie that had begun with a cat and mouse, had followed with the dogs of *Hundejahre*, and had produced, five years before *Der Butt*, the diary of a snail. Moreover, the opening page of the novel hints at continuity of a different kind when the narrator flashes back to an earlier life lived at the mouth of the Vistula. It is the first pointer in the novel to what, by 1977, had clearly become the sole essential landscape in Grass's fiction. Yet, for all the apparent continuity, to read that first page with Grass's earlier fiction in mind is to be made aware more of new emphases than of familiar landscapes: 'Und wie wir uns heute, bevor es Hammel zu Bohnen und Birnen gab, über ihre und meine Kinder mit immer kürzeren Wörtern stritten, so zankten wir uns im Sumpfland der Weichselmündung nach neolithischer Wortwahl' (7/3). The historical span is new. To the Oskar of *Die Blechtrommel* history was a modest but essential step back to his grandmother: 'denn niemand sollte sein Leben beschreiben, der nicht die Geduld aufbringt, vor dem Datieren der eigenen Existenz wenigstens der Hälfte seiner Großeltern zu gedenken' (12). History in the *Hundejahre*, seen on the first page as 'vor vielen vielen Sonnenuntergängen', turns out to mean the nineteenth century. In *Der Butt* a vast span of time is involved, millennia which in the course of the novel are peopled not only by past generations but by a narrator and his wife for whom 'unsere Geschichte'—as the wife terms it in the second sentence of the novel—implies a history lived in, possessed, not a remote prehistory.

  With the 'so zankten wir uns' in this opening episode, another theme is introduced, the central theme, indeed, of that history: the unresolved conflict between man and woman. It is a theme which has no obvious precedent in Grass's fiction. Moreover, the mediators of the history, and its protagonists, are a narrator and his wife who, living through a pregnancy whose nine months structure the novel, tilt history towards the present ('heute', with its mutton, is as important as, and inseparable from, neolithic intimacies and antagonisms). And—to add further to the new emphases already hinted at in the early stages of *Der Butt*—that present is shot through with autobiography.

There had, indeed, been tantalizing overlaps between Grass and his fictions before. He was, for example, born in the same year, 1927, in which Oskar called a halt to natural growth, and in the same town; *Aus dem Tagebuch einer Schnecke*, immediately prior to *Der Butt*, had attempted a quite explicit integration of fact and fiction. But autobiographical fact, the circumstances of Grass's domestic life, informs fiction in *Der Butt* on a wholly different scale. For *Der Butt* is, at one level, a work of intense, sometimes claustrophobically confessional self-preoccupation on the author's part. It is, first and foremost, the anatomy of an unsatisfactory marriage; not some invented one but recognizably Grass's own. And it is provocatively presented as such. Although the source-experience is rehearsed in many historical guises and explored from a variety of vantage-points, its treatment remains conspicuously anchored in autobiographical detail. Alongside the modish clichés and abstractions of gender-conflict and the newly acquired jargon of the Feminal's sexual politics, we encounter—in at most semi-fictionalized form—the raw nerves of the author's own marital predicament. Yet at the same time, and as a counterbalance to this self-lacerating inward turn, *Der Butt* owes as much to a fairy-tale by the Brothers Grimm ('Von dem Fischer un syner Fru') as to its author's own personal circumstances. Indeed, it is the inventive way in which Grass plays with the tale of the fisherman and his wife (Ilsebill, in both Grass's work and that of the Grimms) that opens the novel's psychological horizons archetypally outwards and chronologically backwards, taking it beyond vitriolic domesticity and contemporary sexual warfare into a rich panorama of history, both invented and real. All this serves as a counterbalance—and relates in a variety of complex ways—to the world of a modern marriage breakup, sexual infighting, and male self-doubt.

It is, of course, not for the first time that fact and fantasy, history and myth, have rubbed shoulders in Grass's fiction. But here the pattern is both more powerfully exploited and richer in ambiguities than was the case in the earlier work. Grass himself cited the introduction into his 1972 novel *Aus dem Tagebuch einer Schnecke* of an explicitly autobiographical dimension—concerning, *inter alia*, his political campaigning for the SPD and his relationship to his children—as one of the more daring features of his later narrative strategy. Hitherto Grass had not himself been present as a figure within his own writings. But this and the following novels were to be characterized, to a greater or lesser extent, by that preoccupation with 'subjektive Authentizität' (to use the fashionable phrase of the time) which could be found in much German writing of the 1970s and early 1980s. Whether as a form of identity-quest, a strategy for coming to terms with the skeletons left in the family cupboard by the Third Reich, or as part of the growing exploration of the intimacies of marriage, childbearing, and parenthood which received its impetus from the feminist cause, such a preoccupation appears in the work of writers as varied as Peter Handke, Max Frisch, Christa Wolf, Karin Struck, and Thomas Bernhard, as well as a whole host of lesser figures scarcely known outside Germany. They all began to come out from behind the protective mask of fiction and, in various forms of semi-autobiographical and confessional writing, to dissect their childhoods, to explore memories of Nazi fathers or school experiences, to chart unsatisfactory marital histories—in sum, to try to illuminate both recent history and contemporary social problems within the context of their own personal lives, painful though the process might be.

In this respect, the post-mortem on a marriage (on marriage itself, even) that *Der Butt* primarily represents, as well as the inclusion of such biographical details as a recent visit to Gdańsk and the 1975 trip to India (in connection with his New Delhi speech 'Nach grober Schätzung'), and the documentation within the novel itself of aspects of the work's own writing would seem to be as much part of the much-vaunted contemporary cult of subjective authenticity as Frisch's *Montauk*, Wolf's *Kindheitsmuster* or Handke's *Wunschloses Unglück*. Although, as many of the essays in the present volume show, such surfaces can often be deceptive. Indeed, as most of the novelists of the 'Neue Subjektivität' have illustrated, the result of such a quest for autobiographical authenticity was usually a complex interplay between openness and dissimulation, or what Christa Wolf refers to as 'Diskretion' and 'Indiskretion'. And what is true of the novels of 'Neue Subjektivität' of the time is observable in an even more complex form in the case of *Der Butt*, a work which can in no way be simply equated with the trend of the moment. Grass's novel, although it may share certain thematic concerns with the fiction of the 1970s, is a far richer work than any of the examples of the new 'authenticity' one might choose to set alongside it.

Levels of irony, complex refractions across a whole variety of historical periods and across a galaxy of personae, and the kind of self-doubt that means that, even when 'Grass' speaks, he speaks with more than one voice, all combine to ensure that the very honesty which became the currency of the new feminist era would remain an elusive goal within this work—and not to its aesthetic disadvantage.

Grass's concerns in *Der Butt* are, as this context suggests, not simply grounded in his earlier novels; and the thematic configurations in the work, although unique in his writing, touch on issues central to the 1970s. But sexual warfare, whether in the microcosm of Ilsebill's pregnancy or across the vast continuum of history and prehistory, is more than a matter of surface theme. The interchangeability of present and past, signalled from the very start of the novel ('Ich, das bin ich jederzeit. Und auch Ilsebill war von Anfang an da'), the shedding and the assuming of previous identities, is achieved in a narrative in which the boundaries of time and those who inhabit time can be suspended in mid-sentence, as when Martin Opitz watches Agnes Kurbiella crossing the square—'jetzt am Rathaus vorbei, in dem wir dreieinhalb Jahrhunderte später auf den Hauselektriker warten' (117/113). After Oskar Matzerath, a singular hero in more than one sense, or the multiple but still tidily arranged narrators in *Hundejahre*, *Der Butt* offers its readers not only more history and more narratives but fewer fixed points. It is a novel whose sole, relatively stable centre lies not, so to speak, within the fiction but partly outside it in the narrator/author Grass, 'nicht nur als Autor, sondern auch als Mann betroffen' (150/147). There at least, between the man who cooks mutton in the first line to the man who, a year later in the last line, runs after Ilsebill, there is coherence and development. One of Grass's supreme achievements in this work is to have successfully captured in telling detail the male chauvinist on the defensive, the pathetic, assertive, obsessive, self-pitying male whose creativity and imagination are not an antidote to his rampant maleness but expressions of it. It is a piece of characterization which becomes all the richer because it expands ironically and ambiguously into the speeches of the one character in the novel who does not fit into the sexual warfare because he has no woman: the verbose fish himself.

The one figure that haunts almost all the contributions to the present volume, though he is the subject of none of them, is the flounder which gives Grass's novel its title. As the *genius loci* of the tale, as well as one of its most ambiguous characters—certainly when compared with the transparency of much of the modern male protagonist's behaviour—he is both more physically concrete and yet open to abstract misrepresentation, more seemingly honest yet often as devious as any of his male puppets.

The Grimm Brothers' dialect fairy-tale to which so much of Grass's novel serves as a *Kontrafaktur* mentions only 'The Fisherman and his Wife', whereas Grass's novel refers repeatedly to the *flounder*'s tale ('Ach Butt! Dein Märchen geht böse aus'). Nevertheless, the fish already had a crucial role to play even in the Grimms' story, namely as the familiar granter of wishes in the fairy-tale, although in this case without exacting the kind of exorbitant price that Rumpelstiltskin or his kind might

demand. Each time the fisherman catches the flounder he is forced to
make further requests of the obliging creature on behalf of his apparently
insatiable wife. Over and over again, we hear the fisherman chant his

> Manntje, Manntje, Timpe Te,
> Buttje, Buttje, in der See,
> myne Fru, de Ilsebill,
> will nich so, as ik wol will.

The fairy-tale flounder's leitmotif as he is bombarded with wish after
greedy wish emanating from Ilsebill—'Na, wat will se denn?'—admittedly communicates a sense of male impatience at woman's materialism,
at her dissatisfaction with her lot, and ultimately her disappointment
with her menfolk. But the Grimms' fish does not appear to take sides
according to the crude dictates of gender. He listens and grants the
various increasingly unreasonable wishes, and more than once, and not
unreasonably, certainly appears to sympathize with the poor husband—
until, that is, the point where the wife's requests reach the level of
religious hubris ('se will warden as de lewe Gott'). At which juncture
both are summarily returned to the state of humble poverty which was the
tale's starting-point. The male is punished as much as his wife.

For much of *Der Butt*, on the other hand, Grass's flounder seems to be
firmly established as counsel to, and secret weapon of, the menfolk. In
Edek's words, 'Seitdem er mich berät, hat die Männersache Fortschritte
gemacht' (15/11). It is he ('der Herr Butt', 80/76) who reveals to them
the secrets of fire-making and at various stages in the history of mankind
reinforces the 'Männersache' and the aggression, domination, and callous
progress that it at least nominally represents. Whether, with his air of
'allwissender Überlegenheit' (26/23), he is to be taken as some teutoni-
cally conceived spokesman of the 'Weltgeist', as is suggested at one point
(151/148), or, as Sieglinde Huntscha would have us believe, 'ein Knecht
der jeweils herrschenden Klasse' (145/142), whether he is correct in
claiming that the menfolk have abused the power he gave them (153/149),
or whether he personifies 'das männliche Herrschaftsprinzip' in all its
ugliness (180/177), must remain a matter of interpretation. What is
important for any reading is that it is the fish, not the character Grass or
any of his other male doubles, who is on trial before the Feminal for
much of the narrative (although this may to some degree be an ironically
protective displacement on the author's part, as he sits in the stalls of
the disused cinema witnessing his own vicarious indictment). And for
whatever motives, it is of signal importance that the fish changes sides
near the end to become, in the male protagonist's words, 'nicht mehr
mein Butt, ihr Butt' (556/547). And the women certainly seem to believe

him: 'Zukünftig soll er frei sein nur noch für uns. Wir werden ihn rufen' (542/533). But as *Die Rättin* goes on to show, they may find themselves calling in vain. And even when he does, earlier, come and speak his words of advice to the menfolk, as so often through the various periods of history until he ends up in his glass tank before the Feminal, he does so with such a disconcerting variety of voices and ironic undercurrents, and so often says (and by that token caricatures) what he assumes his audience wishes to hear, that he becomes as ambiguous as any of the other figures in the text.

Yet, however central the narrator and his fish, it is above all the parade of cooks and their attendant males that makes up the richness of this complex fiction. No other novel of Grass's synchronizes so many disparate times and persons, none asks its readers to keep in mind so many strands of narrative. To make matters easier for these readers the flounder ventures briefly into literary genealogy: 'Denn uns fehlen weibliche Literaturpersonen in komischer Hauptrolle. Ob Don Quichotte oder Tristram Shandy, Falstaff oder Oskar Matzerath: immer sind es Herren, die aus ihrer Verzweiflung komisches Kapital schlagen, während die Damen in ungebrochener Tragik verkommen' (223/218). But the flounder has only Gret in mind, and Gret is one of many women, most of whom endure fates hardly productive of comic effects to set them alongside the likes of Tristram Shandy. The flounder's wishful thinking merely reminds the reader of what *Der Butt* lacks—not comedy but a central comic female character.

In Grass's work, *Der Butt* has no obvious antecedents, nor indeed obvious progeny. Outside Grass, as the flounder's brief survey implies, there is no historical tradition into which it can be securely placed. Whether the distinctive, seemingly unrelated character of *Der Butt* accounts for the wary reception of the novel is difficult to say. Talk—and there was plenty—of the baroque and the Rabelaisian, of gourmandizing and phantasmagoria, reflected more a response to the complexities than any attempt to unravel them. The English-speaking world has been warier still; in that world Grass remains essentially a one-novel author. In that single case, *Die Blechtrommel*, barriers of language presented little hindrance to the translation both of a central grotesque creation (the diminutive Oskar) and of events, notably the Hitler years, which were far from remote. Moreover, if German readers were encouraged to see in Oskar a latter-day Simplicissimus and thus to take their bearings from a family resemblance, English readers, unaware of Grimmelshausen's masterpiece, were at least familiar with the picaresque mode. In *Der Butt* there is no figure as powerfully attractive, or, one might add, as eminently filmable, as Oskar. And there is no familiar narrative mode. Certainly, its theme, inasmuch as it concerns the breakdown of communication and even open hostilities between the sexes, is topical; but it is topicality of a different order from the world of Hitler which impinges upon Oskar.

Approached via *Die Blechtrommel*, *Der Butt* seems, in sum, less accessible. Evidently, Grass's achievement in this novel lies not in the creation of a dominant character, nor in a grotesque 'Verfremdung' of recent history, but in his control of a richly complex narrative rooted—directly, but not simply—in nine fraught months of sexual tension. That complexity is reflected in, and mediated by, a language of exceptional richness and variety, which both challenges and on occasion defeats Grass's English translator. Contrasting registers may be muted: the reader of *Der Butt* in translation must forego, for example, Amanda Woyke's dialect and Martin Opitz's seventeenth-century locutions; the friction—often to ironic effect—between formality and colloquialism, between the dead pan and the highly charged, may be less pronounced. And, if it is difficult to render in English the concentrated, elliptical ambiguities of the poems, it is even more difficult to shape and place them as tellingly as does Grass. The richness and complexity of Grass's novel is not least a richness and complexity of language.

To trace the sources of all this complexity and to analyse some of the interlocking and interacting themes and forms of Grass's novel is, therefore, not simply an act of elucidation, it is an attempt to determine the exceptional artistry that has created this exceptional work. The essays collected in the present volume address themselves to this task. They are intended as a collective contribution to an understanding of *Der Butt*, but no more than that. Each of them is the responsibility of a single author, but they share a common origin which, we believe, imparts to the volume a greater degree of unity and coherence than is normally the case with assemblages of essays devoted to a single author or work. In 1985 and 1986 the authors regularly met in a series of seminars, in the later sessions of which the first drafts of the essays contained in this volume were subjected to critical discussion. Major differences of approach and, indeed, of critical judgement about a number of the more controversial topics remained, and it would have contradicted the spirit of the enterprise to have tried to iron them out in any retrospective attempt to produce a single viewpoint. These differences will be apparent to every reader. At the same time, certain themes tended to assume a recurrent significance and prominence in our deliberations, and some of these are for that reason present in more than one of the contributions that follow. We believe that these recurring emphases give a certain unity and enhance the collaborative character of the present volume. We also believe that they are of more than accidental significance for an understanding of the novel; indeed, they play a major part in substantiating the case we are advancing for its stature.

P.B.
T.McF.
J.J.W.

I

The Dualistic Unity of *Der Butt*

RONALD SPEIRS

The subject-matter of *Der Butt* is unusually diverse. The novel encompasses the conception, gestation, and birth of the narrator's latest child and the simultaneous breakdown of the marriage of which the child is a product; an account of how the flounder is arraigned before a clearly fictitious feminist tribunal in Berlin; and the narrator's experiences of travelling to a very real-seeming India, and of meeting in Gdańsk the widow of a friend killed during the revolt of shipyard workers in Poland. All this is intermingled with a (purported) history of sexual relations—particularly his own—since neolithic times, a history of the city of Danzig and its environs, a history of diet and cooking, myth, religion, fairy stories, poetry, reflections on art, politics, writing, language—the list could be extended. That the novel, despite its epic diversity, does not simply fall apart is due on the one hand to the emotional and intellectual intensity of the narrator's engagement with a few central themes—love, death, creativity—and on the other to Grass's peculiar imaginative and compositional gifts. Grass's work, convoluted and rich in thematic variation, makes one think of the art and writing of the Baroque (a period to which much of the fourth section of the novel is devoted), particularly as these qualities are conjoined with a habit of thinking in antitheses while yet holding together imaginatively, in a conceit of *coincidentia oppositorum*, things that are usually kept physically, mentally, or emotionally apart. Equally important in this regard is Grass's double talent as a graphic and a literary artist, which often produces work of an emblematic-allegorical character[1] moving freely between abstractions, word-play, and physical forms which need to be apprehended by the visual imagination.

What follows is an attempt to map in a rudimentary way the symbolic terrain of *Der Butt* by tracing out the main lines of association running from one such area of imagery to another.

[1] The division of Grass's own talent is reflected in the self-division of the novel's narrator into a poet, Opitz, and a painter, Möller, of whom it is said 'Ihm wurde alles zur Allegorie' (279/273).

The setting for the narrator's first and fateful encounter with the loquacious flounder who becomes his mentor throughout the ages is the estuary ('Mündung') of the river Vistula. This is also the place where the narrator has his *last* sight of the flounder, now talking not to him but to Maria. As far as the plot is concerned, then, the estuary is a place of beginning and ending. It is a place, too, of departure and return: it is from here that Edek (as the narrator was known in prehistoric times) sets off, urged on by the flounder, to take his place in the march of history; and it is to this place (or the 'Mündungen' of other rivers)[2] that he returns throughout the centuries, either as a resident of the evolving settlement on the Vistula ('Giotheschants, Gidanie, Gdancyk, Danczik, Dantzig, Danzig, Gdańsk', 112/109) or (in the present) living with his wife Ilsebill at the estuary of the Elbe, close to where it is joined by another river, or settling on the gulf of Cochin during his incarnation as Vasco da Gama, or visiting Calcutta (on the Ganges delta) in his present-day role as celebrated writer. The estuary is also a place of opening, and thus of meeting and mixing: 'Dort, wo sich der Fluß Wistulle immer verändert gebettet mit der offenen See mischte' (24/21). By the same token it is a border, a place of separation where the land ends and the sea begins. Just these few observations of the shape of the estuary and the events and actions associated with it should have made it clear that this is no mere neutral, accidental location but that it has been transformed from a geographical 'given' into a place of the imagination, a focal point for a number of related themes with extensive symbolic overtones. Complex as it is in itself, the image of the 'Mündung' becomes even more so when one considers that it in turn functions as part of a larger network of leitmotifs. The various features of this important, complex image, which, with its extensive ramifications, is one of the most powerful integrative forces in the novel, are worth examining in some detail, and separately, to the extent that this is possible.

At the point when, with the meeting of fish and narrator, the historical action of the novel commences, the image of the 'Mündung' is invoked, not only as the place where this beginning occurs but also as the active agent of initiation, for it is only when the 'Schiefmaul' of the flounder speaks to him that the narrator's self-awareness is awakened: 'So von ihm angesprochen, fühlte ich mich. Mir kam Bedeutung zu' (28/24). It is allegedly also from the mouth of the flounder that the 'Märchen' of the fisher and his wife first emerged to be passed down through history by the 'Volksmund' (47/44). The flounder's mouth also brings about the

---

[2] The interchangeability of these estuaries is made explicit during the narrator's visit to India: 'Das spiele alles im Weichselmündungsgebiet. Aber eigentlich könnte es auch im Mündungsgebiet des Ganges, etwa hier am Fluß Hooghly spielen' (187/183).

feminist hearing in Berlin when, in another 'Bucht' on the Baltic (Lübeck rather than Gdańsk), he attaches himself by it to the nail-scissors cum fishing-hook wielded by a trio of holidaying lesbians and then speaks to them as he had once spoken to the narrator. The trial of the fish in turn initiates the narrator's own confessional telling of his story to his wife Ilsebill:

weil aber der Butt nicht freigesetzt . . . wurde, kam alles raus, ist die mündende Weichsel der exemplarische Ort, wurde ich beispielhaft, muß ich mich häuten, beichte ich Ilsebill, schreibe ich auf, steht hier geschrieben (43/40).

When the narrator then begins to write down the story, the first three activities he mentions—eating, sex, and narration—are again all functions of one 'Mündung' or another:

Ilsebill salzte nach. Bevor gezeugt wurde, gab es Hammelschulter zu Bohnen und Birnen, weil Anfang Oktober. Beim Essen noch, mit vollem Mund sagte sie: 'Wolln wir nun gleich ins Bett oder willst du mir vorher erzählen, wie unsre Geschichte wann wo begann?' (7/3).

If the physical form of the 'Weichselmündung' relates it, on the one hand, to the mouths that open to begin telling of the events that ultimately originated there, its shape points no less clearly to its connection, as a place of origin, with the bodily site of conception and birth. Hence the aptness of the ambiguity when the narrator says of his sense of belonging to the city on the Vistula estuary: 'Von da komm ich her. Da fing alles an. Da wurde ich abgenabelt' (553/544). The link between the estuary and female sexuality is developed by Grass's (and his narrator's) visual imagination into a fantastic word-drawing of the pregnant Ilsebill *as* an estuarial landscape:

Weil ich Agnes nicht fassen kann, lege ich Ilsebills Leib hochschwanger auf das Werder zwischen Käsemark und Neuteich, wo die Weichsel mit ihrem Himmel drüber freie Luftbilder erlaubt, oder hier, zwischen Brokdorf und Wewelsfleth, auf die eingedeichte Wilstermarsch. Im Rücken immer den Fluß, liegt meine Ilsebill. Ein träges Strandgut nach weiblichem Maß. . . . So lagert sie, aus allen Zeiten gefallen. Wo die Weichsel, die Elbe münden und münden wollen (523–4/514–15).

These various associations of the 'Mündung' with conception, birth, and other forms of beginning have as their converse—or rather their inseparable obverse—the equally powerful connotations of ending and death with which such imagery is stamped. In the poem 'Hasenpfeffer', for example, the subject of the poem runs like (or as) a hunted hare back down the mountain of history until he reaches its beginning and his goal, a female figure stirring a pot:

Sie hob den Deckel und rührte im Sud.
'Was gibt's denn, was gibt's?'
'Hasenpfeffer, was sonst. Ahnte ich doch, daß du kommst.'
(228/223)

Here the 'Mündung' has become the opening of a cooking vessel, its maw seemingly destined to welcome the expectant eater as something to be eaten. A like fate awaits the eels which swim, foraging for food, into the estuary of the Vistula, where they in their turn are trapped for food in the conical 'Reuse' fashioned by the great neolithic matriarch, Aua, in the image of the estuary, of an open mouth—and of her own sexual organ. Here, as in the marvellous description of eel-catching by means of a horse's head in *Die Blechtrommel*, the various connotations of the 'Mündung'—eating and copulation, birth and death—are imagined not simply as different aspects of a phenomenon but as interrelated, even interchangeable elements in a complex *unity*. The eels have migrated to the rivers to feed, so that they can return, mature, to spawn, so that their young in turn can migrate to the rivers to feed and return to spawn—and so on, *ad infinitum, ad absurdum*. Because each element in the compulsive, self-renewing, and hence ultimately static cycle of generating and sustaining life implies the other (procreation follows feeding, feeding follows procreation), each element can represent the other metaphorically or metonymically: the eels trapped in the 'Reuse' are simultaneously hunters and prey, phalluses and semen, life beginning in the womb and ending in the tomb.[3] So impressed was the neolithic artist-fisherman by the sight of the squirming eels that he felt moved by an urge just as compelling ('zwanghaft', 25/22) as that governing the movements of the eels to capture the multiple suggestions of the image by drawing it in the sand; the present-day narrator, plagued by the self-same pressures of appetite, sexuality, transience, futility, is still elaborating and varying that self-same artistic vision as he writes his novel.

The meeting, mixing, and merging of the elements of life that is associated with the 'Mündung' is a notion which pervades the novel. The waters of the estuary are brackish from the mingling of river and sea (24/21), and murky ('trüb', 38/35) with suspended sand and alluvial mud, while the 'Sümpfe der Weichselmündung' (15/11) are only a marginally more solid mixture of the same elements, providing men with an unstable

---

[3] Grass's fascination with the multiple suggestions of particular images generates lines of association not only within individual works but between different works. Thus, 'jene zur offenen Seite verengten Körbe' which make up the eel-trap in *Der Butt* recall not only the eel-fishing scene in *Die Blechtrommel* but also the coffin of Oskar's mother, who kills herself with a surfeit of fish-eating after witnessing that scene: 'Er verjüngte sich auf wunderbar harmonische Weise zum Fußende hin' (*Die Blechtrommel*, 189).

basis for their settlements: 'so daß sich die Hauptpfeiler der auf Moddergrund gebauten Johanniskirche ... bis heutzutage senken' (124–5/121). The turbid 'Brühe' (38/35) around the Baltic coastline is the equivalent in nature to the many pots, bowls, and plates of soup that are an important element of culture in all the epochs lived through by the narrator. Yet, though the 'sämige Sud' (14/11) in the soup-pots is a mixture produced by long, slow cooking ('bis zum Zerfall gekocht', 8/4), the process of blending generally does not go so far as to eliminate all trace of the individual ingredients. Thus the narrator, supping Ilsebill's potent fish soup, looks down to see milky fish-eyes staring back at him from its surface, a *memento mori* that is paradoxically understood to betoken 'Glück' (8/4). Similarly, the poor children sustained by Lena Stubbe's never-empty stock-pot cannot be sure which of the soup's more solid elements they will find at the bottom of their mugs or bowls (411/405). Although soup is ubiquitous, not all soups are the same. Not even all potato soups are alike, as Amanda Woyke points out angrily to Count Rumford, as she protests against his 'pampige' adulteration of her own recipe for it: 'Dem Deiwel mecht son Kleister schmäcken' (329/322). The narrator is similarly chided by Ilsebill for his inept attempts at soup-making: 'Nicht die Möhren zerschnibbeln! Und auch die Schwarzwurzeln bleiben ganz. Typisch Mann: will alles mit allem verkochen, bis nichts mehr seinen Geschmack hat' (347/340). Amanda's secret was her ability to combine consistency with variety:

Auch hat sie die alltägliche Kartoffel an Abwechslung gewöhnt, indem sie ihr mit Kümmel, Dill, Senfkorn, Majoran und Petersilie immer neuen Geschmack abgewann. Amandas Kartoffelsuppe jedoch blieb sich, mit Speckschwarten gekocht, im Grundgeschmack treu, weil ihr täglich zugeschält wurde: nie war sie alle (312/306).

Here, as elsewhere in the novel, the notion of unity invoked is not one that smothers individuality but one that depends rather on each element in the whole asserting its particularity even as it blends with others.

If Grass's pots of 'soup', both in nature and in culture, provide repeated reminders of the mixing of substances in life, they equally draw the reader's attention to the inseparable mix of good and evil, creativity and destructiveness in the world. On the one hand, for example, there are the life-sustaining soups prepared by Agnes Kurbiella, Amanda Woyke, and Lena Stubbe, but there is also the pot of soup into which Dorothea von Montau's daughter fell, her screams unheard by her praying mother, or the fish soup laced with amber (initially by accident, but later by design) which, when fed by Mestwina to the ascetic Bishop Adalbert, make him as randy as a devil's goat—'stößig wie ein Bock aus Aschmateis

Stall' (15/12). Mestwina's act of love has terrible consequences, for
Adalbert, guilty at succumbing to the temptations of the flesh, orders the
suppression of the ritual processions celebrating the pagan, sexual deities,
Aua and Ryb. This in turn provokes the pagan priestess, Mestwina, who
had been perfectly willing to blend ('versuppen', 88/84) Adalbert's
Christian religion with the indigenous rites, to murder him with a cast-
iron spoon, for which act of revenge she is then beheaded. This is only
one of numerous instances in the novel when love reveals its 'Unterfutter'
(423/416) of hatred.

   In addition to its metonymic function as an *example* of a whole
composed of a mix of elements, the imagery of soup and soup-bowls is
repeatedly used to metaphorical effect in the novel. As he contemplates
the flat landscape around his home, for example, the narrator sees a
'Teller mit Himmel drauf. Niedriges Regengewölk und ähnlicher Ein-
topf. Schon rollen die Augen von Rand zu Rand' (523/514). Daily
existence is referred to as 'den täglichen Brei' (12/9), while verbal
creativity, in the mouths of Margarete Rusch and her lover–antagonist
Hegge, is also given a culinary designation as 'Silbengeköch' (232/227).
The process of soup-making is used repeatedly to describe cultural
change by amalgamation: Mestwina, 'weil Köchin, auch Priesterin . . .
hat . . . das Heidnische mit dem Christlichen so lange verkocht, bis es
katholisch wurde' (15/12); the indigenous population around the Vistula
estuary was augmented by 'ziemlich mit uns zur Suppe verrührte
gepidische Goten' (111/107). The same image serves on the one hand as a
simile of Lena Stubbe's inexhaustible compassion ('Dagegen Lena
Stubbes unerschöpfliche Liebe, die dem großen, nie leeren Suppentopf
in der Wohnküche glich', 417/410), and on the other as a reminder of the
nauseating circularity of existence, when the narrator, suffering from
diarrhoea in Calcutta ('diese . . . ihren eigenen Kot fressende Stadt', 185/
181), describes the effect graphically: 'Doch noch scheißt er senfblond
flüssig. Die Suppe schlägt Blasen' (184/180).

   Most importantly, the imagery of soup is used as a metaphor for the
self of the narrator:

Mich hat die große, alles verrührende Köchin gegen die Zeit gerührt. Wie sie
mich (immer noch) mit der Schaumkelle klärt. Wie sie mich austeilt gerecht. Wie
ich gesäuert ihr mürbe bin (512/503).

The complex unity of the narrator's personality is expressed, then, by his
being 'ausgeteilt' amongst the characters of his novel by his muse, the
self-perpetuating cook who is supposedly the 'real' writer of his story: 'So
hockt sie in mir und schreibt sich fort' (217/212). Actually, he has nine
muses (and more) in the cooks who are his female partners throughout

the ages and who, like him, are both many and one. Not only does the narrator have various incarnations throughout history, from prehistoric fisherman to medieval swordsmith, from poet to priest (he is Catholic Bishop Adalbert of Prague in one century and renegade Reformation preacher Hegge in another), from kitchen-boy to estate manager, he is different, often mutually antipathetic characters at one and the same time.[4]

In the seventeenth century, for example, he is both the young poet Andreas Gryphius and the older poet and diplomat Martin Opitz, who is in turn a *double* agent working for opposing sides in the Thirty Years War, but with the *single* aim of securing peace. This pairing of a younger and an older man recurs in other historical periods but it is re-doubled in the seventeenth century in Opitz's relationship with the (yet older) painter Möller. These two men dislike one another ('Dem Opitz war der Möller zu derb; Möller sah Opitz als dünnbeinige Theorie', 283/277) but they are simultaneously and equally loved and cooked for by the gentle Agnes Kurbiella (to whom the narrator then applies particularly guilt-ridden variants of the 'Mündung' imagery: 'Sie war der Kübel, in den wir unser Elend erbrachen. ... Sie war das Loch in das wir uns verkrochen', 272/266).

Within such individuals in turn one meets a mix of contradictory characteristics. Gryphius, for example, keeps harping on the vanity of earthly things but wants his poems published as soon as possible and consumes the food he is served at Opitz's table with great gusto: 'Zuerst hörte man nur das Schmatzen des Poeten, der bald wegen seiner wortgewaltigen Todessehnsucht und Absprache aller irdischen Lust berühmt sein sollte' (251/246). In his incarnation as the painter Möller, the narrator mirrors himself repeatedly—but in contrasting aspects—in Agnes, first drawing a picture of himself in coloured chalk on her swollen, pregnant abdomen, and then painting an oil-portrait of her, within which yet more mirrorings take place:

Danach malte Möller die hochschwangere Agnes, wie sie seine gesunde Physiognomie vor sich hertrug, lebensecht mit Ölfarbe auf Leinwand, ließ aber auf der rechten Bildseite Platz. Gleich nach der Geburt—das Mädchen wurde kein Jahr alt—kreidete er sich zuerst auf den eingefallenen Leib der jungen Mutter, dann

---

[4] The division of the narrator's self began supposedly with the arrival of Christianity amongst the heathens: 'Der Schäfer—der Bischof: Zum ersten Mal zeitweilte ich doppelt, war ich gespalten und dennoch ganz heidnischer Schafshirt, ganz christlicher Eiferer' (108/104). As Christianity worships the 'Herrgott', the onset of self-division is thus linked to the assertion of the male will to power against the female. Just as Grass freely varies the mythical material discussed by Claude Levi-Strauss (in *Le cru et le cuit*), he seems to be offering here, as in other details, an alternative psychohistory to Freud's emphasis (in *Totem und Tabu*) on the male rebellion against the *father* figure as the source of inner conflict.

setzte er Agnes mit seinem leberkranken Ausdruck auf die noch leere Bildfläche neben den hoffenden Leib (drauf sein Spaßvogelgesicht) in Öl: der pausbäckige und der grämliche Vater (278/273).

The various incarnations of the narrator across the ages are also paired with those of a 'friend', identifiable by the syllable 'Lud' in his (or her)[5] name. Although generally treated as if they were separate individuals, he and his friend are again aspects of a single whole, as becomes clear in the last section of the novel, in a paragraph beginning with a denial—'Und ich? Ich bin nicht Jan. Ich bin Marias Halbcousin', but then going on to concede, 'Im Zweifelsfall ich: spätversessen und aufgehoben. Neben mir ich. Außer mir ich', and ending with an explicit confession and identification: 'Jan, das bin ich, Maria, nach deinem Rezept' (512/503).

Crucially, however, this dispersal of the narrator's identity through a multiplicity of roles is not restricted to his assumption of male personae but extends also to the female characters in the novel and can even be said to cross the divide between men and other creatures. His identification with women is suggested, for example, by numerous parallels revealing the same (conflicting) characteristics in his womenfolk as the narrator exhibits in his various male roles. His capacity for ascetic 'Weltekel', for example, evident in his 'Zeitweil' as Bishop Adalbert or in his contemporary response to overpopulation and disease in India ('mit Eiter schreiben, Schorf kratzen', 190/186; 'Sich in Kalkutta ... den Schwanz abhacken', 191–2/187) parallels that of Dorothea von Montau—as does his tendency to neglect his *own* children (so Ilsebill complains) when preoccupied with spiritual or altruistic concerns of one kind or another. Conversely, his sensuous revelling in the physical pleasures of life is projected on to the adored (but deeply feared) Margarete Rusch, a figure whose political, commercial, and personal behaviour bears a markedly 'male' (i.e. ruthless, exploitative, chauvinistic) stamp. His drunkenness and violence as the proletarian Stubbe (or Stobbe) in the nineteenth century is replicated in the behaviour of Mestwina in the Iron Age and Ruth Simoneit in the present. At times the women's affinity with 'masculine' aggression becomes so marked that they would like to adopt a male identity: during the Napoleonic wars the patriotic Sophie Rotzoll was so infatuated with 'Säbelhieb Peitschenknall Freiheitsdurst Todeskuß' (20/17) that she 'wollte partout ein Mann sein' (19/16), an ambition that takes on a grotesque aspect in the eighth Month, 'Vatertag', where a group of lesbians carry 'male' chauvinism to the point of raping one member of the group. Conversely, the conciliatory side of the narrator's personality is to be found as much in Vasco da Gama's attempts to run a

---

[5] One of the lesbians in the eighth Month has the name of Fränki *Lud*kowiak (465/458).

multiracial ménage in India or Martin Opitz's attempts at mediation in the Thirty Years War or the narrator's present-day, social-democratic dislike of political disunity, as it is in the gentle humour of the organist Ulla Witzlaff, in Lena Stubbe's 'Stammtisch', or in Bettina von Brentano's ability to accommodate the divergent desires of individuals within their romantic coterie.

Imagery relating to a male figure can parallel the way a female figure is imagined. Thus the mythical 'Himmelswolf', from whom the female Prometheus, Aua, reputedly stole fire, finds its counterpart in Ilsebill, cast in the role of the Big Bad Wolf by the narrator, who wants to punish her by having 'Wackersteine' (545/536) placed in her belly before it is sewn up after the Caesarian. Similarly, the doubling and multiplication of the male personae has its counterpart in the characterization of the women as multiple refractions of a single being. This is most evident when the narrator summons them all to a meal: 'Alle waren mit allen gedoppelt . . . Und irgendwo, nein allgegenwärtig war Aua, das dreibrüstige Prinzip' (401/394). Thus, if the narrator's restlessness sets him at odds with the stable, even static disposition of his earliest women, Aua and Wigga, his counterbalancing desire for stability, expressed in the dream of withdrawal with Ilsebill into the 'Kürbishütte' of perfect parenthood, is frustrated by the discovery that Ilsebill is far from willing to provide him with 'einen Pol . . . einen ruhenden' (152/148) in his life, and is indeed bent on exchanging the joys of infant care for those of the Lesser Antilles as soon after the delivery as possible. The conflicts *within* the narrator, then, are frequently dramatized in this way as conflicts *between* the narrator and another person, who may or may not be his sexual partner: just as Gryphius and Opitz, or Möller and Opitz, express tensions in his personality, the pairing of the idealistic Sophie Rotzoll with the cynical General Rapp is no less a projection of such inner conflicts.

Another important, if confusing, device by which Grass draws the reader's attention to the common identity shared between the central male figure and the female figures in the novel is his habit of identifying the origin of the narration differently at different times. At one moment the narrator describes himself sitting at his desk and writing his story about the nine and more historical cooks. Yet he then speaks of the female cook crouched within him who 'schreibt sich fort' (217/212), and reconstructs the chain of female narrators who have passed down to one another (299/293), and to him, the stories which serve as the basis for 'his' history of them—stories in which he, necessarily, has the status of a character and which link him to them as by an umbilical cord: 'Es sind aber Amandas Kartoffelschalen zurückerzählt die gewundene Strecke bis

Weißtdunoch, späte Erinnerungen an meine Nabelschnur, die aufgewickelt zu ihr führt' (296/290). The notion that the cooks originate
from within the narrator while the narrator originates from within the
cooks is reinforced in the following passage:

Die Köchin in mir und ich, wir schenken einander nichts. Zum Beispiel hat
Ilsebill einen Koch in sich—der werde wohl ich sein—den sie bekämpft. Unser
Streit von Anbeginn, wer als Komplex drall oder mager in wem hockt, fördert
neue Gerichte oder alte, die wieder beliebt sind, seitdem wir historisch bewußt
kochen (346/339).

There is a suggestion of Chinese boxes in this idea, but with the added
complication that each contains the other.

  The process of giving birth—one of the variants of the 'Mündung'
imagery—further serves Grass's purpose of mixing up the identities of
the narrator and the cooks. At the beginning of the story—after a good
meal, that is—the narrator lies down with Ilsebill to conceive the child
that is born in the last, the ninth chapter of the novel. At the same time,
however, a role-reversal occurs, by virtue of which Ilsebill fertilizes the
narrator's imagination with the story being told:

Doch weil wir in Liebe zeugten, waren unsere Gefühle so allumfassend, daß
ihnen im erweiterten Raum, außer der Zeit und ihrem Ticktack, also aller
irdischen Bettschwere enthoben, eine ätherische Nebenzeugung gelang; wie zum
Ausgleich drängte ihr Gefuhl stößig in mein Gefühl: doppelt waren wir tüchtig
(8/4).

The idea is varied in the narrator's dream in the 'Vatertag' episode:

So träumte ich kürzlich: ich bin eine hochschwangere Frau, die vor dem
Hauptportal des Kölner Doms, zu Füßen der Türme, nachmittags, während der
Hauptgeschäftszeit, mit einem Mädchen niederkommt, das gleichfalls schwanger
ist—meine Ilsebill—und knapp nach mir aus schwieriger Steißlage einen
Knaben gebiert, der jedoch buttköpfig ist: schiefmäulig glubschäugig quersichtig
... Worauf der buttköpfige Sohn meiner Tochter aus mir zu den Passanten
spricht (494/485).[6]

Whereas the novel began—parthenogenetically, one might say—with the
narrator's being impregnated by one of his female characters (Ilsebill)
with the very novel in which they will act out their roles, the later passage
has the male narrator dream *himself* into a female role in which he–she
gives birth to the character Ilsebill, who in turn is credited with giving
birth to the novel, the 'buttköpfigen Sohn'.

  It seems more than likely that *Der Butt* has one of its points of origin in

---

  [6] There is yet another variant on this theme of role-reversal in the eighth Month, namely
when the lesbians dream of fathering a child (495/486).

the non-fictional relationship of two people, Günter Grass and Veronika, the mother of his daughter Helene. Yet this speculation (or fact even) should not be permitted to constrict our understanding of the peculiar way reality is constituted within the novel. Rather, we need to consider *why* the identities of the characters are so thoroughly intermingled in the fiction.

One implication of the novel's play with the characters' identities is that to live in human society is to live in a world partly constituted by fictions: the narrator's wife bears the fictional name 'Ilsebill' because, as far as he is concerned, she *is* as he *sees* or imagines her to be.[7] Conversely, the narrator knows that his own personality has been shaped by women's images of him: 'Jan, das bin ich, Maria, nach deinem Rezept' (512/503). But a further effect of the novel's technique of identity-dispersal and multiple mirroring is to set up a tension between the argument from gender running through the novel—that mankind's problems are attributable to the oppression of one sex by the other and the other's resentment of it—and a quite different argument, namely that it is the mix and conflict of the elements in *human* nature that is at the root of such problems. Finally, the principle of dispersal and mixing at work in the novel suggests a model of the world similar to the one entertained by Schopenhauer and Nietzsche, namely one in which, below a surface of appearances governed by the *principium individuationis*, there lies a common essence or 'Will' in which all phenomena share.

This interpretation of reality suggested by the novel's play with the narrator's protean identity is supported by a number of details. There is, for example, the narrator's experience that India is indeed, as he has been told, a perplexing unity, despite the glaring differences between the lives of different classes: 'wie unfaßlich vielgestalt Indien dennoch eine Einheit sei' (182/178). Moreover, a deep impression is made on the narrator's mind by the 'unfaßliche' (180/176) goddess Kali. This ferocious but devoutly worshipped being with many names ('Sie kann auch Durga, Parvati, Uma, Sati oder Tadma heißen', 180/176) fits easily into the novel's gallery of 'doubled' characters of shifting sexual identity, for she is a 'weiblicher Aspekt des Gottes Shiva' (179/175), at the same time exhibiting a gentler aspect in the figure of the goddess Durga (183/180); within German thought the best-known example of this notion of the

---

[7] The imagery of eyes and seeing forms an extensive complex in the novel which cannot be dealt with in detail here. One way in which it seems to relate to questions discussed in this essay is by association with Apollo (a favourite of the flounder), the god of seeing, contemplation, and reason, whose twin and antagonist is Dionysus, the god of the will. The figure of Ludwig Schrieber, sculptor *and* destroyer of graven images (503–5/494–6) embodies both principles.

divinity as one but divided is probably Nietzsche's discussion of the Apolline[8] world of appearances as an aspect of the Dionysian world of suffering.

When the narrator's child is eventually born, it is not the boy so confidently predicted by its mother but a girl 'mit jenem Spalt, der offen blieb, als uns die schöne Aussicht vernagelt wurde' (543/534). The term 'Spalt', which belongs to the image-complex of the 'Mündung', leads into the word-field, so characteristic of Grass's work, of 'Gespaltenheit', 'sich abspalten', 'Spaltung', 'Teilung', 'teilen'. It is a sign which inscribes into nature openness and division as fundamental features of existence, and it is a sign which is thoroughly ambiguous in its associations. In the narrator's reflection on his baby daughter's sex, for example, 'Spalt' carries the positive connotation of the open-ended flow of life linking mother to daughter to grand-daughter as the bearers of successive generations. Division, too, was initially a positive experience for the narrator. Until the flounder entered his life, Edek, knowing only Aua's matriarchal regimen, had been reasonably content, though not without some feelings of resentment at the repressive, constricting features of her 'allumfassende Fürsorge' (66/62). Through contact with the flounder, however, he experienced the thrill of incipient self-awareness: 'So von ihm angesprochen, fühlte ich mich. Mir kam Bedeutung zu. Dieses Übersichhinauswachsen. Dieses Sichbewußtwerden' (28/24), which, like all reflection, involves division, the acquisition of the 'Distanz zu sich' (34/31) that is one of the most striking characteristics of the knowing flounder.

Significantly, one of the first pieces of knowledge imparted to Edek by the flounder is that fire is able to separate metal ore from other stone, a technique which, by giving men the capacity to create new artefacts, takes the separation of culture from nature a large step forwards. Smelting then serves the didactic flounder as a metaphor for the way the mind develops by separating idea from matter, possibility from fact:

Dieses und mehr ausgeschmolzen, und ihr habt nicht nur Kupfer gewonnen, sondern obendrein dem Feuer einen weiteren, einen fortschrittlichen, scheidenden, entscheidenden, einen männlichen Sinn gegeben. Feuer, das ist nicht nur Wärme und Garküche. Im Feuer züngeln Visionen. Das Feuer reinigt. Dem Feuer enteilt der springende Funke. Feuer, das ist Idee und Zukunft (29/26).

Inevitably, the 'Fortschritt' advocated by the fish is a 'Fort-schreiten',

---

[8] The flounder, who promoted the education of the Edeks by bringing them accounts and examples of the more advanced cultures of the Mediterranean, boasts to the Feminal that he 'der apollinischen Vernunft Geltung verschaffte' (50/46). The fact that so much suffering ensues on the illusions he nourishes in his clients suggests that, in the guise of being an agent of Apollo, he in fact does the destructive work of Dionysus.

involving the narrator's emotional separation from Aua and his exit from her encircling care: 'Weg von der Brust. Ihr müßt euch entwöhnen' (36/31).

Hardly has the fish begun to expound his emancipatory plans for the narrator when their violent aspect is revealed. The flounder demands that the Edeks kill Aua in order to break the hold of matriarchy on their imaginations. He pleads, too, for the division of labour, of peoples, and of land, so that the arts of war may develop: 'Aus Horde und Sippe gliedern sich Stämme ... Reich grenzt an Reich. Und in Waffen stehen die Männer' (35/32). At first the Edeks are slow to realize the fish's dreams, but in the course of history their descendants carry his principle of division to its perhaps final stage, the splitting of the atom (403/396). At every level that same principle entails destructive consequences. In the public domain history has turned out to be a succession of territorial wars ('die Teilung Polens' becomes a kind of historical refrain), religious intolerance (the subjugation of paganism by Christianity, the schisms in the Church resulting in wars of religion), class oppression and class warfare, political splintering and fratricidal sectarianism, particularly amongst the forces of change. Those *holding* power, by contrast, generally continue to do so by closing ranks when challenged from below.

In the private sphere the consequences of 'Spaltung' are similarly unacceptable. The characters experience self-division:

> und wäre nicht doppelt, weil üblich gespalten
> und hätte nicht zwischen die Wahl ...
> und trüge dem Zwilling nicht nach
> und bliebe ohne den übrigen Wunsch ...
> Mein übriger Wunsch ist üblich gespalten.
> Und auch ganz bin ich halb nur und halb.
> ('Aua', 22–3/19)

A pathological form of this dividedness is migraine: 'Helene Migräne| Sitzt im gespaltenen Baum' (143/139). Self-awareness can make the personality seem like a montage of clichéd poses acquired in the cinema:

> Zwischendurch möchte sie rothaarig sein
> oder ein bißchen tot oder Nebenrolle
> in einem anderen Film.
>
> Jetzt zerfällt sie in Ausschnitte und Textilien.
> Ein Frauenbein für sich genommen.
> ('Wie im Kino', 154/151)

For the male figures, too, the result can be alienated self-disgust: 'Manchmal ist einem die eigene Morchel zuwider, lästig, fremd geworden, das störende Anhängsel zwischen den Beinen' (69/65). Conversely,

the tendency of characters to be attracted to their opposites—or seeming
opposites—appears to be an attempt to overcome the divisions in human
nature by the principle of complementarity: hence the narrator's (and the
fish's) recurrent attraction to a strong-willed type of woman 'mit ihrer
trägen, wie ungenutzten Kraft' (152/148), or Lena Stubbe's 'Hang zu
starken Männern mit weichem Gemüt' (425/419). The hope is to achieve
the wholeness of love ('vielgliedrig dennoch ein Schlaf', 144/141), but
this appears to offer only a temporary refuge from the sense of
separateness:

rauchten wir im Bett unter einer Decke jeder seine Vorstellung von Zigarette
(8/4).

> Als es noch die Musik gab,
> konnten wir Gleiches zusammen verschieden hören.
>   (508/499)

Dein Abwasch und mein Abwasch sollen und wollen nicht unser Abwasch
werden (133/130).

The flounder's words to the primeval Edek ('Weg von der Brust!') are
repeated in the penultimate chapter of the novel: 'weg von der Brust, raus
aus der Möse, frei vom Strickstrumpf, dem Abwasch, dem Haar in der
Suppe' (461/455). In this instance they express the ambition of a large
part of the male population of Berlin, bent on indulging, for one day in
the year at least, in the fondly remembered self-sufficiency of bachelor-
hood. But on this particular 'Vatertag' a parallel celebration of separateness is staged by four lesbians who, rebelling against their sexual
exploitation by males, 'sich . . . ins eigene Geschlecht verkrochen hatten.
Jetzt wollten sie anders, unbedingt anders sein' (462/456). These
attempts at dealing with the irritations of heterosexuality by excluding
the opposite sex have disastrous consequences. The same structures of
dominance and submission which these women have rejected in their
heterosexual relationships have been replicated *within* the lesbian circle,
where the individuals evince a tendency either towards 'male' or towards
'female' patterns of behaviour. Sibylle (alias 'Billy') in particular has not
escaped the conflicts of sexual difference but has internalized them in a
'Zustand molliger Zwiespältigkeit' (471/464). Because Billy is the one
with the most 'womanly' body and habits (she cries herself to sleep after
a fight with the others), she becomes the focus of the others' male-
chauvinistic fantasies and thus the object of a group rape. Yet not only
does the attempt at self-enclosure within one's gender offer no refuge
from the problems of *human* difference (domination/submission), in this
instance it has the effect of exacerbating these problems, for the lesbians'
behaviour in turn awakens the aggressions of a group of young 'schwarze

Engel' (487/478) who avenge the lesbian travesty of their own self-enclosure in their buttoned-up male arrogance ('Denen löste keine Pointe das Häkchen', 487/478) by surrounding Billy ('da hatte sich schon der Kreis geschlossen. Schnapp! machte die Falle', 501/492), repeating the rape ('Dich reißen wir auf, du Sau!', 501/492), and then churning her body to a pulp beneath the wheels of their motor bikes. The tragic irony is intensified by the fact that this happens to Billy just after she has separated herself from the other women ('Sie hatte sich in ihre Einsamkeit eingepuppt', 500/491), and decided to have nothing more to do with lesbianism ('Da brauch ich doch die nich. Das sind doch nur Verirrungen, durch die man durch muß. Ich will. Und zwar als Frau. Und zwar eindeutig', 500/491).

The 'Schnapp' made by the trap closing just before the Black Angels 'aufreißen' Billy echoes the term 'Schnappmöse' (or *vagina dentalis*, 302/296), a coining that expresses male fear of female sexuality.[9] When the motor-cyclists surround Billy, they are clearly seeking an aggressive outlet and compensation for their castration fears in an act of symbolic revenge: they entrap the female 'trap'.[10] The same kind of symmetry is to be found in inverted form in Sophie Rotzoll's attempt to murder General Rapp by feeding him a calf's head stuffed with poisonous fungi. The phallic significance frequently assigned to mushrooms throughout the novel[11] is emphasized by the fact that one of the most poisonous of the fungi used by Sophie carries the name *Amanita phalloides* (392/385). Her intended revenge would have taken the form of making Rapp perform an act of self-castration by putting into his own mouth a symbol of what he has been vainly trying to force into the steadfastly 'closed' Sophie ('zeitlebens ein siebenmal verschlüsseltes Mädchen geblieben', 20/16); ironically, the plot fails because he nibbles only a tasty morsel of the calf's *mouth* and none of the stuffing!

If these fierce reciprocal parodies of sexuality stress the feared aspects of both the closing and the opening functions of the 'Mündung', they are counterbalanced by other instances where enclosure and openness are seen in a positive light. Enclosure, for example, can afford protection,

---

[9] Although the preacher Hegge is the only man literally to be castrated in the novel (when Gret Rusch bites off one of his testicles in order to help him climb over a wall), this incident provides the paradigm for various male experiences of female power.

[10] It has been argued (Friedrichsmeyer 1983, 151–62) that this whole episode is a male-chauvinistic fantasy of revenge on the part of the narrator, who doubly vents his spite on women: once by imagining them aping the male capacity for atrocity, and once by subjecting them to male retribution for so doing.

[11] In Grass's graphic work, however, mushrooms can also represent the female sexual organ. For a visual parallel to the unity in contradiction characteristic of the verbal imagery of the novel, see Grass's drawing of 'hermaphroditic' fungi (cf. *Ach Butt*, 29).

whether in the form of the primitive 'Hakelwerk', which 'aus Weiden geflochten vor pruzzischen Einfällen Schutz bot' (15/12); or the dikes built to turn the estuarial floodlands into productive agricultural land— 'Ich kam . . . durch das (nach den Hungerjahren) neu eingedeichte Land zwischen Nogat und Weichsel' (120/116); or the womb which the child in the novel is reluctant to leave ('Nur ein Kind . . . ruft: Da will ich nicht runter. Will nicht runter', 45/42) and which the narrator still dreams of nostalgically ('und um dich wölbt sich feuchtwarm die Höhle', 395/389). With hindsight the narrator now has sympathy for the attempts of his women to block the flow of history:

Ob Aua oder Wigga oder noch später Mestwina: sie verhinderten sagenhafte Züge und Fahrten. Sie überlebten ohne besondere Zeichen, sie legten, wenn wir Geschichte oder Geschichten machten, ihre Natur quer (103–4/100).

In his mythical vision of her, the narrator sees, with admiration, Ilsebill doing the same as her primeval sisters: 'Quer liegt sie allen Plänen' (523/ 515).[12]

However, such dreams of protective enclosure or attempts to achieve it result in what is at best a temporary or an illusory state of security: the 'Pruzzen' are not kept out for long—history has not been sealed off; the dikes are threatened even today by the combination of a spring tide and a swollen river; the reluctant child may adopt the breech position in order not to leave the womb, but in the end 'es muß' (45/42). Though he may at times dream of a return to the womb, the narrator is also aware that such enclosure is a form of imprisonment. Of his time as kitchen-boy to the voluminous Gret Rusch, for example, he says, ambiguously: 'Sie hielt mich unter Verschluß. Sie war das deckende Fett' (17/14); later he recalls the case of the patrician Ferber (himself again, of course) who died in bed, smothered by Gret's enveloping form (205/201). Equally, the womb-like existence provided by Aua was eventually felt to be an intolerable restriction: 'Du wirst zugeben, Ilsebill, daß so viel mütterliche Fürsorge, auch wenn sie mich warm und in Unschuld hielt, langsam zum Zwang wurde' (33/30). This 'memory' of Aua is presumably coloured by his contemporary experience of Ilsebill's restrictive protectiveness: 'Dicht hält sie, dicht: kein Ausblick ins Ungefähre bleibt dir erlaubt'

[12] There may be poetic irony in the fact that Gret Rusch, with her 'masculine' restlessness and desire to profit from historical change (she supports the *opening* of the trade routes to India), dies because her throat is *blocked* by a pike's bone. The narrator suggests that it is in fact, an unwelcome turn in the course of history that causes her to choke: 'Der alten Nonne hat wohl mehr als die Hechtgräte quergelegen' (216/211). Maria, too, experiences a choking-fit after the death of Jan—whose involvement in the fateful strike against price rises *she* had encouraged: 'Als das Gedicht rezitiert wurde, mußte Maria, die etwas im Hals hatte, kotzen' (518/509).

(410/403). Conversely, Ilsebill rejects as a 'Scheißidylle' the narrator's dream of their confinement within a 'Kürbishütte': 'Eher treib ich das ab, und zwar in London, eh ich mich von dir einranken lasse. Ist doch der alte Männertrick. Goldener Käfig und so' (98/94). Maria, too, 'wollte keine Kette, keinen geschliffenen Anhänger' (127/123).

Closure then, repeatedly figures in the novel as a state that demands to be ended by an act of opening. The writing of the novel itself is thought of as bringing relief from a painful blockage: 'Wer von so viel Vergangenheit verstopft ist und endlich zu Stuhl kommen möchte, den drängt es, von Mestwinas Bernsteinkette zu erzählen' (22/19); or there is the case of 'Dorothea ... die seit dem vierzehnten Jahrhundert meine Galle preßt und raus soll endlich, das Miststück!' (132/129). Conversely, the citizens of beseiged Danzig are granted respite from starvation when the river floods, carrying fish *into* the streets and breaking open the 'Ring um die Stadt' (373/367). Bottled-up emotions demand to be brought out into the open: 'Und die restliche Schande? Kreuzweis verschnürte Pakete, die aufgedröselt sein wollen' (110/106); 'verkapselte Gründe' (132/129), too, underlie Ilsebill's onslaught on the narrator's precious collection of hand-blown glasses—reasons which are not difficult to deduce from the shape of these objects—'Mündungen' one and all, with their historical origin in the 'handlichen Steinmösen als Trinkschalen' (68/64) manufactured by the primeval artist Ludek.

The spread of culture, too, depended on abandoning the state of 'Abkapselung' (62/59), opening new horizons: 'Immer habe ich Ziele hinter den Horizonten gesucht. Gott wollte ich durch nautische Kunst erreichen' (183/179). In retrospect, however, such attempts to open new historical possibilities seem tainted because the flounder, who first held out the prospect of 'einige über den jungsteinzeitlichen Horizont weisende Erkenntnisse' (27/23), urged the murder of Aua as a necessary step towards emancipation, and because history as it has actually turned out has been a succession of acts of hubris and cruelty. As he tries to ingratiate himself with the women whom he now (purportedly) believes to be the creators of new possibilities for humankind, the flounder remains the advocate of historical openness: 'Man dürfe die Schöpfung nicht als abgeschlossen werten' (42/39). Yet in order to take this position the flounder has to undertake a quite illegitimate act of historical foreclosure by denying any responsibility for the worst excesses arising from the historical process he once set in train:

Ihr könnt mir Alexander und Cäsar, die Hohenstaufen und Deutschherren, auch noch Napoleon und den zweiten Wilhelm anlasten, aber nicht diesen Hitler und diesen Stalin. Die liegen außer meiner Verantwortung. Was danach kam, kam

ohne mich. Diese Gegenwart ist nicht meine. Mein Buch ist geschlossen, meine
Geschichte ist aus (460/453).

There speaks the flounder *as* Kaiser Franz Josef with his self-exculpat-
ing, 'Ich habe es nicht gewollt.'[13] What the flounder refuses to acknowledge is that the very openness he advocates can be something to be
feared as much as closure: Lena Stubbe's arrest (and subsequent murder)
by the Nazis comes about because she 'kindisch wurde und nur noch
offen sprach' (458/451); as he describes a primitive religious procession
the narrator recalls that, 'ungetauft glänzten die toten Augen der Fische.
Starre Blicke in den Himmel gehoben. Das offene Fangmaul. Kiemen-
flossen gespreizt' (89/85)—eyes, mouth, fins, all open, but each a sign of
death.

The 'Mündung', it has been argued in this essay, is a complex,
'polysemic' image that binds together much of the novel's thematic
material in an extensive network of parallels and antitheses. It has also
been suggested that the writing of the novel itself is characterized by
metaphors drawn from this complex of imagery and thereby related to
the other life-processes that it describes. Furthermore, the shape and
functions of the 'Mündung' serve as emblems of the way the fictional
world is organized, namely as a world divided but one, and as a place
where the most diverse things, times, places, persons can mingle and
merge. By way of conclusion, then, let us consider a few examples of the
novel's language and composition which can be subsumed under this
same complex of diverse but unifying imagery.

The linguistic equivalent of the 'Spaltung' of the estuary, and of the
events and people associated with it, is ambiguity, many instances of
which have already been cited in the discussion of the narrator's
suggestive metaphors (e.g. the mushrooms, eels, nails, swords, rockets
which all mean both themselves and the male sexual organ). Although the
narrator, in his neolithic guise, was already intuitively aware that things
may contain more than one possible meaning, linguistic ambiguity is
something he first encounters in the unsettling manner of speech used by
the flatfish: 'Während du, Butt, mich nervös machst. Du redest so
zweideutig. Was sind das: Informationen? ... Und hat das, was ist, auch
noch einen anderen Sinn? Zum Beispiel das Feuer?' (28/25). Thereafter
he meets the phenomenon recurrently throughout history as a feature of
female as much as of male language. Dorothea von Montau, for example,
whose mouth became 'schief' like the flounder's after being kissed by it,

---

[13] Ironically, the words of the Kaiser are put into the mouth of Billy: 'Das habe ich nicht
gewollt' (497/489).

sublimates the sexual desires that she refuses to satisfy in her earthly marriage by chanting lascivious–mystical love-songs to Christ, which the clerics bent on canonizing her have to render unambiguous for their own purposes: 'Zwar sei in den Wortgebilden der alles reimenden Dorothea die Grenze zwischen Fleischeslust und Seelenfeier nicht immer deutlich, aber die Liebe zum Herren spreche sich dennoch zweifelsfrei aus' (160/157). The narrator still lives daily with equivocation in the mouth of his present Ilsebill: 'Nein, sagt Ilsebill, was Ja heißt' (133/130).

The narrator has in turn cultivated the art of ambiguity for his own purposes, perhaps in emulation of Gret Rusch's 'unterschwelliges Gebrabbel' (198/194), with which she simultaneously entertains her guests and pursues her personal/political interests: 'Und doch fand das Aftersinnige ihrer Tischreden jedermanns Ohr ... und brachte auf lange Sicht einzig dem Kloster der Heiligen Brigitta Nutzen' (198/194). Rather like Gret when she is trying to stave off her father's execution, the narrator is supposedly seeking to hold the interest of Ilsebill with his 'hovering', suggestive brand of story-telling, in order thereby both to hold together their crumbling marriage and to provide an account of male–female relations that will do justice to their complexity.

Responsibility is another subject on which the narrator tends to equivocate. Ostensibly, the main drift of his account of life with Aua is to praise the primeval matriarchal system. On the other hand, he wants to insinuate that his rebellion against Aua, however much it involved *him* in guilt, was partly attributable to *her*. Thus, when speaking of Aua's theft of fire, he says, 'Es kam ja alles von ihr, nicht nur Reuse und Angelhaken' (31/28). On the surface these words pay tribute to Aua, the Great Provider, but the generalization also carries the implication that the responsibility for everything consequent on the acquisition of fire (i.e. the creation of metal objects and hence the development of deadly weapons) lies with Aua, a suggestion strengthened by Aua's secret fascination with, and continued use of, a metal knife after she has outlawed such objects (30/27).

If the narrator uses ambiguity to disclose divergent meanings in a single state or action, he will use paradox to throw into question normal assumptions about separateness and difference. Thus he has the flounder say of Ilsebill, 'Manch eine Frau ... steht durchaus ihren Mann' (36/33), implying that gender does not simply and conveniently divide the human race into warlike males and peace-loving females. The converse of this paradox (or the case of Sophie Rotzoll) is to be found in the fact that German, curiously enough, uses the word 'milk' for the semen of fish: 'Man erkennt die Milch, den Beweis seiner Männlichkeit' (519/511).

The thematic association of the 'Mündungen' of the novel with

enclosure ('die Aalreuse', 'die Schnappmöse') and circularity (as a place
of departure and return for eels and narrator alike) finds its *narrative*
equivalent in the recurrence of seemingly stereotyped forms of action
throughout history.[14] When Billy is crushed to pulp by the Black Angels,
for example, the scene is a rerun of the one in which old Lena Stubbe was
beaten to pulp by a thug in a concentration camp, the parallel being
emphasized by the detail that beside each corpse lie the victim's broken
spectacles (458/452, 502/493). Similarly, Billy's rape by the motor-
cyclists repeats her rape by the lesbians, which in turn repeats the rape of
Agnes by marauding Swedish soldiers after the battle of Wittstock (an
event specifically recalled in the 'Vatertag' episode, 473/466). In the
political sphere the suppression of the dock-workers' protest in Gdańsk
by the Communist authorities in the twentieth century repeats the
patricians' suppression of the revolt of the guilds there in the Middle
Ages: 'Seit 1378 hat sich in Danzig oder Gdańsk soviel verändert: die
Patrizier heißen jetzt anders' (123/120). In the slum streets of Calcutta
the narrator believes he is witnessing the return of the Stone Age:

Nachts hocken sie um Feuerstellen vor jeder Papphütte und kochen, was sich im
Abfall fand. Zum Schluß bleibt der Sammeltrieb. Kohlenstaub mit Stroh zu
kleinen Küchlein geformt oder getrocknete Kuhfladen unterhalten die Feuerstellen. Die Steinzeit will zukünftig werden. Schon beginnt sie, die Stadt zu
erobern. Schon sehen die Autobusse aus, als seien sie archäologische Funde (186/
182).

In the face of these unremitting cycles of poverty and cruelty the
novel's characters repeatedly feel that everything that happens follows
a pre-established pattern: 'Alles was ist, ist schon vorgeschrieben'
(473/466).

Finally, however, since nothing in this novel is without an antithesis
that is also its complement, the tendency to narrative circularity needs to
be seen in relation to a narrative openness comparable to the ever-
shifting, ever-open estuary of the Vistula. Early on in the novel, for
example, the narrator describes how he fashioned a necklace for Mestwina from pieces of amber gathered by the sea-shore. This necklace then
supposedly becomes involved in the chain of events leading to the deaths
of Mestwina and her lover Adalbert, for it comes apart while she is
cooking, and the melted amber in the soup has an ultimately disastrous
aphrodisiac effect on Adalbert. At a later point, however, the novel offers
a quite different account of the undoing of the necklace. According to
Amanda Woyke, the necklace was severed along with Mestwina's neck by

---

[14] For a detailed and illuminating study of such patterns, see Reddick 1983, *passim*.

the executioner's axe, at which point the pieces of amber flew off into the fields where they can still be gathered today (304/298).

The novel similarly contains several competing versions of the *Märchen* 'Von dem Fischer un syner Fru'. Apart from the 'standard' version enshrined in the Grimms' collection, an alternative version was supposedly told to Philip Otto Runge in which exorbitant desires were ascribed to the fisher rather than to his wife; there is also the narrator's interpretation of the fairy-tale, which casts the flounder in the role of a seducer and *fabricator doli*, and there is the tale of specifically sexual insatiability told by Mäxchen to Billy (491–3/483–5). The narrator also toys with three different stories which might account for the loss of Aua's third breast: according to the first it fell off when the flounder slept with Aua; according to the second it may have disappeared when the Edeks terrified the womenfolk with a huge statue of a male with three 'Stinkmorcheln'; while according to the third story the third breast was still possessed by Wigga but disappeared when she prohibited the use of an hallucinatory plant or 'Wunschkraut', with the result that the men 'sahen ... nicht mehr wirklich, was uns Wunsch war. So riß der Film lebhafter Vorstellung. So verloren wir unsere Unschuld. Weg war die dritte Brust' (72/69).

The narrational openness with regard to this supposedly crucial event at the beginning of history is matched by the contradictoriness of the novel's ending, or rather endings. In its penultimate section the narrator, depressed by the stale warfare of marriage and man's history of failure, sees only a gloomy future: 'Ach, Butt! Dein Märchen geht böse aus' (552/543). Yet the very last scene of the novel has the narrator watching Maria-cum-Ilsebill as she walks up the beach past him, and then getting to his feet to follow her once again:

Ilsebill kam. Sie übersah, überging mich. Schon war sie an mir vorbei. Ich lief ihr nach (555/547).

But in what direction, one might ask, and with what prospect of breaking out of the cycles of destruction in nature and history?

The tension between narrative openness and fateful, cyclical closure in the novel corresponds to a conflict in Grass himself. In conversation he has stressed the openness of the ending, the hope that accompanies each new life, in contrast to the shocking finality of Billy's fate in the 'Vatertag' episode:

Alle meine Bücher haben einen offenen Schluß, und im *Butt* kann es gar nichts anderes als einen offenen Schluß geben. Die Schwangerschaft löst sich in Geburt auf—das Leben geht weiter. Der letzte Fall der Maria Kuczorra, der Kantinen-Wirtin auf der Leninwerft, bleibt auch offen; zwar wird der Streik und Aufstand der Arbeiter zusammengeschossen von der Volksmiliz in Polen, aber die Forderung nach mehr Freiheit und Selbstbestimmung bleibt in den kommunistischen Staaten bestehen, auch dort geht das Leben weiter … Zum Schluß stehen der Mann, der Ich-Erzähler, und das Autoren-Ich in einer Person da, haben den berühmten Informationsvorsprung der Männer verloren, der Butt spricht zuerst mit der Frau, mit Maria Kuczorra, dann kommt sie zurück und entpuppt sich als Ilsebill, beide sprechen, beide lachen, er versteht kein Wort, sie übergeht ihn, er läuft ihr nach—ein offener Schluß. Ich habe diese Steigerung vor dem Schluß gewollt. Ich hätte niemals mit 'Vatertag' aufhören wollen, dann wäre das ein effekthafter Schluß gewesen, der nicht in meiner Absicht lag (Arnold 1978, 30).

Yet the very words Grass uses in this interview to suggest openness in the direction of hope ('das Leben geht weiter') are an echo of the last bitter twist in the tail of 'Vatertag':

'Und nach fuffzig Schritt liegt da paar Schritte links ab ne nackte Frau tot. Jadoch. Richtig. Sag ich ja.' Danach ging das Leben weiter (502/493).

2

Future Imperfect: Time and the Flounder

JOYCE CRICK

Wir haben das so in der Schule gelernt: nach der Vergangenheit
kommt die Gegenwart, der die Zukunft folgt. Mir aber ist eine
vierte Zeit, die Vergegenkunft geläufig. Deshalb halte ich auch die
Form nicht mehr reinlich. Auf meinem Papier ist mehr möglich.
Hier stiftet einzig das Chaos Ordnung. Sogar Löcher sind Inhalt
hier.

Kopfgeburten, 102

Ever since a glimpse of the future caused Oskar Matzerath to stage-
manage his own retardation by falling down the cellar steps, temporal
patterns in Grass's novels have been problematic. *Der Butt* is no
exception. Indeed, it outdoes any of its predecessors in the variety and
vastness of its historical and pseudo-historical material, the evasiveness of
its omnipresent narrator, and above all in its play with the logic of time,
its illusory subversions of chronology, and the multiplicity of its shifts
from the narrative time of Ilsebill and 'ich' to the manifold narrated times
of the nine and more cooks and their reincarnations in the Feminal. And
back. And forwards. And round about.

This essay proposes to look at the notions of time and history with
which the novel operates, and at how the narrative form acts as their
vehicle.[1] But first, by way of clearing the ground, we should remind
ourselves of the classic proposition of Enlightenment aesthetics which
Lessing put forward in *Laokoon*: as the dimension of painting is space, so
the dimension of narrative is fundamentally that of time. This holds good
for the oral teller of fairy-tales, for the time/space sequence of the printed
page, for our own life-stories from birth to death, and for the very
utterance of language itself.

Of course, ever since Laurence Sterne at least, the conjurers of the

---

[1] It is a topic which has made its way into a number of earlier studies of the novel; cf.
Koopmann 1983, Demetz 1983, O'Neill 1982, Stern 1982, and Williams 1980.

imperfect have cast their doubts upon this stable proposition, and have represented the passage of time in convoluted patterns which pretend to movements quite contrary to the linear sequence that takes the reader from the morning of the First Day to the evening of the Sixth, and from page one to page five hundred and fifty-six. 'Vorwärts? Das kennen wir schon,' exclaims the lyric I of *Der Butt*, 'Warum nicht rückentwickeln' (57/54). But Grass himself finished the novel five years older than he began it, and operated with a many-layered open scheme which allowed him the opportunity to develop.[2] Nevertheless, it is also a novel which quite remarkably invites a to-and-fro, backwards-and-forwards reading; and Grass as author is on record as having to a large extent composed it in this way.[3]

For we may distinguish, over and above the endemic linear movement, other kinds of temporal patterning at work in the novel: cyclical, suspensive, synchronic, and—for want of a better word—disruptive. Not that it will be entirely possible to discuss these separately and sequentially, for they often overlap one another, and are mutually determining.

Firstly, there is the progressive linear movement of those implacable nine months from conception to birth which form the temporal frame of the work and give headings to the 'chapters'. Within this narrative time, Ilsebill gestates her daughter and the narrator generates his rival brainchild, the history of the cooks: 'Gleichberechtigt sind uns Fristen gesetzt' (14/8); concurrently the flounder, as the spirit of history, is put on trial by the Feminal. These nine months represent a line of biological development with a sequential pattern which also matches that grand stage-by-stage progressive philosophy of history of the kind which Lessing put forward in his *Über die Erziehung des Menschengeschlechts*,[4] and which Heine distinguished, on the whole with approval, in his *Verschiedenartige Geschichtsauffassungen*, but which the lyric voice of the novel now attributes to the destructive 'Endzielmänner', linear to a man, of the key poem 'Am Ende' (99/95–6). Analogous linear patterns are to be discerned in certain ways of making intellectual order of the world: in the processes of logical thinking and of secure historical periodization. Cause follows effect and conclusion derives from premiss as surely as the Reformation follows High Gothic and the twentieth century follows the nineteenth. What, darkly, may follow the twentieth, is left to Grass's following novel,

---

[2] 'Ich bin der Überzeugung, daß jemand, der vor hat, über Jahre—das Ganze hat fünf Jahre beansprucht—einem epischen Stoff nachzugehen, ein Konzept haben muß, das offen ist, das ihm erlaubt, sich in dieser Zeit selbst zu entwickeln' (Arnold 1978, 32).

[3] 'Und dann [gegen Ende des ersten Arbeitsjahres] begann ein zügiges, fortwährendes Schreiben, nicht im linearen Sinn, sondern in all den neun Teilen, die schon da waren' (ibid., 31).

[4] For Grass's bitter *revocatio* of this once-noble vision, see *Die Rättin*, 188–9.

Die Rättin, to explore. The narrative analogies to these teleological movements are to be found both in the naïve consequentiality of the fairy-tale ('Und dann? und dann?' ask the listening children),[5] and in the chronological sequence which the rational fish, as the patron of progress and order, advises the narrator to employ in telling his tales ('Doch weil mir der Butt zur chronologischen Folge rät . . .', 22/18), even though two late tales urgently demand to be told: 'Billy und Maria drängen' (ibid.). And indeed, in a very broad sense, the narrator does take this advice, presenting the nine months and twenty centuries with their pre-liminaries and pre-histories in the proper pre-position. In this way he can hold off telling the painful stories of the birth, of the end of his marriage, of Billy and violence, and of Maria and the redundancy of men. But in doing so he also implicates his story-telling in the doomed historical/psychological complex of progressive masculine rationality represented by the fish. Progressive rationality is designated 'masculine', because, as the very premiss of his novel, not just as the *parti-pris* attitude of the Feminal, Grass has ironically pre-empted the feminist-apocalyptic version of the 'Dialektik der Aufklärung': rationality—here, masculine rationality—has overreached itself and turned destructive.

Accordingly, the narrator also subverts the linearity of the novel again and again with contrary temporal patterns which are the correlatives of a scepticism of all the flounder stands for. Progress is called into question by a cyclical movement which operates with a view of history as repetition-compulsion; positivism is doubted when the fiction-maker claims greater truth than the historian[6] and when the suspensions of fiction nullify the world of fact; the power of consciousness is queried by the emergence of unconscious neurotic factors not subject to change and time; a priori particulars have the rug pulled out from under them as a synchronic arrest operates to transform ongoing narrative into the illusory effect of spatial graphics. The bankruptcy of the fish's values is demonstrated above all in the disruptions of linearity which occur with the three urgent, tragic tales of Vasco in India, of Maria and Jan in Poland, and of Billy's death in the Grunewald on Ascension Day, 1963. In different ways, political and personal, all three demonstrate the narrator's human impotence at man-made horror.

The narrative, then, also operates in repetitions and prefigurations

---

[5] *Aus dem Tagebuch einer Schnecke*, 191, 159; *Die Rättin*, 382.

[6] In any case, Grass is suspicious of the apparently 'factual' historian as a tendentious purveyor of fictions; that is, not as a novelist and honest illusionist but as a liar—'Ich sehe mich in der Lage, genauere Fakten zu erfinden als die, die uns als angeblich authentisch überliefert wurden' (Arnold 1978, 31). Grass the poet agrees: 'Erst Mönche, Stadtschreiber später,| Schriftführer heute halten die Lüge in Fluß' ('Geteert und gefedert', 208/203).

which match a cyclical view of history quite other than that progressive forward movement initiated when the flounder first came on to the scene, and which now, the novel proposes, is coming to an end. This cyclical view of history is not new in Grass's works: it was particularly discernible in *Die Blechtrommel*, where the nightmare cycle was at work both in history and in Oskar's psyche: on the one hand, there was the terrible roundabout of invasion/repulsion/invasion in German/Polish history; on the other, there were the neurotic fears which returned to Oskar in the shape of the 'schwarze Köchin'. It is also present on both levels, historical and psychological, in *Der Butt*, voiced by the narrator sometimes in panic, sometimes in resignation. There are, for example, the two different occasions when the Gdańsk shipyard strike calls from him the same observation: 'Seit 1378 hat sich in Danzig oder Gdańsk soviel verändert: die Patrizier heißen jetzt anders' (123/120). And again, looking back from 1970: 'Man muß das historisch sehen. Das hört nie auf. Auch nicht im Kommunismus. Immer die Niederen gegen die Oberen. Damals hießen die Bonzen Patrizier' (515/506). Not only the narrator but Ilsebill and Lud too enjoy multiple historical incarnations. The members of the Feminal have their prefigurations among the cooks. Looking for fantasy models around the camp-fire on that catastrophic Father's Day, Billy, Siggi, and Mäxchen find theirs as soldiers after the battle of Wittstock in *Simplicissimus*: 'Alles was ist, ist schon vorgeschrieben,' says Siggi (473/466). The flounder himself, talking for his life, now revalues the forward march he had previously advocated in terms of repetition-compulsion, 'eine zwangsläufige Folge von Krieg und Frieden, Frieden und Krieg' (530/521), and offers the women the flattering opportunity to enter history themselves, thereby rescuing the world—and the flounder. What may, ironically, be going on here, is a kind of higher repetition-compulsion in which women now re-enact the historical fall of men. If this is so, then what the narrator fears is true: 'Ach Butt! Dein Märchen geht böse aus' (131/128; 552/543).[7]

The novel's treatment of time also operates quite counter to *any* temporal movement, whether it be history as progress or history as cycle, to arrest time and to present figures and events not successively but simultaneously and spatially. 'Auf unserem Papier findet das meiste gleichzeitig statt' (127/123). All the cooks in history may well be located very exactly in 'männlich datierter Geschichte' (227/221) in the sequential centuries, but they are all in Danzig, the place where the narrator was born and where it all began (553/544); they are all Aua; they are all Ilsebill. And not only are they all in Danzig; they are all in the narrator,

---

[7] It is not necessary for me to pursue this part of the argument further, as it has already been developed by O'Neill 1982.

who is synchronically and historically omnipresent—'Ich, das bin ich jederzeit' (7/3). 'Wann' turns into 'wo' (363/356). Time turns into place: 'Ich lief, die Zeit treppab, davon' (8/4); 'ich lief . . . Geschichte bergab' (100/96; 227/222). Arbitrary and totally ahistorical syntactical simultaneities are established with Grass's old trick of a straight-faced 'Als . . .' or 'Während . . .'.

There is, of course, a sense in which these two temporal patterns, the cyclical and the synchronic, can be thought of as identical, for if events are only repeated, then there is stillness in the movement. There is no change, only a very elaborate kind of arrest, 'gestauchte Zeit' (436/429). The cycle is self-cancelling:

> Zweitausendfünfhundert Jahre Geschichte,
> frühe Erkenntnis und letzte Gedanken
> lecken einander, heben sich auf.
> ('Leer und alleine', 245/239)

Now there are three aspects of psychic experience where we may say that temporal movement appears to be suspended: religious, aesthetic, and neurotic. Time is suspended in mystical contemplation, but in this most secular of novels, we may scarcely expect to find this aspect except as occasional subject-matter, and then ironically. More importantly, time is also suspended in that condition of secular mysticism, the contemplation of the work of art. Moreover, story-telling casts its spell on the listener/reader, who for the space of the telling/listening/reading abandons his own time and willingly follows every twist and turn and loop in the narrative line so adventurously invented, and accepts the curious perspectivism which lies in the nature of the activity.[8] In the making of the work too, time is suspended:

> Noch und wieder: Federn blase ich leicht
> und behaupte, was schwebt.
> ('Wie ich mich sehe', 95/91)

In the state of creative dream, all things are present: the lyric 'I', the narrator, the several figures both in their distinctiveness and in their fluidly merging identities. Much of the novel itself is told as a merging and emerging of reality and fantasy in and out of each other, and in dream the principles of time and individuation are inoperative. The unconscious knows no tenses. Ilsebill is represented as a primeval landscape (523/514). 'Das Ganze ist mehr ein Traum,' the narrator protests from the start (10/6).

Thirdly, the rules of temporal sequence do not apply in neurosis.

---

[8] Cf. Käte Hamburger, *Die Logik der Dichtung*[3] (Stuttgart, 1980), 65.

Ancient traumas are re-enacted. The unhappy subject, 'gegenwarts-
müde' (99/95), longs to regress to an infantile condition where stress is
absent. As hidden guilts play bo-peep in concealment and revelation,
repressed fears return compulsively in symptom after inventive symptom:

> Ich schreibe gestauchte Zeit. Ich schreibe, was ist, während anderes auch,
> überlappt von anderem, neben anderem ist oder zu sein scheint, während
> unbeobachtet etwas, das nicht mehr da zu sein schien, doch, weil verdeckt, blöd
> dauerte, nun einzig noch da ist: zum Beispiel, die Angst (436/429–30).

This is a very exact built-in abstract of the spatial-temporal scheme of the
novel, and of the narrator's psychological motivation too: here its multi-
layered synchronicities ('während anderes auch') are conceived in terms
of place ('neben anderem') and of time ('nicht mehr ... schien'),
perpetuating hidden fears.

There is a fourth, artificial suspension of time which also has a place in
this novel: that of the unreal fantasies which come from eating the right
kind of mushroom, as Bettina assures Arnim—'Sie wisse, daß der
Fliegenpilz ... Träume mache, die Zeit aufhebe, das Ich erlöse' (359/
352).

Of these aspects of temporal suspension, the ones which appear to
offer the most useful avenues of interpretation are the neurotic and the
poetic: on the one hand, the permanent present of the unconscious, the
regressive flight from the present, repetition-compulsion; and on the
other, the spell cast by story-telling, and the effects of spatial graphics
upon ongoing narration.

They all work against the linear tendencies in the novel. The spell of
story-telling—'in Küchengeschichten Zeit aufzuheben' (11/7)—the
flights into the past, and the permanent present of the figures in the
creating mind run counter to the nine months of the developing foetus.
The regressiveness and repetition-compulsion work against what I take
to be the fundamental theme of the novel, namely, in the long perspective
of satisfactions and deprivations, glut and famine, cooks and eaters,
mothers and children, women and men, the theme of emancipation.
Emancipation, that is, first by way of man's entry into the freedom of
history, but now, since his time has run out, by way of the emancipation
of women (see the poems 'Am Ende' 99/95–6, at the beginning, and
'Mannomann' 547/538–9, at the end).

Now emancipation too, as part of a progressive view of history, implies
change, development, growth, and hence assumes a linear concept of
time. The same linear temporal pattern appropriate to the development
of the embryo towards birth is also appropriate to the development of the

infant into independent adult, and also to the transition from Adamic prehistory—'eine angenehm geschichtslose Zeit' (14/10)—into the freedom to act autonomously in history. Some might call this the Fall; the voice of the Enlightenment called it 'der Ausgang des Menschen aus seiner selbstverschuldeten Unmündigkeit'.[9] But mankind's freedom to act in history has now overreached itself; his enlightened rationality has now produced not full autonomous human beings but clever automata, whose greatest inventions are the instruments of destruction which will suspend time once and for all. Death is at the end of the line. This is the Feminal's argument; the flounder is ready to adopt it to save his skin, and humankind's skin too, of course. And it is the ironical premiss of the novel itself, countered only by the nugatory dream of 'Was Drittes' (10/7). Mitigated by irony after irony, the flounder's final self-accusatory speech for the defence appears to be the—deeply undermined—value-centre of the novel.

There have been many stories of the Fall into freedom and history, from Eve's apple to Freud's band of brothers. Grass adds his version in *Der Butt*. They all entail pain and guilt. In *Genesis* and in *Totem und Tabu*, woman comes off very badly. In the one case, Eve is the agent of temptation, and Adam can blame it all on her. In Freud's 'Just-So story', woman is not even an agent; she is merely the passive object of the primordial rivalry and the occasion rather than the cause of the murder of the Ancient Father.

Mythologically-minded feminists[10] have rejected both myths in favour of the benevolent authority of the Ancient Mother, under whose fruitful sway the masculine combination of rationality with power had no place. There are regressive and non-emancipatory implications in this myth which Grass seizes on. Ironically, he takes over the feminist myth of the golden age of the Great Mother complete with dependent young. No band of murderous brothers these, but a horde of clinging children maintained in contented infancy by the tyranny of gratification. The benevolence is despotic, the place of shelter timeless. This is certainly no place for emancipation and change, but when history and the present and the pressures of adult masculine will and responsibility grow too great, it becomes a safe place of retreat (see the poems 'Gestillt', 70–1/67–8; 'Was uns fehlt', 57–8/54–5; and the last stanza of 'Wie ich mich sehe', 96/92).

---

[9] Immanuel Kant, 'Beantwortung der Frage: Was ist Aufklärung?', *Werke*, ed. Ernst Cassirer, iv (Berlin, 1922), 169. Cf. the flounder's command: 'Ihr müßt Euch entwöhnen' (36/33). Kant's categorical imperative is listed among the destructive 'Ersatzgeburte der Männer' (403/396–7).

[10] See, e.g. Marilyn French, in *Beyond Power* (London, 1985).

Womb modulates into tomb when Ilsebill is represented as the Earth (524/514–15).

Freud designed his myth of the Fall of Man so as to follow the same pattern as the development of individual guilt in the infant's rivalry with the father to possess the mother. And although Grass's fictional anthropology is rather different from Freud's, he too shapes the phylogenetic development of his prehistoric humans as analogous to stages in individual human development. He too represents the paradisal gratifications of prehistory and the subsequent deprivations of the entry into history in terms of the process of infant maturation. And he tells them on the whole developmentally, chronologically, as the flounder advised: from Neolithic to Iron Age, and from oral to anal. No further. There cannot be a defiant Oedipal stage, because there is no Great Father to rebel against. This role is taken by the flounder in his very first words to Edek: 'mein Sohn' (26/23), and it is the flounder as the Great Stepfather who encourages rebellion against Aua. In her golden day, the equation between sexual gratification and nourishment was perfect. Man is represented as an infant dependent on Aua's abundant three breasts. (This imaginative regression is ironized at once, of course, by the adult Ilsebill's tart comment 'männliche Wunschprojektion' (9/5). One of her functions is to act as a reality principle when the more labile narrator wants to regress.) The first step in an ineluctable development takes place when Aua gives way to Wigga, and oral satisfaction gives way to the more contemplative pleasures of the anal stage: making objects, giving gifts, and devotedly defecating in congregation. Again, the imaginative regression to this stage on the part of the narrator is offensive to the adult Ilsebill—'zu gut erzogen', he sighs (244/239). Archaic and infantile levels of experience, no longer available to the emancipated adult, are nevertheless at the call of the imagination still. But the fall from timelessness into history does come—though in *Der Butt* it comes gradually. Since there is no Oedipal Father, there is no revolution, but a series of stages of escape under Wigga and Mestwina, told in the main chronologically. It is accomplished not by a single act but by an evolutionary series which take us into the twilight of the Dark Ages: with Edek's epoch-making discovery of paternity, when man discovers that he too has a place in the life-cycle; with his first attempt at autonomy, when he runs away to join the Goths but comes limping home to Mother, hurt and violated; with his exploitation of metal—Aua may have discovered fire, but Edek put it to use; with his developing skills and sign-making.

The first Month, then, is devoted to the tales of prehistory. In the second Month, man is in history, indeed in civilization: the opening section is actually headed 'Wie wir städtisch wurden'. The primitive satisfactions are over, and with the entry into history the deprivations begin—with Dorothea. Good breasts give way to bad, earth mother to saint, or witch. What is striking, however, is that in this very first *historical* month, where historical sequence has begun, Grass works out the basis of that synchronic view of events and identities which runs counter to the progressive linear development of history as seen by the flounder, and after him, by the 'Endzielmänner'. Similarly, within this very first linear 'chapter', where the second month follows the first, the narrator stages a major disruption in the narrated time: as soon as he brings Edek—himself—into history and chronology, he arranges that his way of telling his story should act to disturb them.

'Im zweiten Monat' has a particularly important function in upsetting both the linear (= progressive, masculine) view of history and any hopeful, forward-looking view of personal relations. The historical deprivations begin with Dorothea; on the narrator's time-level, the last love-affair ends with Maria; and in the history of humankind, the flounder deserts the men for the women, leaping into Maria's arms as once he had into Dorothea's. And at the very stage where the second month should follow the first, Grass makes a huge, hidden, temporal detour into the future—though still, of course, evasively and confusingly employing the narrative past—to a stage much later in the 'now', and identified very late in the novel indeed, only five pages from the end, as 'drei Monate nach der Geburt unserer Tochter' (552/543), i.e. to a time wholly incongruent with the apparent time of this Month, which arithmetic tells us should be November 1973. What he does is to slot into the present narrative time an account of his own return to the place where it all began and where it all so obsessively takes place, to the town, which for all the historical tranformations of its name and appearance, retains, like Aua–Ilsebill, a constant fictional dream-identity: 'Mein Giotheschants, Gidanie, Gdancyk, Danczik, Dantzig, Danzig, Gdańsk' (112/109). That visit will not in fact (fiction?) have taken place until September 1974—the future perfect is an appropriate tense for 'Vergegenkunft'—but this is something the narrator half conceals, quarter reveals. We are led to believe it is November—but the sun is warm. Time appears to be playing tricks—or rather, Grass is playing tricks with time. The return to the new old town is itself upsetting to an orderly sense of chronology. Past and present, change and non-change coincide in the rebuilding 'des historischen Danzig als polnisches Gdańsk' (114/110). Equally unsettling is the utterly arbitrary appearance and disappearance of Prince Philip, prompting the untimely observation that it could just as well have been Schopenhauer! The temporal dimension of the entire episode appears to be Grass's fourth time of 'Vergegenkunft'.

Two factors, psychological and aesthetic, contribute to this sense of temporal insecurity, to the way in which time past and time future are devoured by ever-present place in the Danzig scenes. There is the syndrome of repressed guilt on the one hand—of which more later—and there is the presence of other artistic media through which to view Danzig past and future. Grass/the narrator has returned to make a television film for the thirtieth anniversary of the burning of Danzig in November 1944. But television, with its sequence of immediate images, operating in the dimensions of time and space, has the effect of making everything 'flach gegenwärtig' (114/110), even Möller's seventeenth-century painting of Danzig. This is not the narrator's way, who escapes into past time by way of place:

ich verkrümelte mich ... geschichtlich treppab, bis ich im fortgeschrittenen siebzehnten Jahrhundert die Küchenmagd des alternden Stadtmalers schwanger über den Langen Markt kommen sah (116/112).

And so these pages go on in the fourth time of 'Vergegenkunft'. Embarking in a narrative time which is ten months ahead of the chapter-heading on a story about the fourteenth century, Grass anticipates the seventeenth-century material of the fourth Month, peppers his account of Agnes and Gryphius with present-day language (Opitz is 'ein Doppel-agent', 117/113) as much as with archaic (see Dorothea's rhymes *passim*), and can go back a moment later to 1308, using the present, which is really (really?) the future, only as a point of orientation:

Als der Elektriker endlich kam und unsere drei Lampen ... wieder ... Anton Möllers Zinsgroschenszene auf dem Langen Markt ausleuchteten, hatte ich gerade das siebzehnte Jahrhundert und dessen religiöse Vielfalt verlassen, um zu Beginn des vierzehnten Jahrhunderts—genau: am 17. Mai 1308—der Hinrich-tung der sechzehn pomerellschen Ritter ... zuzugucken ... (117/113–14).

This passage achieves not only a shift in time but also a shift in identity, from narrator to ancient Kashubian groundling. And the shifts continue as the narrator-persona re-emerges to identify that ancient outrage with a modern one close to his heart: the shooting of his friend Jan in the Gdańsk shipyard strikes of December 1970. From then on, the story of Schlichting, the later fourteenth-century swordsmith, and his anorexic wife is shot through with memories of the strike, and also with the account of the current encounter with Jan's widow Maria four years after, and with further episodes of the filming.

This overlaying and overlapping of 1308 with 1632, 1970, and 1974 is summed up in Grass's conversation in the course of filming with the Polish painter and draughtsman Richard Strya, who had also done a series of prints of Dorothea: 'Auf unserem Papier findet das meiste gleichzeitig statt' (127/123). We recall from the orderly lucidities of *Laokoon* that painting is an art in the dimension of space, narrative in the dimension of time. The film, which occupies both, only has the effect of robbing the present of its depth and the past of its existence. But the painter and teller of tales dwell in the present only as one possibility: 'Wir sind immer nur zeitweilig gegenwärtig' (ibid.). It is the graphic artist in Grass, I would suggest, who conceives the possibilities of an ongoing narration which produces the illusion of the simultaneity of art in space. The passage on Ilsebill as landscape is illuminating here. Unobtrusively, Grass turns her into a drawing—though not without other (utopian? obsessive?) resonances; 'Jetzt füllt sie meinen Entwurf' (523/514),[11] and in doing so does not, at first, 'narrate' the picture dynamically. It was an important illustration of Lessing's argument that in representing Achilles' shield Homer did not describe it statically but narrated the process of its making.[12] Grass, on the other hand, describes. The verbs are mainly static—'liegt', 'neigt sich', 'stützt'—and tend to turn into participles—'gelagert', 'gebettet' (523-4/514-5); what movement there is in the paragraph, from item to item, resembles the movement of an eye across a canvas. Might there have been such a drawing, perhaps, among the paralipomena to *Der Butt*? Lessing's categories have been defied. However helpful their clarity may have been in identifying the problem, based as they are on an Enlightenment paradigm of representation, they cease to apply to the text that Grass has written. This very fact is a built-in signal that the reign of the flounder is at an end.[13] Small wonder too that the narrator observes of his seventeenth-century incarnations: 'Ich wollte ja Maler und Dichter zugleich sein' (283/277).

The merging of time into space, then, is one important contributory factor to unsettling any clear sense of sequence in the second Month. The

---

[11] Manheim's translation is less than helpful here. Not implausibly, his knowledge that Grass was once a sculptor makes him translate 'Entwurf' as 'mock-up'. 'Draft' or 'sketch' would fit my argument better. This is not the only occasion when interpretative, loose, or colloquial renderings, or sometimes mere under-translation on Manheim's part, are inadequate to support my argument, which is based on Grass's distinctive German. Distinctive in the sense that, for a fat novel, *Der Butt* has all the density, precision, and large-scale cross-referencing of motif and phrase characteristic of poetic language. The scepticism of the 'Erziehung' motif is blurred, for example, when Manheim translates 'zu gut erzogen' (244/239) as 'much too genteelly'. And he loses the implication of linearity in destruction when he omits the key word from the fish's protest: '*Was danach kam*, kam ohne mich' (460/453), over-interpreting it as: '*Their crimes* were none of my doing.'

[12] G. E. Lessing, 'Laokoon: oder über die Grenzen der Malerei und Poesie', *Werke*, vi (Munich, 1974), 119–23.

[13] Cf. David E. Wellbery, *Lessing's 'Laokoon': Semiotics and Aesthetics in the Age of Reason* (Cambridge, 1984), 245–6.

other is the premature narration of future events: the 1974 visit to film Gdańsk and to meet Maria. Here, I would suggest, the deforming factors are personal and historical grief and guilt and impotence. The two modern episodes in the second Month, Jan's death remembered and the meeting with Maria anticipated, are heavy with them. It is as much from these as from Ilsebill that the narrator is running away into history here. He is pulled obsessively back to them again and again, but there remains something hidden, unspoken, 'etwas, das . . . weil verdeckt, blöd dauerte' (436/429–30). The large-scale temporal diversion is part of a strategy of mystification and evasion which allows guilty omissions to go unnoticed. What is hidden at this stage does not get revealed until the story is retold a second time in its more appropriate temporal position at the end of the novel, three months after the birth, this time with Maria, no longer with Ilsebill, as its recipient.

Now such repeated narrations are frequent in the novel, and they have a number of functions. Some act as résumés, reminders, or as advance surveys of what is to come. The introductory list of 'Neun und mehr Köchinnen' (13–22/9–19), the cheese-making sequence (59–60/56–8), and the summarized deaths of the cooks (455–8/449–52) are of this kind. They are local attempts to hold the vast material together, and they do on a small scale what the nine months do for the novel as a whole. As such, they support its linearity. But some résumés are represented, like so much else, as existing intensely within the present consciousness of whoever-it-is-who-is-telling-the-story—the author-in-distress or his angst-ridden persona, the narrator. This is particularly noticeable in the panic-stricken rehearsal to Maria of his own time-suspending roles, here not as consumer but as consumed:

Neben mir: ich. Außer mir: ich. Mir (als Bär) aufgebunden: das folgsam brummende Ich. Immer entlaufen, zeitflüchtig, hinterrücks. Wo der Geschichte die Latte im Zaun fehlt. Hör mal, Maria: Das war, als Mestwina von mir gelöcherten Bernstein am Hals trug. Von ihren Töchtern und Tochtertöchtern leiten sich Sambor, Mestwin, Swantopolk und die Prinzessin Damroka ab. Nein, das bin ich gewesen, der sich den sprechenden Butt fing. Ich auf der Zunftbank, als die Gewerke aufständisch wurden. Ich saß im Stockturm und löffelte meine letzten Fleck. Und als mich die Pest im Vorbeigehen grüßte. Und als die Kartoffel über die Hirse siegte. Mich hat die große, alles verrührende Köchin gegen die Zeit gerührt. Wie sie mich (immer noch) mit der Schaumkelle klärt. Wie sie mich austeilt gerecht. Wie ich gesäuert ihr mürbe bin. Liebstock und Kümmel, Majoran, Dill. Abgeschmeckt ich. Jan, das bin ich, Maria, nach deinem Rezept (512/503).

Such a catalogue, in reminding us of the dreamer, serves to reaffirm the dream, and once again to suspend time: 'Ich bin der Einschluß. Im Zweifelsfall ich: spätversessen und aufgehoben' (ibid.). In addition, there is another kind of repeated narration: partial and imperfect accounts— 'woran ich mich nicht erinnern will' (99/96)—to which the narrator returns again and again, each time successively dredging up more and more of the story. The tale of Mestwina's execution, for example (91/88), has to be told a second time (107/103) for the narrator to be able to say outright that Edek had betrayed her. The Goths' departure (84/80) is part of the established tribal story before it emerges (106/102) that Edek had gone after them and come limping back, assaulted. And it is long after the celebration of Aua's abundance that the reader learns how in time of famine the Edeks had eaten their Überaua and thereafter ritually repeated the act (267/261); longer still (300/294) before the narrator can bring himself to tell the version in which they killed her with the newly-forged iron urged on them by the Wolf-Butt. The narrative movement in these guilty stories is repetitive, but the circle is not closed; a kind of spiral progress of 'Sich-frei-Erzählen'[14] is under way, an emancipatory process which, unlike the fish's, is not simply linear. It is to this last group, but on a far more overriding scale, that the repeated narration of the Maria episode belongs. It is in the late, second account, 'Dreimal Schweinekohl', that the omissions of the second Month are made good: more of the friendship with Jan, more of the events at the strike that made Maria a widow, the final escape from Ilsebill, the joyless coupling with Maria, the shift of the flounder's allegiance from men to women. However late it comes, all the exuberant tales of the cooks have not been able to hold off for ever the story of personal and historical failure which wanted to be told: 'Ich gebe zu: Billy und Maria drängen.'

Billy too. The events in the second Month are not the only ones to break the holding temporal framework. And India. Both are associated with comparable upsets to the flounder's chronology. Because on the whole the novel maintains a large-scale congruence, not only between the succession of months and the succession of historical periods but also between the months and the sequence of external events in the narrator-author's lifetime,[15] the *in*congruence of the time-scheme in the second

[14] 'Schreiben Sie sich frei' is the advice given the guilt-ridden narrator of *Katz und Maus* by his confessor. A similar would-be therapeutic unburdening is the aim of Oskar Matzerath in *Die Blechtrommel* and Walter Matern in *Hundejahre*, and determines the nature of their story-telling.

[15] The narrator's visit to the Socialist conference at Bièvres in the fifth Month (February, 1974) corresponds to one made by Grass in that month, though not without some temporal track-covering: 'behauptet der Februar, er sei März' (343/336). See 'Sieben Thesen zum Demokratischen Sozialismus', speech held at Bièvres, 24 Feb. 1974, in *Denkzettel*, 189–93. The Guillaume scandal, which culminated in the resignation of Willy Brandt as Chancellor at the beginning of May 1974, is located at the end of the seventh Month (April/May 1974) (450–1/443–4). The baby is born towards the end of June when, according to the novel, representatives of the two Germanies signed an agreement about fishing rights in the Baltic, consequent on the establishment of Permanent Delegations in each state, which were set up in March and opened in June of that year.

Month, with its loop into the future, is a signal of deep disruption. So is the even more upsetting diversion into the past in the eighth Month— seemingly, if fictional arithmetic serves us right, May 1974—with its account of the traumatic events of Ascension Day 1963.[16] The experiences represented in both cannot be accommodated by the flounder's bland progressiveness. The two chapters in question concern Maria and Billy, the two women in his life whom the narrator cannot fit into his series of invented cooks. The painful stories of his personal involvement with them, and their political associations—the politics of Poland and the politics of gender, the guilt of Germany and the guilt of men—are also being held up and held off and held at bay by the invented telling, just as the birth of his daughter and the end of his marriage with Ilsebill are. Billy's story is held up until the eighth Month, Maria's not finished until the ninth.

There is a further episode, of a different order but equally disturbing, which disrupts the congruence between month and datable external event: the visit to India. With the account 'Vasco kehrt wieder'—an unsettling title again, for the first Vasco's departure has yet to be told— Grass makes a temporal leap forward, incorporating his own visit to India in early 1975 into the third Month, seemingly December 1973. Vasco holds the speech 'Nach grober Schätzung' (179/175) which Grass will not have held until February 1975 to the Council of Cultural Relations in New Delhi. Just as the visit feeds the novel, so Grass's speech is nourished by the themes of the longer work:

Ich bin Schriftsteller von Beruf. Ich versuche, gegen die vergehende Zeit anzuschreiben, damit das Vergangene nicht unbenannt bleibt. Zur Zeit sitze ich über einen Manuskript und mache Wörter, die weit ausholen, ins Mittelalter, in die Vorzeit zurücklangen und von essenden, kochenden, hungernden Menschen handeln ... Vergangene Hungersnot sucht ihren Ausdruck. Doch die Zukunft hat uns schon eingeholt ... Die Zeiten sind wie aufgehoben: vergangene Barbarei kommt uns spiegelverkehrt entgegen. Wir meinen zurückzublicken und erinnern dennoch bekannte Zukunft. Der Fortschritt, so scheint es, liegt hinter uns (*Denkzettel*, 217).

Author and narrator were never so close as in the Indian episode, where Grass/Vasco encounters his theme of privation in the flesh. Compelled to relativize the frivolity of his profession against the monstrous reality of the Calcutta slums, he is shocked out of his customary linguistic

---

[16] Of all episodes in *Der Butt*, 'Vatertag' has received most critical attention. See Thomas 1980, Reddick 1983, and other contributors to this volume. I do not propose to add to these here, beyond emphasizing that the sheer monstrosity of what it represents is important to my argument. It too disrupts the linear sequence of time and the rational progressiveness of the fish.

exuberance into the tact of plain prose and the muted discretion of bare, sparse verse. Fictionality recedes. The horror of this episode too is as resistant to accommodation by the flounder's chronology as the Billy and Maria episodes are. All three embody loss and guilt and failure on personal and political levels, which are so traumatic as to defy a rational time-scheme. The Indian famine declares Western political impotence and lays bare the sheer irrelevance of Grass the novelist; Billy's vandalizing represents the most extreme instance of female emulation of male violence and male revenge for the transgression. In her loss, the general and the particular—the narrator is representative man, and he is this man, once engaged to this woman—are horrifically united. Maria's demonstration that she scarcely needs the narrator as a lover leaves him bereft of his manhood, while the appearance of the fish with his message for the women appears to confirm this in more universal terms. The story-teller's occupation's gone.

This last episode raises a further problem related to the convolutions and disruptions which have played havoc with the linearity of the story: the nature of the end. The flounder's sequential relation assumes a beginning, a middle, and an end: a beginning, as Aristotle put it, 'which does not necessarily come after something else' and an end 'which . . . is not itself followed by anything'.[17] Neither formulation is appropriate to *Der Butt*. Aristotle proves as redundant as Lessing. Its very first line, 'Ilsebill salzte nach' (7/3), certainly comes after a great deal else, at the very least the narrator's cooking and her dissatisfaction. And it is the Aristotelian flounder, not the narrator, who demands an end. Recoiling at the end of the seventh Month from the account of Lene Stubbe's death in the concentration camp, and protesting against Billy's story to come, he disowns the men's cause. 'Wissen und Macht habe ich euch verliehen, doch nur Kriege und Elend habt ihr bezweckt . . . Die [Hitler and Stalin and what followed] liegen außer meiner Verantwortung. Was danach kam, kam ohne mich. Diese Gegenwart ist nicht meine. Mein Buch ist geschlossen. Meine Geschichte ist aus' (459–60/453). But the narrator dreams a dream to counter this: men's history may be written off, but the flounder will pass on his wisdom to the women. 'Das Buch geht weiter und die Geschichte auch.' And it does. Even to further horror ('Was danach kam, kam ohne mich' protests the fish), for the eighth Month is 'Vatertag'. But history and the book can go on, past even that: 'Danach ging das Leben weiter' (502/493). Part of the irony here lies in the way 'Danach' restores linearity to the novel and simply enables the ninth

[17] Aristotle, 'On the Art of Poetry', in *Classical Literary Criticism*, tr. T. S. Dorsch (Harmondsworth, 1965), ch. 7, 41.

Month to follow the dead end of the eighth. For despite its internal endings—Jan's death and the end of love between Ilsebill and the narrator—this is above all the month of the birth and the chapter when the forward-looking dream is enacted and the flounder does speak to the women—to Maria, who merges into Ilsebill: 'Schon war sie an mir vorbei. Ich lief ihr nach' (556/547). 'Danach' continues, and history too can go on.[18]

To sum up: the broad chronological line of the novel necessarily implicates the narrator in the men's story and men's historical guilt, but the novel also includes multiple pressures which contribute to subverting the fish's rational chronology and the naïve sequential narrative which depends on a mere 'danach'.[19] This is a modern fairy-tale and therefore 'anders erzählt' (555/545). The complexity of temporal structure is the correlative of loss of masculine nerve and loss of historical faith in all the fish stands for. Grass writes 'gegen die Zeit' out of personal pain and historical failure, setting up a complex temporal system whose manifold devices I have scarcely begun to identify in this essay, and which upsets the advancing successions of linear history, of the nine months' unfolding of the foetus, and of the narrator's advance to emptiness. It is a system which represents events in terms of repetition and suspension, synchronicity and disruption. Past, present, and future coexist as 'Vergegenkunft' in the imagination; infantile levels of experience and archaic identifications persist in the unconscious of the not-so-mature adult; guilt at betrayals past and future insists on being both hidden and revealed. The moral and psychological triggers are guilt and failure, the fear of time, and the death of love. The political premiss is that time has run out for modern, emancipated, well-fed man; its aesthetic rationale lies in the ambitions of Grass the graphic artist to produce in writing, an ongoing art in time, the effects of simultaneity and extra-temporality characteristic of painting as an art in space; and in the aim of Grass the teller of

---

[18] Grass has himself taken pains to point out how each strand of the narrative is open-ended (Arnold 1978, 30).

[19] The idea of linearity is an analytic tool dear to feminist critics, who employ it straight, though Grass in his practice employs it ironically and guiltily. Linear, to Christa Wolf in her *Kassandra* lectures, for example (Darmstadt and Neuwied 1983, 117), means the forward march of the heroic epic, all clashing arms and plotted narrative: sequence is compromised by the need for glory. Instead, she proposes the open, cross-referencing narrative web as the appropriate form for humane (= feminine) values, and the rediscovery of the hidden toils of everyday, 'wo der Geschichte die Latte am Zaun fehlt'. And Grass has provided these too, in abundance. The persiflage of the Feminal should not blind the reader to the fact that Grass has written—monstrously, ironically—a text which has strong feminine characteristics as well as masculine. The feminine, as I have shown, undermines and subverts the masculine, but it is from the union of the two that the text itself is begotten and born.

fairy-tales to suspend time—temporarily—by casting the spell of story-telling.

But for it to be possible for the story to be told at all, 'danach' has to be rescued from the manifold temporal upheavals occasioned in the marriage-story, the nourishment-story, and the men's story by the break-up-story, the famine-story, and the women's story. There is no going back. The answer to the question without a question-mark 'Warum nicht rückentwickeln' is that it can only be done experimentally, in a novel, and only then as—temporary, partial, nine-month, five hundred and fifty-six-page-long—escape from the demands of the present and the future. *Der Butt* sets up an elaborate illusory representation of 'Vergegenkunft' but still exists in the real dimension of linear time. 'Danach' also leads on out of the novel and into the world.

3
Conceptions of History

DAVID JENKINSON

I

There has been considerable disagreement, in the critical and scholarly reactions to *Der Butt*, regarding the role and status of history in the novel. Large claims have been made: Gunzelin Schmidt Noerr, in a largely hostile feminist critique, defines the subject of *Der Butt* as 'die Geschichte der Zivilisation, der Ernährung, der Beziehung von Mann und Frau' (Noerr 1978, 92). Other critics have tended to see the historical episodes either as an aspect of the narrator's self-characterization or as a battleground for the marital warfare that the novel is presumed to be principally about. Some readers have found little interest at all in the historical episodes: Marieluise Janssen-Jurreit likens them to a circus performance (quoted in Arnold 1978, 27), whilst Ronald Hayman—who regards *Der Butt* as a 'ragbag' and its author as being 'like a careless cook, throwing in a little of every ingredient that happens to be at hand'— asserts that 'the attempt to evoke contrasted historical backgrounds is an almost total failure' (Hayman 1985, 65–7). Grass himself appears to deny that the novel has any real historical perspective—'Auf unserem Papier findet das meiste gleichzeitig statt' (127/123), the narrator notes, and 'ich schreibe gestauchte Zeit' (436/429). Yet these and other similar remarks indicate not that *Der Butt* lacks a historical dimension but rather that the historical subject-matter is present in its entirety in the—highly egocentric—consciousness of the narrator, without constituting a continuous narrative into which any development, let alone teleological significance, can be read, and that this subject-matter provides an organizational principle, inasmuch as no historical episode is wholly self-contained. The division of the novel into nine Months does not entail nine neatly separated historical sections: although there is a central core devoted to each 'cook', there is also constant overlap, anticipation, backward reference, and résumé. It will be argued in this essay that, although the larger claims made for the novel's historical content cannot be upheld, and although some of Grass's own statements on the matter need to be treated with caution, the historical subject-matter of *Der Butt* is an important and interesting component of the novel in its own right.

It has been widely assumed that *Der Butt* is at least partly about the history of the emancipation of women, although Grass himself has claimed only that the novel is concerned with the largely anonymous role of women in history, which is not at all the same thing (Raddatz 1977[1], 30). But the novel cannot convincingly be seen as dealing with the progressive emancipation of women from male domination. Rather, the historical episodes serve two purposes. First, they are intended to convey the essential quality of particular historical periods. Second, these episodes dramatize a series of ahistorical variations of basic 'constellations' (Arnold 1978, 28), principally that of an aggressive/inadequate man and an oppressed/rebellious woman. The various cooks both function as focal points and metonyms for the evocation of what Fernand Braudel would call the 'collective mentalities' of various historical eras, and represent basic female types, and they all have exact and explicit correspondences in the members of the contemporary Feminal—correspondences which Grass does not even leave the reader the pleasure of discovering for himself, such store does he set by our being fully aware of them.

Anyone interested in writing a systematic history of the emancipation of women would have, at the very least, to look closely at the progress, in the nineteenth century, towards the reform of divorce and property laws, towards access for women to higher education and the professions, indeed towards any paid work outside the home, at the ideas and influence of such women as Helene Lange and Clara Zetkin, and very much more besides. Whatever Grass's purpose is in his depiction of Sophie Rotzoll and Lena Stubbe, it is clearly not this. Nor are the cooks always seen primarily in terms of their relationships with men: Amanda Woyke and Margarete Rusch in particular have a significance far transcending their relationships with men. In the case of Lena Stubbe, on the other hand, the relationship with her two more or less identical husbands is clearly much more central, serving to indicate the still very subservient and powerless position of women within a political movement purportedly committed to their emancipation.

There are, of course, many different kinds of 'history', ranging from history as biography, which is very easily assimilated into fiction, to quantitative, statistical economic history, which is much more resistant to such assimilation. History as (invented or adapted) biography figures very prominently in *Der Butt*, with its wide spectrum of mythical, invented, half-invented, possibly real, real, and famous characters. Grass both subverts the traditionally popular genre of the historical novel by means of an all-pervading irony, and reasserts it by virtue of organizing almost all his historical material around individual historical or quasi-historical characters. Economic history, on the other hand, with its interest not only in statistics but, more importantly, in the large-scale general patterns of development in economic life, is not only very difficult to fictionalize, it may well also be uncongenial to Grass because of its close association with Marxism, which aims to relate, dialectically, all social phenomena to the base of material production, and which sees conflicts of economic interest as the essential motor of history. The only historical event in *Der Butt* which would be grist to a Marxist mill, the fourteenth-century revolt of the Danzig guilds and its crushing by their patrician rulers, is repeatedly set alongside the events in Gdańsk of December 1970, which constitute for Grass bitter proof that Marxist socialism is a continuation of oppression, not a liberation from it. (It is worth noting here that whereas much of the historical material of *Der Butt* sets out iconoclastically to challenge and subvert received notions such as that of the beneficent rule of Frederick II of Prussia, where the events of December 1970 are concerned, Grass shares the orthodox West European perception.) For the rest, Marxism figures only as one of the numerous varieties of feminist rhetoric which are so exuberantly satirized throughout *Der Butt*, as a closed system of manipulative concepts utterly impervious to counter-indicative facts, however obvious and irrefutable. Hegelian dialectic is similarly dismissed, in occasional references, as yet another rhetorical construct. The stance throughout is that with which Karl Popper has made us familiar:[1] Hegelianism and Marxism are merely two of the many intellectual nostrums generated by the flounder's naïvely mistaken belief in the possibility of linear progress, his invention of 'Götter . . . von Zeus bis Marx' (153/150).

Since today almost any book concerned with history is likely to take at least some account of the analysis of social class and class conflict, Grass's consistent indifference—with the one special exception noted above—to this aspect of history can be seen as part of a more general refusal to write what he regards as school-book history, the 'Unsinn, [den] die Schulbuchgeschichte uns überliefert hat' (91/88). Grass has recorded that during his preparatory research for *Der Butt* he came to realize 'wie sehr unsere Geschichtsschreibung, die sich als authentisch ausgibt, weil sie auf Dokumenten fußt, Fiktion ist: nicht zugegebene Fiktion' (Arnold 1978, 31) and there are numerous references in the novel to the inadequacies of historiography as we know it.

This is not to say that Grass does not sometimes write passages that

---

[1] Karl Popper, *The Poverty of Historicism* (corrected edn.; London, 1961).

accord with generally accepted views of history, most notably perhaps the fictionalized account of the 'revisionist debate' in the SPD in the late nineteenth century (see Tudor, 1988). He is also fond, overfond perhaps, of detailed, densely factual narrative history, thick with names and dates, concerning his beloved Danzig (just as he tends to assume a limitless interest on his readers' part in the minutiae of foodstuffs). Grass's attitude towards Danzig and its past is here, as in so many of his works, what Nietzsche, in one of his *Unzeitgemäße Betrachtungen*, called 'pietätvolle Historie': an affectionate, even reverent celebration of his own roots. Elsewhere Grass offers us potted history in comic-strip style, especially in the early prehistorical sections: individualized characters and simplified action are used to evoke, in a flippant, facetious tone, an image of what one might, in the absence of any real evidence, more or less plausibly imagine life to have been like at that time. Other occasional passages seem, in their disingenuous simplicity, to be intended as parodies of conventional structured narrative history; they are reminiscent of Maria, Lady Callcott's nineteenth-century patriotic classic *Little Arthur's History of England* (first published in 1835). They suggest the view that such history so oversimplifies the chaos and complexity of the real world as to be childishly simplistic, and furthermore always serves a crudely didactic intention. Some examples from *Der Butt* are the first page of the section 'Wie wir städtisch wurden' (111/107–8), the decision to canonize Dorothea von Montau (161/157), and Bürgermeister Ferber's naval expedition to Denmark (231/225–6).

The most striking manifestation of Grass's hostility to conventional historiography is his consistent marginalization of what we normally think of as major historical characters and events. Examples are the very fleeting references to famous women in history, such as Cleopatra and Joan of Arc (49/46), the destruction of Rome as the end result of the migrations of races (105/101), the Black Death of 1347–8 (169/165), the sinking of the Spanish Armada (205/201), Luther's nailing of his Theses to the door of the church in Wittenberg in 1517 (mentioned only as the year in which Margarete Rusch takes her nun's vows). The Seven Years War is scarcely mentioned in the episode of Amanda Woyke's meeting with Frederick the Great, just as the Thirty Years War plays only a very shadowy role in the background of the Agnes Kurbiella section. It is perhaps in the same spirit of provocative indifference to textbook history that the narrator here and there gives slightly incorrect dates (though never in his lengthy accounts of the history of Danzig). Thus the French Revolution is playfully concealed in the date on which the flounder is first caught by Edek, 3 May 2211 BC, four thousand years earlier, *almost* to the day (it was on 5 May 1789 that the Abbé Sièyes demanded that the States

General be declared a National Assembly and thus started the Revolution). Similarly, the history books give 23 April 997 as the date of the assassination of Adalbert of Prague (it is his day in the Saints' Calendar); the novel has it variously as April 994 (15/12)[2] and 997 (91/87). These (presumably intentional) 'errors' may be intended to indicate the narrator's deeply interested but somewhat cavalier (because egocentric) attitude to history, which can also be seen as one motive for the far more significant alteration to the historical record in the Adalbert von Prag episode, viz. that in *Der Butt* the assassin is a woman, Mestwina, not a male priest as history, written by men for men in the interests of male domination, has recorded (109–10/105–6).

Describing the genesis of *Der Butt*, Grass has stated:

> Zu Anfang wußte ich nur eins, ich will über die Entwicklung oder die Geschichte unserer Ernährung schreiben; bei dieser Arbeit bemerkte ich, daß ich einen zweiten Bereich geschichtlicher Entwicklung mit berichten mußte, nämlich den anonymen Anteil der Frauen an unserer Geschichte (Raddatz 1977[1], 30).

It was not until a year later that Grass conceived the idea of using the tale of the fisherman and his wife as a structural element of the novel. The narrator makes an identical statement to Sieglinde Huntscha (150/147), and the opening of the novel precisely reflects this genesis: Ilsebill and the narrator eat before they do anything else. The view that the theme of the novel is the history of food *tout court* has remained Grass's (no doubt convenient) stock response to interviewers, to whom he is fond of claiming that he is filling a gap left by historians; he has even used some of his substantial earnings from *Der Butt* to fund a literary prize to 'encourage the writer's historical and prophetic role' of exploring 'areas of the past that the historian is powerless to reach' (Smyth 1978, 37).

Things are, however, not quite what they seem here. The reader of the interview with Robin Smyth may become suspicious when Grass claims that the history of food includes the history of excretion ('The turd also has its place in the cycle of eating'). The notion of a history of excretion is a manifest absurdity, and although Grass may succeed in extracting a certain interest from the theme of changing *attitudes* towards excretion, the reader may well suspect that this statement is no more than a rationalization, the purpose of which is to allow Grass to pursue those anal and faecal interests (clearly erotic rather than historical or anthropological) which he is as determined to share with the reader as the narrator is to share them with Ilsebill, on equally spurious grounds.

The role of food in *Der Butt* is in fact less prominent than Grass is fond of asserting. The degree of attention paid to it is very variable, and it

---

[2] The English translator has 'corrected' the error here.

clearly often has metaphorical rather than literal-historical significance, for instance in the case of Amanda Woyke's potato soup, though Grass does of course give us a great deal of authentic information in that episode about the spread of the potato. His thesis that changes in eating habits have had a substantial effect on history is indeed at its strongest here, though Grass is by no means the first to realize this: Redcliffe Salaman established it irrefutably in 1946.[3] For readers interested in pepper and spices, the details given by Grass in connection with Margarete Rusch are confirmed and supplemented by Henry Hobhouse,[4] who, like Grass, attributes the post-Renaissance European expansion largely to the effects of the pepper trade (he also examines the role of quinine, sugar, tea, cotton, and potatoes). But elsewhere in *Der Butt* the inclusion of details of foodstuffs does not remotely amount to a history of nutrition, nor demonstrate any substantial effects of changes in nutrition on the course of history. We are told that the flounder gives lectures on 'Die Zusammenhänge von Hungersnöten, Heeresbewegungen und Epidemien' (293/287), but these lectures are not included in the text. Grass has moreover built into the novel a clear admission that he was in fact deluding himself in his original belief that his prime interest was anything other than aesthetic: in the section 'Vasco kehrt wieder', which gives the genesis of *Der Butt* in some detail, against the background of the hell of starvation in present-day Calcutta, Vasco reflects on the book which one *ought* to write (179/175), i.e. a history of famine, but the episodes which he envisages there are not in fact elaborated in the novel, and Vasco admits that his real aims are less lofty than he would like to believe himself and have others believe. The whole section emphasizes the illusoriness of Vasco's belief that his aim is to enlighten, and thus perhaps to help, a suffering humanity; his real interest, in matters of nutrition as elsewhere, is aesthetic and creative, verging on an aestheticism which does not stop short even at the spectacle of mass starvation: 'vergeblich verbietet sich Vasco . . . Schlafleichen schön zu finden' (181/178). The tension expressed here is of course familiar to all students of Grass's works, and we should not be surprised that Grass, for whom a recipe is a fit subject for a poem,[5] occasionally parodies and ironizes his own rationalization of his voracious interest in food into a supposedly historical interest. The narrator notes: 'Als der Butt nun steinzeitliche Gerichte hersagte . . . schrieb das Publikum eifrig mit' (52/48); old recipes are modishly adopted by various factions of the feminist gather-

---

[3] Redcliffe Salaman, *The History and Social Influence of the Potato* (London, 1946).

[4] Henry Hobhouse, *The Seeds of Change* (London, 1985).

[5] The dish of lamb with pears and string beans described on the first page of *Der Butt* is also the subject of one of the poems in the collection *Die Vorzüge der Windhühner* (p. 7).

ing; and the flounder reduces even Christianity to an episode in the history of eating—'die [christliche Religion] gründe nun mal auf Fastenzeit und Fresserei im Wechselspiel' (135/132).

The history of nutrition is part of that history of material life which has long been the concern of the 'nouvelle histoire' associated with the French historians Fèbvre, Le Roy Ladurie, and above all Fernand Braudel (of whose work Grass does not appear to have been aware).[6] To read *Der Butt* is in places, e.g. in the account of 'Schwadengrütze' (82–3/79), very like dipping into Braudel's inexhaustibly interesting book, where one may read in some detail about the history of pepper, and where the role of the potato, the 'miracle crop', and its early success in Germany (and Ireland) are briefly documented. Braudel's stance towards his material may assist us in the evaluation of *Der Butt*. He stresses the difference between 'material history', which is concerned with the concrete specifics of food, clothing, etc., and economic history, with its much more abstracting, conceptualizing, and organizing approach to its material. Braudel claims a humanizing potential for the study of material history: it reminds us of our common humanity; it implies a critique of contemporary consumerism by reminding us of the very modest standards of material life of most people at most times in history, including the present; it helps to relativize the widespread limitation of the notion of cultural history to the history of the creative arts; it sensitizes us to the fact that in our own time material life is the area of the most sweeping, speedy, and still accelerating change—far more so than the economic, political, or cultural spheres.[7] The first poem in *Der Butt*, 'Worüber ich schreibe' (11–13/8–9), establishes precisely these Braudelian perspectives.

At the opposite pole to Braudelian micro-history are those broad philosophical patterns into which Schiller (in the essay 'Was heißt und zu welchem Ende studiert man Universalgeschichte?') claimed that the facts of history must be organized before they can satisfy the human spirit. All critics have agreed that in *Der Butt* any teleological conception of history is unambiguously rejected; history is here seen as a Nietzschean 'ewige Wiederkehr des Gleichen', a cyclical process of unending violence

---

[6] Fernand Braudel, *Civilisation matérielle et capitalisme 1400–1800* (Paris, 1967); English edn. *Capitalism and Material Life 1400–1800* (London, 1973); did not appear in German until 1985.

[7] Braudel makes the point memorably by inviting the reader to imagine a visit to Voltaire at Ferney: 'The men of the eighteenth century were [our] contemporaries on the level of ideas. Their minds and passions were the same as ours or at least near enough to prevent total disorientation. But if we spent a few days with the master of Ferney, all the details of material life, even his personal hygiene, would shock us' (Braudel, *Capitalism and Material Life*, x.).

created and sustained by men, who lack the wisdom to remain in the
ahistorical realm of women. The narrator's first bid to be part of history
by participating in the migration of races leads to his being sodomized by
a toothless Goth, and subsequent consequences of that ambition are no
less distressing. From the perspective of the 'Kürbishütte' the Thirty
Years War has never ended, history is, as it is for James Joyce's Stephen
Dedalus, 'a nightmare from which I am trying to awake'. Noel L.
Thomas spells out this conception of history, and makes the important
point that the section 'Vatertag', to which there has been so much
objection for its appalling and allegedly gratuitous violence, is to be seen
as the culmination of that conception (Thomas 1980, *passim*). On all
levels, trivial or momentous, life is cyclical recurrence: on the first page of
the novel Ilsebill and the narrator quarrel just as men and women
quarrelled four thousand years ago; even the glaciers that once covered
the Danzig region will, the narrator assures us, return one day (64/60), a
return which is also forecast in the second, suppressed version of the
Märchen (356/349). Just as patriarchy succeeded matriarchy before the
dawn of recorded history, so matriarchy may well, with the flounder's
help, re-establish itself at some future date.

It is, however, worth pointing out that the reiterated contrast of
masculine 'history' and feminine 'Geschichtslosigkeit' is ironically
undermined from the outset. It is Aua who brings fire from the wolf in
heaven in her 'Tasche', just as the flounder brings a rock sample from
Sweden in *his* 'Kiementasche', and women are no less vulnerable than
men to the lure of material progress: Aua uses the kitchen knife in secret,
Ilsebill craves the dishwasher. And as if to prepare for that distant day
when the political world will be controlled by women, Aua already uses
the language of political repression when she bans mathematical research:
'Sie werde jegliche Spekulation unter Strafe stellen. In seinen Anfängen
müsse man den Irrationalismus bekämpfen' (33/29–30). Mestwina's
assassination of Adalbert, Margarete Rusch's vengeance for her father's
execution, and Sophie Rotzoll's patriotic francophobia likewise give the
lie to any easy equation of 'feminine' with 'peaceable'. What the flounder
sees in Ilsebill is not a repository of gentle, peace-loving femininity (it
would be hard indeed for anyone to see this) but 'soviel unverbrauchter
Wille zur Macht' (153/150).

Grass has included in *Der Butt* a brief discussion of the Snail's
philosophy of slow progress, and the dangerous lure of the Great Leap
(336–8/330–2), taking up ideas familiar from *Aus dem Tagebuch einer
Schnecke*, but with considerably less acrimony towards the Great
Leapers. (This may perhaps be connected with Grass's withdrawal from
active politics during the writing of *Der Butt*.) But the overall impression

of pessimism left by the novel is more in accord with Grass's recent pronouncement: 'Heute weiß ich ... Die Schnecke ist uns zu schnell.'[8] At the point in human history which we have now reached, the best we can hope for is no further change at all. The flounder may, with his irrepressible optimism, look forward to 'eine neue Phase der Humanent-wicklung' (42/39), now that he has decided to switch his allegiance to women, but by the end of the novel any grounds for such optimism have been wholly eroded. What good to us will be a shift of power from men to women, which is all that Grass appears to expect from the further liberation of women? Grass may repeatedly assure his interviewers that 'das Leben geht weiter' (e.g. Arnold 1978, 30; Casanova 1979[1], 179), as if this mitigated the novel's pessimism. But the closing sentence of 'Vatertag' does not allow us to see any such mitigation in that statement.

We must not make the mistake of identifying Grass with either the flounder, the narrator, or the Feminal; all three have a vested interest in a particular, limited conception of history. The flounder is on trial for his life and hence interested principally in 'einen ihn entlastenden historis-chen Zusammenhang' (174/171). He can thus conceive of history only as progress, led by men but to the advantage, by and large, of women also. He is a rational humanist, opposed to revolutionary violence and firmly believing in non-violent progress through technology, changing social institutions, and the evolution of ideas. This belief has led only to one disillusionment after another, but the flounder remains incorrigible.

The narrator, for his part, sees himself and his problems as the real subject of history. He has undoubtedly a genuine passion for history, a passion which is an essential part of his make-up, but at the same time history is for him principally a circuitous route to get closer to Ilsebill (cf. the poem 'Ilsebill zugeschrieben', 167/163–4). 'Denn eigentlich, Ilsebill, ging es immer um mich' (95/91) he insists, a perspective no less restricting than that of the flounder, and the product of an infantile narcissism which the following poem 'Wie ich mich sehe' articulates. This is the narcissism of the self-aware man who supports the cause of women—notwithstanding his ironic awareness of the deficiencies of the more strident varieties of feminism—but is more interested in his own complex ethical-psychological insights than in actual women—a failing of which women readers have not been slow to accuse Grass himself. But it cannot be Grass's intention that he should be identified with this devious, self-serving narrator; a reader who did this would get the novel badly out of focus. The Grass who wrote the 'Danzig Trilogy', to say nothing of the active political campaigner, has a greater interest in the

---

[8] Günter Grass, 'Die Vernichtung der Menschheit hat begonnen', *Die Zeit*, 3 Dec. 1982, 45.

world and its history than simply as a reflection of his own problems with women. The insistence, which pervades this entire novel, that history is real, that it exists in its own right and demands to be taken seriously by any educated person,[9] is not undermined by the philosophical common-place that history, like all human knowledge, is ultimately the creation of a human mind which selects, organizes, and evaluates data within a particular paradigm of background assumptions.

The Feminal insist on seeing the entire past only in relation to *their* present aspirations, struggles, and resentments. They smother all history in shrill ideological rhetoric, subordinating it, like the flounder and the narrator, to their own special pleading. Their crude poster, which turns Sophie's involuntary virginity into a desire to castrate men, indicates the level and quality of their 'interpretations' of history. The very conception of the Feminal may, of course, appear to reduce all history to a vast battleground for the sexes, on to which the author projects his own marital disputes, ranging from the migraine which fills the house when a dinner party has to be cancelled and the apocalyptic ferocity unleashed by the absence of toilet-paper, to the argument over the prehistoric process, speculatively charted by Bachofen and Bebel, of the transition from a matriarchal to a patriarchal society.[10] Marital disputes do of course loom large in *Der Butt*, and both partners regularly seek support in history for their various points of view, but one can no more equate the author with the wholesale reductionism of the Feminal than with the position of either the flounder or the narrator. The feminist perspective is seldom absent for long, but it is subverted throughout by sustained satire: the members of the Feminal can never agree on their interpreta-tion of any historical episode, nor on any conception of what history might have been like if they had had the making of it (50/47–8); all they can agree on is a handful of female-chauvinist platitudes to the effect that women are more peace-loving, sensitive, fair-minded, serene, and genu-inely creative than men—none of which superior qualities are visible in the novel any more than they are in the real world. The members of the Feminal do not, of course, lack articulacy or eloquence, and for much of the time they succeed in imposing on their audience their view that their disputes over the interpretation of history are of greater interest than

---

[9] For Starusch, in *örtlich betäubt*, the teaching of German logically entails the teaching of history: he is 'Studienrat für Deutsch und also Geschichte'.

[10] This interpretation appears at its crudest in Hellmuth Karasek's reference to: '*Der Butt*, wo die ganze gute alte Kaschubei herhalten muß, um ein heutiges Wehwehchen zu übertönen, den Ärger mit den Frauen, die Misere mit der Ehe' (Karasek 1977, 103).

history itself (93/89). Not a few readers of *Der Butt* have been similarly persuaded, including Eva Figes and, less predictably, Neal Ascherson.

The reader is, however, not tied to any such limiting perspective. The most cursory reading of *Der Butt* suggests that there is so much history in it, so massively *there*, that it must have a significance over and above these prejudiced appropriations. There is in fact a fourth perspective, Grass's own, that of the author who, through narrative invention, metaphor, and symbol, offers us the distilled essence of various historical eras. The narrator's question in the poem 'Aufschub': 'welches|Jahrhundert spielen wir jetzt?' (216/212), indicates this central concern. Contemporary reality is too close at hand for this 'playful' metaphorical distillation to be possible; hence, as the narrator admits, Billy and Maria, the two extra 'cooks' added to the nine principals, although they urgently demand attention, are 'noch ungenau, weil mir die beiden zu nahe bekannt wurden' (22/18). But past historical epochs which have played a major part in shaping contemporary civilization can be thus evoked, and it is to Grass's treatment of these past epochs that the remainder of this essay will be devoted.[11]

II

Three principal aspirations may be said to have set their stamp on the modern world since the end of the Middle Ages: the liberation of the body, the liberation of the mind, and the liberation of human society. We may loosely but conveniently associate these aspirations with the Renaissance, the Age of Reason, and the Age of Revolution. In the episodes concerning Margarete Rusch, Amanda Woyke, and Sophie Rotzoll together with Lena Stubbe, Grass offers us images of these three strands of our history: secular humanism, applied rationality, and political idealism.

The Liberated Body: Margarete Rusch

The major historical events that come immediately to mind when considering the period of the Renaissance, viz. the Protestant Reformation and its consequences, are, like so many major historical events in *Der Butt*, relegated to a very marginal position, indeed offhandedly dismissed as 'die Wortspalterei der Reformationszeit' (123/119). Far more important for Grass is the fact that 'dicke Gret' is born in the same year (1498) in which Vasco da Gama discovered the sea-route to India: the date signals the beginning of an age of expansion and discovery of both the

---

[11] For Grass's fictionalization of prehistory and the Gothic Dorothea von Montau see the essays in this volume by Joyce Crick and Timothy McFarland.

world and the individual personality, where new continents are discovered and where the wealthy learn languages, collect works of art, and
cultivate music as part of a secularized conception of the good life. A
contemporary of Rabelais, Gret embodies the new humanism, with its
celebration of the individual and his carnal existence. Joyously she
drowns the Pope and Luther alike in her laughter (17/13), indifferent to
history, living entirely in the present (301/295), but also inexhaustibly
interested in the life going on around her, involved in administration,
politics, and far-sighted enterprises involving the vital pepper trade. To
the narrator, in the poem 'Wie ich ihr Küchenjunge gewesen bin' (176–7/
172–3), she appears to embody an ideal blend of security, in her massive
maternal femininity, and purposiveness, in her all-embracing delight in
human life. In Margarete Rusch the deep contradictions and oppositions
that had marked medieval man's view of himself are unified: life and
death, sex and spirit. At the 'Henkersmahlzeit' for her father she boldly
sets life against death, preparing the meal in the executioner's kitchen
and serving it in the dungeon; her dishes 'lullen die Todesfurcht ein'
(195/191). Her semi-castration of Hegge, carried out 'nur aus Not und
verzweifelter Fürsorge' (302/296), saves his life; on the other hand it *is* her
favourite story—unlike Amanda Woyke, whose stories are always 'von
anderen und deren Mühsal' (303/297). Similarly her ministrations both
reduce the narrator to impotence and restore his potency, and although
she dies by choking on a fish-bone, she reaches a ripe old age first.

Gret's overwhelming vitality always purports to serve life, but it has
severe limitations for all that. In her religion of sex, with its extremes of
cheerful blasphemy, there is no place for love, 'dieses Wimmergefühl'
(201/197). The loss of love is a high price to pay for the liberation of the
body and the secularization of the sexual mystery; Grass has lamented
this loss in our own time, whilst expressing scorn for the alternative
notion of 'Partnerschaft' propagated by what he calls the 'theologisch-
soziologische Trivialliteratur' (Raddatz 1977, 30). Margarete may appear
to represent a beneficent regression to Aua's comprehensive gratification
of masculine needs, but this return to an effective matriarchy entails an
indifference to notions of commitment, fidelity, and paternity which
anticipates a widespread attitude among self-styled liberated women of
our own day. Gret stands at the beginning of a development not only
towards the uninhibited enjoyment of physical pleasures but also towards
a much more problematic cool hedonistic permissiveness. This flatulent,
gluttonous, sexually voracious nun is a profoundly ambivalent figure.
Her cultivation of a wholly uninhibited polymorphous perversity, especially in the orgy of liberated anality 'Der Arsch der dicken Gret', with its
ecstatic 'wer küßt hier wen?' (209/205), a line which occurs also in both

Hundejahre and the poem 'Kirschen'[12]—all this clearly appeals deeply to the narrator and, it can scarcely be doubted, to Grass. 'Endlich will ich die dicke Gret, wie sie in mir hockt, freisetzen' (210/206), the narrator exclaims, in the same spirit as his admission of sadistic fantasies of torturing Ilsebill: 'Ach, die Gedanken! Endlich ausgesprochen' (291/285). Whether we are dealing here principally with a strategy in the narrator's marital warfare or whether Grass is giving free rein, in fantasy, to his own darker desires, we have in a more general way an image of where the total freedom from sexual restraints can lead. Grass does not pursue this idea (as does for example the film *Last Tango in Paris*) to the point of the tragic insight that a man can be driven to make sexual demands of such an appalling nature that no woman's love can accommodate them; nor is the point made anywhere in *Der Butt* that these demands alone would be sufficient to explain the breakdown of the narrator's marriage. Grass does, however, take Margarete a considerable distance along the path towards the Marquis de Sade in the episode in which (with a Kafkaesque literalization of the notion of 'Schweinerei') she substitutes a pig for herself, dressed in her nightshirt and filled with hot bricks, for the benefit of Moritz Ferber, who is thereby rendered impotent for life (though he becomes a rich bishop by way of compensation). The enforced three-day orgy of eating and defecation which is Hegge's punishment for iconoclasm is a similarly alarming extreme, where a direct linguistic link is made between Gret's behaviour and the disastrous lesbian activities of 'Vatertag': Gret is credited with having created the freedom within which 'weiblicher Humor ... die ganz große Sau loslassen darf' (224/219; cf. 462/455 in 'Vatertag'). It is neither surprising nor reassuring that the women in the audience at the flounder's trial take to Gret enthusiastically, several of them seeking positions as prioresses after the discussion of her case is concluded.

Religious Tolerance and the 'Dialektik der Aufklärung': Amanda Woyke

If Grass has far-reaching doubts about the liberation of the body, his allegiance to the enterprise of the liberation of the mind is firmer, though by no means unreserved. The Agnes Kurbiella section, with its contrast between the witch-burning fanaticism of the religious warfare which engulfed Europe in the early seventeenth century, and the first tentative pursuit of religious tolerance in the devious diplomatic activities of Martin Opitz, is thematically thin in several respects. It is possible that

---

[12] Cf. the discussion of 'Kirschen' by Leonard Forster in Hilde Domin (ed.), *Doppelinterpretationen: Das zeitgenössische Gedicht zwischen Autor und Leser* (Frankfurt, 1974), 227–9.

Grass already had his next novel, *Das Treffen in Telgte*, in mind and was hence inhibited from offering a full portrait of the seventeenth century here. But this section serves at least as a prelude to the far more detailed and interesting evocation of the Age of Reason in those parts of the novel organized around the figure of Amanda Woyke, who memorably embodies the rational concern for human welfare of the Enlightenment at its best, a motherly sustaining concern for her fellow human beings. Grass clearly has nothing but sympathy for Amanda's anguish at the death of her three young children from starvation (there is none of his usual omnipresent irony here), and nothing but approval for her vision of a global war against poverty. Indeed, he points out that the survival of the human race may well depend on the willingness of the world's rulers to wage such a joint war. But he is also well aware that such a project must depend on the very unreliable support of voters whose limited vision is bitingly satirized in the poem 'Übers Wetter geredet' (317–8/311): 'Bei uns bleibt genug zu tun. | Die vielen kaputten Ehen.' Measured against this complacent myopia, Amanda's vision has a heroic grandeur. On a less elevated plane, her fruitless defence of the notion of small lease-holders with incentives to produce, against greedy and short-sighted enclosure policies, likewise commands assent as a genuinely progressive notion. Furthermore, Amanda's rationalism is genuinely liberating in that it aspires to the only genuine freedom that there is: freedom for everybody, not just for women.

But the 'Dialektik der Aufklärung' is such that belief in the emancipation of the human mind and the solution of material problems through the application of liberated reason and science has produced in our own day 'one-dimensional man' (H. Marcuse) with his 'instrumental reason' (Adorno), devoted to the endless elaboration of a technological civilization deeply inimical to real human needs and posing a threat to our very survival. Rational and humane as she is, Amanda, with her Maoist utopia of a communally fed, classless society, is not wholly free from a spiritually arid utilitarianism. Her belief in the universal panacea of potato flour indicates a proneness to naïvely simplistic thinking (it cures Ilsebill's migraine and exorbitant demands, but only for a week), while her dream of a vast potato field is anticipated in Esau's fantasy of drowning in a sea of lentils (194/190). As George Moore remarks in Tom Stoppard's play *Jumpers*, using an image strikingly close to Grass's, a wholly rational approach to human life would result in the world becoming one vast soya-bean field. In later glimpses of Amanda Woyke, we see her, now literate, reading from the newspaper to Romeike, without comment, the terrible events of the French Revolution, a further product of the Age of Reason, and she is reported to have died with a vision of atomically fuelled 'Großküchen' (456/450), an ominous reminder of the perils to which uncritical belief in technological progress has brought us.

In the main, however, Amanda is seen positively; to suggest that she is 'satirised mercilessly' (O'Neill 1982, 8) is to miss the point of the entire episode. The more negative aspects of the heritage of the Enlightenment are embodied in the figure of Count Rumford (who actually has some claim to be a real benefactor: he was one of the founders of the Royal Institution and invented the Rumford Stove). Rumford not only turns Amanda's splendid potato soup into a dismally stingy and unpalatable 'Kleister', he also develops her charitable and sensible practice of encouraging beggars to work for their soup into the notorious institution of the workhouse, which is scarcely distinguishable from a prison and does indeed within a few years become a prison, a motif which succinctly encapsulates Michel Foucault's critique of the institutionalization of cruelty and inhumanity in the wake of the Enlightenment.[13] Rumford believes that he, like Amanda, is serving 'die große und wichtige Wahrheit, daß keine politische Ordnung wirklich gut sein kann, wenn sie nicht dem Wohl der Allgemeinheit dient' (324–5/318). But his actual, historically authentic, major achievement is the sudden arrest, registration, and incarceration of all the beggars in Munich, including children, in a workhouse, over whose entrance is written in golden letters: 'Hier werden keine Almosen empfangen!' (326/319). Entrances to concentration camps were embellished with a similar slogan: 'Arbeit macht frei'. It is in the arms of Count Rumford, who has debased all her noble ideals, that Amanda dies, passing on knowledge to the last. It is from her that her granddaughter Sophie Rotzoll inherits the belief in the power of reason. What Amanda lacks, however, is Grass's own 'melancholische Einsicht . . . daß der Fortschritt sich immer wieder aufhebt' (Raddatz 1977[1], 30).

The Liberation of Society: Sophie Rotzoll and Lena Stubbe

Amanda Woyke (1734–1806), unlike any of the other cooks in *Der Butt*, makes history by promoting the spread of the potato. But when she dies, with Napoleon at the height of his powers, in the year of the formal abolition of the Holy Roman Empire (which might well be thought of as the symbolic culmination of the Enlightenment), Amanda is still a serf. The *political* liberation of man has, in Germany at least, scarcely begun. Frederick the Great's commitment to the abolition of serfdom is thwarted, for her, by the efforts of August Romeike. Similarly, it is not Napoleon who determines the lives of Sophie Rotzoll and Friedrich

---

[13] Michel Foucault, *Surveiller et punir: La naissance de la prison* (Paris, 1975).

Bartholdy but his one-time adjutant Jean Rapp.[14] Most human lives
depend less on great men and their ideas than on the very imperfect small
men who apply and traduce those ideas in practice.

For all that Sophie inherits her grandmother's belief in reason, she is
herself a romantic rather than a rational revolutionary. The reading of
revolutionary books has left her 'heillos kurzsichtig' (20/17), irremediably
deluded by the belief that it is great ideas that shape the world, and that
freedom is to be achieved by revolution and war. The solitary 'Steinpilz',
to which Napoleon is likened (369–70/363), may stand proudly, 'als gäbe
es unverletzt die schöne Idee' (366/360), but it is always accompanied by
the psychedelic 'Fliegenpilz'. No ideal without illusions, no ceps without
agarica, and for Sophie no revolutionary commitment without sublim-
ated sexuality. A secular equivalent of Dorothea von Montau (20/17), she
derives her ardent idealism from her love for Friedrich, a stuttering
schoolboy who is safe because he is imprisoned and hence unattainable,
'entrückt und nicht abzunutzen' (371/365) like the figures on Keats's
Grecian urn. Friedrich, for his part, draws his inspiration indiscrimin-
ately from Danton, Marat, and Robespierre, and as a result goes straight
to prison for most of his adult life. His story is a poignant tragedy of the
reality of the 'verratene Revolution' (382/375), a reality which is always
personal and individual: looking for mushrooms in the forest, Fritz and
Sophie never meet the 'Weltgeist zu Pferde' (Hegel's description of
Napoleon, also quoted in *Aus dem Tagebuch einer Schnecke*) but 'nur
immer uns' (399/392). As for the French Revolution itself, its dictatorial
savagery and bloodthirstiness are gruesomely enacted by the poisoned
guests at the dinner party which only Jean Rapp, the intended victim,
survives (384/377–8).

Behind the revolutionary rhetoric which they ape lie wasted lives,
betrayed ideals, men rotting in prison from one regime to the next. Like
the deromanticized 'enfant perdu' of Heine's poem, Friedrich remains in
prison, thanks to Jean Rapp's infatuation with Sophie, throughout the
years of the Napoleonic 'liberation' and into another era of reaction, 'so
korrekt wechselten die Systeme' (382–3/376). When he is released, it is,
ironically, by royal pardon. He leaves prison having long since forgotten
the reason for his incarceration, a man old and weary before his time,
with no energy left for either love or revolution. Sophie dies a virgin, her
love remaining unconsummated as her ideal of freedom remains unreal-
ized. Friedrich dies 'im Revolutionsjahr 48, ohne zu begreifen, um
welche Freiheit es diesmal ging' (402/395), Sophie a year later when, with
the dissolution of the National Assembly at the point of Prussian

---

[14] Jean Rapp was Governor of Danzig 1807–9, defended the city under siege 1813–14,
and wrote memoirs (1823) which are known to be unreliable.

bayonets, the aspirations inherited from the French Revolution may be said to have finally died in Germany. By this time Sophie's idealism has been wholly eroded and turned to murderous hatred, the French occupation having replaced her revolutionary internationalism with a fervent patriotism. The long-term consequences of this development are too well known to require elaboration.

From the wasted lives of Sophie, Fritz, and all similar victims of romantic illusions and actual *realpolitik*, something at least is salvaged: a genuine humanitarian concern for the poor in Sophie's feeding of the neighbouring children, her one real achievement (the flounder's intervention having foiled her attempt to poison Jean Rapp). It may be uncertain whether anything is left, by the end, of Sophie's republicanism, whether her last words are 'Es lebe die Republik!', or 'Rehrücken in Aspik!' (456/450), but in the year of her death Lena Stubbe is born; the struggle will go on.

Where Sophie is an idealist, Lena is a sober pragmatist; in the romantic and the realist the two poles of the political life of the nineteenth century are contrasted. Where Sophie dies a virgin and draws inspiration from the realm of ideas, Lena is a war-widow twice over and 'immer von grauer Praxis umwölkt' (21/17). The dates of her life mark, as Grass reminds us, important stages in the history of the working-class movement in Germany: born in 1849, she comes to maturity in the 1860s, the decade of the legalization of German trade unions and the founding of the political parties which subsequently joined together to form the SPD; in the 1880s she is involved in strikes (the unification of Germany in 1871 being passed over with Grass's by-now familiar indifference to the events highlighted by conventional historiography); in 1913, on the eve of the First World War, which will take her second husband from her just as it will mark the demise of socialist pacifism and internationalism, she travels to Zürich for Bebel's funeral; and she dies at the age of 93 in Stutthof concentration camp in 1942, with the socialism to which she has devoted her life at its absolute nadir. Her 'proletarisches Kochbuch', which enshrines all her belief in the working-class movement, is destroyed when Soviet troops occupy Danzig at the end of the Second World War.

Lena's wasted life mirrors, like Sophie's, the relentless attrition of an idea by both its practitioners and its enemies. Saddled with the most wretchedly abject of all the inadequate, violent husband/lover figures in *Der Butt*, she suffers at first hand all the hypocrisy and male chauvinism of the rank and file of the purportedly progressive SPD, whilst tirelessly asserting in her cooking a basic humanity and solidarity which at least temporarily heals the bitter divisions of the 'Revisionismusstreit'. Lena's failure to gain Bebel's support for her proletarian cookery book, which is as much a history as a recipe book, stands as a bitterly ironic metaphor for the general failure to avert the 'Verbürgerlichung' of the SPD, its corruption and assimilation into the capitalist system. Bebel for his part grows rich on the proceeds of *his* book, *Die Frau und der Sozialismus*, and is eulogized at his funeral by Clara Zetkin for his part in the struggle for the emancipation of women. However, the Lena Stubbe section evokes more than just the failures and compromises of the SPD. It also looks back with nostalgic affection to an era of optimistic belief in the eventual victory of socialism, of a genuine working-class culture not as yet submerged in mass popular culture, and to an age in which at least some of the German working class, undeterred by material hardship, took a serious, literate interest in politics, unlike the present-day media-addicted workers who accuse Grass of being élitist and bourgeois (435/429) because his writing makes intellectual demands on the reader.

Lena's life spans almost a century, 'ein Jahrhundert lang wässrige Hoffnung' (458/451). A 'watery hope' is better than no hope at all. In our own day, when even the snail is too fast for us, even such weak hope is something to be mourned. From Amanda Woyke via Sophie Rotzoll to Lena Stubbe there is an unbroken chain of commitment to the belief that the world can be improved. For Grass, any such belief can no longer be sustained. Lena's great-granddaughter is the pitiable Billy, raped as a child, brutally abused by the women to whom she misguidedly turns for support, violated and murdered to salve the outraged sexual pride of mindless hooligans. As Grass puts it in one of his bleakest comments on history: 'So viel gewaltsamer Tod . . . Viel ist da nicht zu beschönigen. Addierte Verluste. Das Konto Gewalt' (458/452).

4

The Transformation of Historical Material: The Case of Dorothea von Montau

TIMOTHY McFARLAND

I. Narrative, Memory, and History

The past as it exists for all of us is history synthesized by the imagination, and fixed into a picture by something that amounts to fiction.

Herbert Butterfield

The past is what you remember, imagine you remember, convince yourself you remember, or pretend to remember.

Harold Pinter[1]

In *Der Butt* the activity of narrating is often presented as being synonymous with remembering: 'Wahrhaftig werde ich, was Philipp Otto Runge als andere Wahrheit mitschrieb, auf meinem Papier erinnern; und müßte ich Wort für Wort aus der Asche lesen' (23/20). From time to time, beginning on line 7 of the first page ('Gegen Ende der Jungsteinzeit erinnere ich unseren ersten Streit'), Grass uses the verb 'erinnern' in the simple transitive form, as above. Although many dictionaries do not regard it as standard usage, it is far from unique in modern writing and colloquial speech. Grass appears to employ the verb in this way in order to stress the element of internalization and creative appropriation which is a necessary stage in the frequently strenuous activity of the writer. He has also drawn attention in interview to the close association of the two activities: 'C'est en écrivant que je me souviens' (Casanova 1979[1], 102). In *Der Butt* remembering takes its place among the many and various groups of metaphors used to highlight

---

[1] Herbert Butterfield, *The Historical Novel: An Essay* (Cambridge, 1924), 22. Thomas P. Adler, 'Pinter's *Night*: a Stroll Down Memory Lane', *Modern Drama*, 17 (1974), 461–5 (462).

different aspects of the writing of fiction, alongside those associated with the preparation of food, such as pounding acorns, plucking geese and peeling potatoes (295–307/290–301), and those associated with pregnancy and delivery and with defecation (13–22/9–19). But remembering is less metaphorical than these other images, and more metonymically associated with the creative process. Memory shares fully in the ambiguity of story-telling: on the one hand there would be no creative freedom and mobility without it, but on the other hand it is deeply implicated in the self-indulgent and evasive escapism of fabulation, and in the narrator's resistance to being nailed down by the real world of the present. Memory gives access to the imaginary world which is being constantly interrupted by the real, as when the narrator says of Agnes: 'Ich erinnere ihre Barfüße. Manchmal hoffe ich, wenn leise die Tür geht: Agnes kommt—aber immer kommt Ilsebill und bringt sich mit' (523/514).

In general the historical material in *Der Butt* is firmly placed in this remembered, imaginary world, in that sphere which the real (usually in the shape of Ilsebill) is constantly interrupting, challenging its validity and dismissing it as mendacious and evasive: '"Du mit deinen historischen Ausflüchten und Lügengeschichten!" schimpft sie täglich. (Ilsebill glaubt nur, was in der Zeitung steht.)' (172/168). But the narrator is well aware that there is an alternative way of presenting history, one to which he frequently alludes. Juxtaposed to his narrated stories is that history which consists of data: 'was sonst noch vorgekaut wurde: datierte Geschichte' ('Worüber ich schreibe', 12/9). The narrator claims, perhaps a little disingenuously: 'Eigentlich wollte ich ... nicht Geschichten erzählen, sondern Zahlen nennen und endlich den kaschubischen Legendensumpf statistisch trockenlegen' (298/292). This is the kind of history that Ilsebill (who is fed up with the narrator's interminable, unreliable, and self-serving stories) says she wants to know. But the attempt doesn't work: 'Doch nicht das Gezählte, das Erzählte hing an' (299/293). The narrator's own incontestable and voracious appetite for documented, statistical history, of the kind written by those academic historians who despise narrative history, is creatively unproductive: 'Doch ... so fleißig ich also das achtzehnte Jahrhundert nach Daten und Fakten flöhe, es will mir kein rückwirkendes Bild geraten: wie hörig muß ich neben Amandas Korb hocken und ihrem Schälmesser wie dazumal zuschauen' (298–9/292–3).

In settling thus for history as narration, he is putting himself on the side of the story-telling cooks, and in one sense also on the side of their primeval matriarch Aua, in her efforts to prevent Edek from learning to count, to calculate, and to master the world with mathematics and money, as the flounder is urging him to do: 'Fortan wird gezählt werden. Und wer zählt, wird bald rechnen. Und wer rechnet, berechnet voraus. ... Bald werdet ihr Abgezähltes gegen Gezähltes tauschen. Wenn nicht morgen, dann werdet ihr übermorgen bezahlt werden und gleichfalls zahlen, bezahlen' (32/28–9). In such passages there is an implicit opposition between 'erzählen' on the one hand, and quantifying verbs such as 'zählen', 'abzählen', 'zahlen', and 'bezahlen' on the other. This certainly reflects the flexible, open-ended quality of story-telling as it is mediated through the subjectivity of a narrator concerned to give both versions of the folk-tale of the flounder, and to tell the 'other truth' about this as about many other matters.

This does not imply that the novel fails to engage with historical ideas, or to use its historical material seriously. But this material is also, in accordance with its location primarily within the imaginative sphere, one of the replacements for Aua's third breast, a source of surrogate satisfaction and at times a favoured infantile playground. The narrator's historical knowledge, his curiosity and appetite for detail are immense, and only barely constrained by the size and themes of his book; but all this material is patient and malleable, available to be shaped and reshaped as required, and not subject to the demands of academic accuracy. It can function as a realm into which the narrator can escape from the boredom or frustration of daily reality: 'In Erwartung des richtigen Elektrikers ... verkrümelte ich mich ... geschichtlich treppab, bis ich im fortgeschrittenen siebzehnten Jahrhundert die Küchenmagd des alternden Stadtmalers Möller schwanger über den Langen Markt kommen sah' (116/112). Once the figure of Agnes Kurbiella has been thus summoned into imaginative existence as the narrator's central point of reference for the Baroque period, she can unite about herself figures who are historically quite widely separated: she can be attached at the age of 14 to the painter Anton Möller (1563–1611), who is allowed to survive into old age; a few years later at the age of 18 she provides for Martin Opitz (1597–1639) during his last years; and finally she is burnt at the stake with Quirinus Kuhlmann in Moscow in 1689. Occasionally the trivial details of the history remembered by the narrator are inconsistent or careless. Adalbert of Prague is first sent to the Vistula estuary by the Polish king Wladislaw (85/82), and a little later (and historically correctly) by 'Polackenherzog Boleslav Chobri' (111/108). Johannes Marienwerder appears first as abbot (156/153) and later (correctly) as dean (169/165). Frederick the Great's visit to Zuckau in 1778 took place after the first Polish partition, and not, as we are twice told (294/289, 310/304), after the second, which was carried out in 1793 after the king's death.

It would be pedantic to draw attention to such details if they did not reinforce the impression that the historical material in the novel is being drawn from the narrator's capacious but not infallible memory. For him as for all of us, memory is the repository not only of what he has himself experienced, but also of the historical knowledge he has acquired and can remember, and within this storehouse the two spheres constantly interact with each other and determine each other reciprocally. He can, of course, (again, like all of us) maintain a broad distinction between what he has lived through himself and what he has learned about the past, and indeed this distinction is fundamental for the organization of the narrative material. Nevertheless, there is no hard and fast dividing-line. The last two cooks in the historical sequence, Sybille Miehlau and Maria Kuczorra, who both belong to the world of his personal experience, are related to the last three historical cooks Amanda Woyke, Sophie Rotzoll, and Lena Stubbe in a complex Kashubian kinship system, which can even be extended to embrace the earlier women: 'Schließlich sind wir Kaschuben alle über paar Feldwege miteinander verwandt' (508–9/499–500). The narrator can remember seeing the aged Lena serving soup when he was a small boy (21/18). Such details blur the distinction between the narrator's experience and his acquired knowledge, and indicate that within his memory the two form a continuum which constitutes his uniquely individual sense of the past and is a potent constituent of his sense of identity.

In this respect the narrator is behaving as we all do. We all recall the past in the form of a personally edited narrative, one which gives us a version of events which helps us to get through our daily lives, whether this memory exists intrinsically in the form of a narrative or whether we merely conjure it up in the form of one. In this edited narrative we have assigned particular importance to specific episodes which we judge to be formative or fateful, and we are tempted to interpret them in a self-justifying light. There is no hard and fast dividing-line in these memory-narratives between what we have personally experienced and what we have learnt—whether about contemporary or past events, or about history, culture, or historical fictions. Thus I may say that I remember Charles de Gaulle or Marilyn Monroe, even though I never met them, although in fact I know of them in the same way as I know of Queen Victoria or Kafka, and I may even feel that I know fictional figures such as Anna Karenina rather better that these historical personages. We attach different kinds of status to the figures and events which stock our memory, but prior to this differentiation the historical figures, fictional creations, and our personal acquaintances are all there cheek by jowl. By their presence in our memory-narratives, and through the way we organize them into significant patterns, they contribute to our personal culture and our sense of identity.

David Lowenthal has claimed that this recognition of the role of memory in constituting identity, and the recognition of the degree of subjectivity in all historical 'remembering', are characteristic insights of the twentieth century; he also suggests that they now inform the writing of scholarly history to an increasing extent and are significant features in much contemporary fiction, for which he cites García Márquez, John Fowles, and others as evidence.[2] We can claim with confidence, I think, that *Der Butt* should be seen in this context, and we should regard the way in which Grass links his authorial, historical self with his narrator-figure as a remarkable example of this mode of fiction. The simultaneity—'Auf unserem Papier findet das meiste gleichzeitig statt' (127/123)—and the complex interplay of temporal patterns embody in the text the complex simultaneity in the narrator's memory.

The many parallels between historical and contemporary events and figures, both great and trivial, exemplify this clearly. The betrayal of Socialism by Robert Michels brings the Guillaume affair to mind (449–50/443); the revolt of the craft guilds in 1378 is compared to the 1970 Gdańsk shipyard strike (123/120; 515/506); a chance encounter with Prince Philip evokes a fourteenth-century visit to Danzig by the English prince Henry Derby, known to the narrator from Shakespeare (115/112). Structurally, this relationship between past and present is most firmly anchored in the correspondences established between the historical cooks and the members of the Feminal. The most fully realized of these is that between Dorothea von Montau and Sieglinde Huntscha. To see these two figures together may therefore be a profitable way to explore how the narrator's personal experience interacts with his extensive historical knowledge.

Much of the historical material in the novel is, moreover, literary in character, whether in the wider or the narrower sense. Is the reading of literature part of our personal experience, or is it one of the ways in which we acquire historical knowledge? Here too the two spheres are totally intermeshed. There is no need to be reminded that the author of *Der Butt* frequently engages with other literary texts and makes extensive use of literary history. Siegfried Mews has drawn attention to a wide range of reading, both primary and secondary, on which the learned flounder can

---

[2] David Lowenthal, *The Past is a Foreign Country* (Cambridge, 1985), 227, 236. The introductory section of my essay is indebted to ch. 5 ('How We Know the Past', 185–259) of Lowenthal's study. See esp.: 'Memory and identity' (197–200); 'History and memory' (212–14); 'History, fiction, and faction' (224–31).

draw in self-defence during his trial (Mews 1983[1], 164) and has commented on the two most prominent examples of literary history in the novel—the treatment of Baroque poetry in the fourth Month, so clearly anticipating the author's extended treatment of the subject in *Das Treffen in Telgte*, and the evocation of the Romantics in the sixth Month (ibid., 169–74). This latter episode provides the basis of Grass's own appropriation of the fairy-tale form. The narrator's declared intention in this matter (23/21) is to draw up from his memory the alternative version, 'die andere Wahrheit', of the familiar fairy-tale, as well as refashioning the received version. This designation of his intertextual procedures can serve as a paradigm for his treatment of other literary material as well, such as his presentation of Margarete Rusch as a female Gargantua in what might be seen (to use Bakhtin's terminology) as a dialogical transformation of Rabelais.[3] But Mews fails to recognize that some of the novel's apparently historical sections are engaged in a similarly intertextual debate with narrative sources which are just as literary as those he considers, even if they do not belong to an established canon.

The 'Ollefritz' episode in the fifth Month affords a good example on a small scale of how the narrator's memory enables him to draw upon a minor literary genre in order to present his 'other truth' about history. The genre in this case is the popular anecdote about Frederick II, handed on and intended to perpetuate the belief in the humanity of the king and his 'common touch'. These anecdotes often tell of encounters with humbler subjects such as the famous miller of Sans Souci. They were collected and edited from miscellaneous, frequently oral sources and achieved a kind of canonical status in Franz Kugler's *Geschichte Friedrichs des Großen* of 1840, a work which became the standard general biography for the nineteenth and early twentieth centuries. It was reprinted numerous times in popular editions and was illustrated with several hundred delightful engravings by Adolph von Menzel, which did a great deal to fix the image of the king in the popular imagination.[4] Once established in this way, the conventional image was further propagated in historical novels and in the visual arts. One typical painting, Robert Warthmüller's *Der König überall* (1866, now in a Hamburg private collection) depicts the king leaving his coach to inspect a potato field, with forelock-touching peasants in attendance, very much as described

---

[3] The critical categories employed in the essays translated and collected in Mikhail Bakhtin, *The Dialogic Imagination*, ed. M. Holquist (Austin, Texas, 1981), esp. 'Discourse in the Novel' (259–422), might be applied to *Der Butt* and other works by Grass with profit. Cf. also Mikhail Bakhtin, *Rabelais and his World* (Cambridge, Mass., 1968).

[4] Eda Sagarra, 'The Image of Frederick II of Prussia in Germany in the Century before Unification', *European Studies Review*, 4 (1974), 23–32, esp. 28–9.

by Grass: 'der Olle Fritz mit Stock im Rock, wie er später auf Bildern in Oel gemalt wurde' (311/305), and it might indeed be a source for this passage.

Such details of the *mise-en-scène* are recreated with great care in the account of Frederick II's unannounced visit of inspection to the Prussian state-farm at Zuckau in October 1778 (310–17/304–10). 'Ollefritz' is a good example of Grass's skill in pastiche, but these conventional elements, which make it a perfectly recognizable variant of the genre, become the instrument whereby the ideological intention is subverted. The king is bedraggled and demoralized, wet through, sniffing and sobbing into his potato soup, while Amanda Woyke, the pioneer in the cultivation of the potato, gives him sound information and maternal advice for which she will receive scant credit. The conventional ending of such stories, designed to glorify the benevolent despot doing good by stealth, is then inverted by an emphatic series of negatives:

Mir, dem Inspektor Romeike, wurde keine Schnupftabakdose geschenkt. Amanda fand keine Dukaten in ihrer Schürze. Den Töchtern Lisbeth, Anna, Martha und Ernestine wurde keine Hand aufgelegt. Kein Choral wurde von der immer noch regennassen Gemeinde gesungen. Kein spontaner Erlaß hob die Leibeigenschaft auf. Kein aufklärendes Wunder geschah unter absolutistischer Herrschaft (316/310).

This simple device is sufficient to give us the other truth, to unmask the myth of Frederick the Great by exposing the genre-specific convention of the happy ending employed in its popular dissemination. This can be done because the 'history', in this case, has been mediated in a literary form which the author-narrator remembers from childhood or school; he is not drawing upon his own reading of letters and other primary sources, as he does in order to debunk Count Rumford, the other popular enlightener from the school history-books.

The history of Dorothea von Montau is the most important example in *Der Butt* of the retelling of history derived from a source which is literary in this sense, and in the remainder of this essay the themes raised thus far will be explored with reference to this figure. Whereas the untrammelled historical imagination of the author-narrator must be held responsible for the other cooks, Dorothea is a figure of considerable interest, the first woman in the history of Danzig about whom a great deal is known. Although we have other sources as well (such as the documents of the canonization proceedings in 1404 and 1405), most of what is known about her is to be found in the extensive writings of Johannes Marienwerder. The most relevant of these to *Der Butt* is his German 'biography', written in the specific form of the saint's life or *vita*. To a more complex degree than in the case of Frederick II, therefore, the story of Dorothea von Montau is the subverted retelling, 'die andere Wahrheit', of a life which in its main source is already mediated through the conventions of an established literary genre.

Although the author-narrator almost certainly knew Marienwerder's *vita* at first hand, his own introduction to the material came from his Latin teacher Richard Stachnik, himself the most zealous interpreter of Dorothea to the modern world. To Marienwerder's medieval version Stachnik added a Catholic and hagiographical commentary for the twentieth century. The history of Dorothea first entered the capacious historical memory of the narrator in adolescence, perhaps in the same class-room in which he encountered the anecdotal history of Frederick the Great, and presumably by the route of oral transmission. Grass's own telling of her life in *Der Butt* must be seen not only as a response to, and a retelling of, Marienwerder's *vita*, but also as a product of his reaction to the modern hagiographical Catholic reading offered by Stachnik.

So what appears at first to be a question of the author's adaptation of historical material turns out on a closer inspection to be a fairly complex case of intertextual responses. Both the original source-material and the manner of its mediation to the author-narrator are interesting enough to shed some light on the novelist's creative procedures. In the light of the historical subject-matter, the feminist theme and the unregenerate male narrator of *Der Butt*, it was the author's good fortune that the early literary history of Prussia provided a remarkably full life of a woman of Danzig by a male author. Altogether, our knowledge of Dorothea is derived primarily from what men have written about her, i.e. from male-determined readings of a female life. It would be superfluous for a critic to provide a fourth male interpretation of Dorothea's biography, in addition to the three we already have from Marienwerder, Stachnik, and Grass. Instead we should look at the relationships pertaining between these three readings and ask whether a glance at the first two can shed any light on the third, present in *Der Butt*. Before looking at the sources, a brief analysis of the strategies adopted by the narrator to integrate the figure into the overall scheme of the novel may help to give sharper definition to the distinctive features of Grass's reading of Dorothea's life.

II. 'Im zweiten Monat': Dorothea, Sieglinde Huntscha, and Ilsebill

The eleven cooks whose stories form the core of the historical strand of the novel are all centrally located in the narrative fabulation of their appropriate Months, but in addition they are related to the rest of the novel by means of a number of distinctive thematic and structural devices. The most important of these is the technique whereby the cook figures on two levels in her own Month, first as narrative and secondly on the level of commentary in the deliberations of the tribunal, most of which is contained in the lengthy exchanges between the prosecutor and the flounder.[5] Secondly, each cook is linked to a specific member of the Feminal, and sometimes to Ilsebill as well, thereby underlining the reciprocal relationship between personal experience of the present and acquired knowledge of the past in the memory of the narrator. Thirdly, she is kept alive, so to speak, throughout the whole course of the novel by means of a good many incidental allusions in the text. Most of these occur in passages in which a thematic motif is explored with reference to several of the cooks in turn, often in a brief imaginative digression on the narrator's part.[6] These three techniques are deployed with sufficient frequency to constitute a kind of system, but with enough selective variation for the technique not to become schematic or mechanical.

Fear is the dominant response of the narrator to Dorothea, as many of these passages scattered throughout the novel demonstrate. The opening and closing references to her stress it: 'Die vierte Köchin in mir ist zum Fürchten' (16/12); 'Doch nicht Maria kam zurück. Es wird Dorothea sein, sorgte ich mich. . . . Ilsebill kam' (556/547). In this negative role of fear mingled with sexual fascination she appears as the converse of her successor Margarete Rusch, a predominantly positive fantasy-image of sexual and culinary indulgence and gratification, tinged in this case with the fear of suffocation or castration. The antithetical roles of these first two historical cooks are reinforced in the passages contrasting their behaviour in respect of love (269–71/263–5) and their culinary sorcery (287–8/281–2). It is the narrator's initial insistence that Dorothea is a witch rather than a saint that identifies her as the representative of her epoch: 'Wenn ich sage, daß sie, obgleich vom Volk wie heilig verehrt, eher hexisch und des Satans Bettstück gewesen ist, heißt das wenig für

---

[5] For a demonstration of how a text may use a second level of narrative as a commentary supplying the meaning of the first level of narrative, see the analysis of the *Queste del saint Graal* by Tzvetan Todorov, 'The Quest of Narrative' in T. T., *The Poetics of Prose*, tr. R. Howard (Oxford, 1977), 120–42.

[6] Dorothea figures in nearly all of these passages, which usually deal briefly with culinary and other domestic matters, such as the manner in which the women served 'Glumse' (60–2/56–8), inspected faeces (241–2/236–7), ate apples (422–3/416–7), or cooked cabbage (548–9/539–40). The longer examples (beginning with 'Neun und mehr Köchinnen', 13–22/12–19) are chapters in their own right. They provide many significant leitmotifs, e.g. the description of the cooks' use of spectacles ('Wo ihre Brillen liegenblieben', 453–5/447–9), which is followed directly, in 'Lena nachgerufen' (455–7/449–50), by the listing of their modes of dying, and is taken up later to invest the deaths of Lena (458/452) and Sibylle (502/493) with pathos.

eine Zeit, die sich, während die Pest im Vorbeigehen raffte, Hexen und
Heilige in Personalunion hielt' (16/12).

   This fourteenth century of saints and witches introduces the era of
patriarchal domination, monogamy, and Christianity, and accordingly
the fear and fascination inspired by Dorothea are related to the two
spheres of marriage and religion. The narrator's first monogamous
marriage is a historical paradigm prefiguring his own relationships, both
with Ilsebill and with Sieglinde Huntscha, whose fanatical Marxist-
feminist ideology is the secularized contemporary equivalent of Dorothea's ruthless mystical piety, and equally repugnant to the narrator.
These three women are all seen in relation to each other more explicitly
than is otherwise the case in the novel (cf. also 145/141–2; 150–1/147;
151–2/148; 153/150):

Auch hat die Anklägerin des Hohen Gerichts erschreckende Ähnlichkeit nicht
nur mit meiner Ilsebill. Beide sind Schwestern der Dorothea von Montau: von
bezwingendem Ausdruck, mit starkem Willen geimpft, der alles engführt und auf
plattem Land Berge versetzen kann. Entsetzlich blond sind sie (alle drei),
strenger Moral verpflichtet und von jenem Mut besessen, der immer nur
geradeaus geht, komme was wolle (138/134–5).

   This triangular pattern is emphasized by the arrangement of prose
episodes in the second Month. These are five in number, alternating with
six poems dealing, significantly, with the growing tensions between the
narrator and Ilsebill and the theme of marital strife. In the first episode,
'Wie wir städtisch wurden', the narrator introduces Dorothea and his
marriage in the context of the visit to Gdańsk in 1974 and his elaborate
exercise in the synchronicity of the city's history. The next two sections
make the contemporary parallels explicit: first with Ilsebill in 'Ein
Abwasch' and then with Sieglinde Huntscha in 'Ähnlich meiner Dorothea'. Only after these correspondences have been securely established is
the way clear for the central exposition of Dorothea's place in a world of
male authority-figures ('Schonischer Hering'), a narrative which concludes the account of her 'Lebenslauf' with a brief notice of her
enclosure, her death, and the abortive attempt to secure her canonization.
The fifth and final passage is the letter to Dr Stachnik which, for this
Month, continues the process of commentary and interpretation which
had been initiated in the account of the Feminal's proceedings and the
narrator's nocturnal visit to the flounder in the third episode.

   The similarity that links Dorothea and her feminist equivalent is of
unusual interest because Sieglinde Huntscha is a major figure in her own
right. As prosecutor she is the most articulate and therefore the most
highly profiled member of the Feminal; she must in fact be regarded as

the representative spokesperson of radical German feminism in the early seventies, as the narrator sees it. We first meet her and her friends because she has been chosen by the flounder to fish him out of the Baltic, as he later admits (140/138), and she takes a leading role in setting up the tribunal (38–44/34–41). This episode prepares the way for the subsequent trial but it also establishes the link, backwards in time but forwards in narrative terms, with Siggi's participation in the appalling events of 'Vatertag'. The frightening aspect she shares with Dorothea is derived from this history, from her fanatical feminism, and from the threat she presents as prosecutor, a threat which certainly affects the narrator but is aimed more immediately at the arraigned flounder, and culminates in her last judicial act, a plea for sentencing him to death by electrocution (533/523–4).[7]

But the satirical treatment of the Feminal subverts the forcefulness of its members in comparison with their historical prototypes.[8] 'Ähnlich meiner Dorothea' emphasizes Sieglinde's vulnerability. Her ideological position does not appear to affect the casual sexual relationship of long standing between her and the narrator, and she is happy to unlock the cinema for him at night. She nearly ruins the prosecution's case by giving a crudely over-simplified Marxist account of the revolt of the guilds which the flounder has no difficulty in refuting (146–8/142–4). But she does introduce the 'Prinzip Hoffnung' into the argument, and thereby enables the exchange which follows between the flounder and Dr Schönherr about Dorothea's desire for freedom to be cast in the terminology of Ernst Bloch—a motif that will assume some importance when later reported by the narrator in his letter to Dr Stachnik.

As for Ilsebill, the reciprocal determination of historical images and the narrator's personal experience is never more explicit than in the opening pages of 'Ein Abwasch' (131–3/128–30), one of the crucial depictions of domestic conflict in *Der Butt*. The narrator's married life with Dorothea, which is then evoked in similar terms, provides a pseudo-mythical account of the origin of this state of affairs: 'Seit Dorothea gibt es das Abwaschproblem' (142/138). The somewhat complicated

---

[7] Thanks to her part in 'Vatertag' Sieglinde is the only person apart from the narrator to be actively present in all nine Months—which even Ilsebill and the flounder are not. She is probably a more central figure in the conception of *Der Butt* than has been recognized. A full discussion of feminism in the novel would have to analyse her forensic strategies and arguments, and also to consider whether the militant lesbian of 'Vatertag' and the prosecutor are the same person in any other than a formal sense.

[8] Michael Minden's argument (p. 196) that the contemporary women are 'defensively imagined' is also relevant here: 'The "I" in the present is forced into positions which deny its protean adaptability, and therefore reinvents the women so as to reduce them (by seducing them) as a compensatory gesture.'

explanation describes a circular movement leading from marital misery back to marital misery, incriminating the craven husband in two acts of treachery in the process. Reduced to a nervous wreck by his inability to cope with marriage (135–6/132), a new institution devised to ensure that male dominance should replace the ancient matriarchy, he first betrays Dorothea by letting the flounder teach him how to transfer his migraine to her (135–7/133). He forfeits the advantage thus gained, however, by then betraying the flounder to Dorothea, thus earning the opprobrium of them both. The flounder's revenge for this act of cowardice is the institutionalized misery of married life: 'Fortan wird dir die Ehe ein Joch sein. Zusätzlich wird der herrschende Mann seinem Hausdrachen Tribut zahlen müssen, und sei es in der Küche beim Abwasch' (138/134). After her two visits to the flounder Dorothea abandons housework, and the pattern already rehearsed for us by the narrator and Ilsebill is established.

The dismal paradigm makes it clear that the fear inspired by Dorothea, and indeed the failure of marriage altogether, are inseparable from the husband's guilt and incompetence. This sense of inferiority is brought out even more drastically in his most disturbing fantasy, the surreal account of Dorothea's second visit to the flounder, in which she first attempts to execute the fish (something which Sieglinde Huntscha will try to bring about later) and then spends a night with him under the sea, from which she emerges claiming a new omniscience (140–2/136–8). The reader is left to make what he or she may of this enigmatic parable until the very last page of the novel is reached, where it becomes apparent that Maria's communion with the flounder has been prefigured in the earlier episode. We are reminded of this by the narrator's final apprehension that the returning woman might, once again, be his threatening witch Dorothea; but it is Ilsebill, and he is content to run after her. He is now well aware of his own inferiority: 'Du bist doch fertig, Mann, und nur noch läufig' (547/538). This suggests that at the end of these eventful twelve months he can accept, albeit with a degree of apprehensive resignation, the flounder's transfer of his allegiance to the female sex and the end of male authority which it signals. But from the beginning of the patriarchal period he was always anxiously aware that this might happen; and in the second Month, as in the fourteenth century, this awareness could only be registered with fear and horror.

Grass's 'other truth' about Dorothea von Montau thus appears, in part at least, to be a deeply compromised projection of the narrator's own fears and resentments about his marriage to a 'witch' and about the threat posed by militant women demanding, like Dorothea von Montau, 'freedom for themselves'. In order to see how far the narrative material of

Dorothea's life offered a basis for his alternative reading, we must now turn to the medieval source from which it was derived.

III. Marienwerder's Life of Dorothea and *Der Butt*

Johannes Marienwerder, dean of the cathedral chapter in his home town, Marienwerder in Prussia, tells us that he began to record the visions, teaching, and autobiographical confessions of Dorothea von Montau in 1392. About a year after her death in 1394 the German Order applied to the Holy See to institute proceedings for her canonization, and Marienwerder's extensive Latin writings were produced to further this end and to propagate the cult of the new local saint. Various short accounts of her life were in circulation by 1396 and the definitive *Vita Latina* appeared about 1398. This and his two books of her visions, the *Liber de festis* and the *Septililium*, constitute the 'große Trilogie' which Dr Stachnik recommended to the attention of the author of *Der Butt* (169/165).[9] Finally, Marienwerder produced his German *vita*, a carefully planned selection from his Latin writings, adapted and translated between 1398 and 1404. Taken together these writings constitute one of the fullest accounts extant of a late medieval life, especially in its psychological and spiritual dimensions. Because the wealth of detail they provide is so characteristic of its period, writes Richard Kieckhefer, Dorothea can be seen to epitomize 'almost all those tendencies that have given the fourteenth-century saints a reputation for idiosyncrasy and disquietude'.[10]

The German *vita*[11] is divided into four books. The first two cover the whole of Dorothea's life except the last year, including her childhood and marriage in Danzig and the pilgrimages to Aachen, to the 'hermits' (probably at Einsiedeln), and to Rome, where she is when her husband

---

[9] Anneliese Triller, 'Marienwerder, Johannes' in *Die deutsche Literatur des Mittelalters: Verfasserlexikon²*, iii (1987), coll. 56–61, is the most useful bibliographical article (reprinted with others in Müller, U., 1985, 119–25). A concise account of Marienwerder's writings is to be found in the introduction to the critical edition of the *Vita Latina*: Hans Westphal (ed.), *Vita Dorotheæ Montoviensis Magistri Johannis Marienwerder* (Forschungen und Quellen zur Kirchen- und Kulturgeschichte Ostdeutschlands, vol. i; Cologne and Graz, 1964), 1–4.

[10] Richard Kieckhefer, *Unquiet Souls: Fourteenth-Century Saints and Their Religious Milieu* (Chicago, 1984), 22. The short account of Dorothea von Montau and her broader historical context in this book (22–33) is the best available introduction to the subject.

[11] 'Das Leben der heiligen Dorothea von Johannes Marienwerder', ed. Max Toeppen, in Theodor Hirsch *et al.* (eds.), *Die Geschichtsquellen der preußischen Vorzeit*, ii (Scriptores Rerum Prussicarum, 2; Leipzig, 1863), 179–350. All references to the text in my essay are to this edition, citing book, chapter, and page numbers. All translations into English are my own.

dies. They contain the narrative biographical material on which the figure of Dorothea in *Der Butt* is based. The whole of the third book is devoted to the last year of Dorothea's life (1393–4), spent as an *inclusa* in the anchorhold built for her at Marienwerder. These first three books are translated and adapted from the *Vita Latina*, whereas the fourth book brings visionary and mystical material from the *Septililium*. That about half of the *vita* deals with Dorothea's year as an anchoress and her spiritual experience demonstrates clearly that her earlier life, including her marriage, is seen as a preparation for this culminating phase.

This is the case in spite of the fact that for the German version Marienwerder omitted much of the visionary material, including the accounts of Dorothea's mystical pregnancy and her experience of being pierced by lances held by Christ or the Blessed Virgin. Similar material does occur in other vernacular lives written for nuns, and its omission here may indicate that the German version was intended by Marienwerder for refectory readings in the conventual houses of the German Order, whose members, being warriors, did not know Latin and, being men, would not be expected to identify with modes of mystical writing specific to women. There is little reference in *Der Butt* to the details of Dorothea's mystical revelations, which supports the suspicion that the narrator's assertion that he learned little Latin from Dr Stachnik (168/164) is no mere humility formula. His knowledge of Dorothea appears to be derived from the German *vita* (which he could have read in the original or in the modern German translation by D. Korioth of 1893) rather than from more recent devotional biographies or from Dr Stachnik's writings.

Like all lives of saints, Dorothea's German *vita* must be read in terms of its generic conventions and the purposes they serve. Marienwerder makes it clear in his prologue that his intention is didactic: 'For her blessed life is a living lesson ('eyn lebende lectio') for those who like to hear it or read it themselves' (1, Prologue. 201). The medieval saint's life or 'legend' consists of episodes designed to be read as such lessons in the *vita christiana*, and arranged within the framework of a life. These episodes may be outward events narrated to show how God's grace was active and made publicly manifest through the saint's activity, in which case the *vita* perpetuates the knowledge and exemplary power of these moments. But in fourteenth-century lives there may also be episodes of an internal, often mystical kind, such as were already familiar in the literature of visions and revelations. In such cases the *vita* is communicating to the outside world for the first time the occasions of divine grace which had been the private and inward experience of the recipient and hitherto known to nobody else. The integration of such episodes into an

organized narrative marks a significant stage in the literary exploration of
the inner life, an area in which the secular narrative genres at this time lag
far behind devotional literature.

It is a distinctive feature of Marienwerder's *vitae* of Dorothea von
Montau that they contain episodes of both the outward and the inward
kind, and episodes which combine the two. In these the narrative
perspective is not aligned exclusively with a transcendental spiritual
reality but encompasses a split world in which the sphere of spiritual
experience is consciously juxtaposed to a concrete, social sphere of
objects and human relationships which retains full reality and exists in a
state of inherent tension with the spiritual sphere.

This is particularly true of the depiction of Dorothea's married life in
its later stages. In its earlier phases (1, 21–4. 218–21) it is described in
idealizing terms, in accordance with that aspect of church teaching which
was concerned to modify the exclusive merit attached to virginity and to
present chaste and honourable marriage as an estate pleasing to God and
blessed in this world with children and the consolations of companionship and fidelity. The excellence of Dorothea's husband is also stressed.
Dorothea grants him his conjugal rights but takes pains to avoid sexual
pleasure for herself. After the birth of their youngest child, husband and
wife agree to abstain 'from marital intercourse in complete chastity, in
order to serve God with a free spirit' (1, 24. 221), and this is maintained
for the last ten years of their married life.

So far so good, but a different picture emerges in the later chapters.
Marienwerder had stated in his preface that among the exemplary
qualities of Dorothea's life was her prodigious capacity for suffering:
'Who has ever heard or read of a person inflicting upon themselves such
intense, bitter, and long drawn-out suffering of so many kinds, and in
such quantity, and with such a good intention, as she inflicted upon her
own [five] senses?' ('Vorrede'. 197). The acceptance of suffering as a
form of *imitatio Christi* is common in saints' lives, and it is a didactic
requirement that Dorothea should suffer progressively more as she
approaches sanctity. Dorothea's sufferings were partly inflicted by her
husband and her fellow-citizens, both lay and clerical, as the response of
the 'world' to the life of grace to which she was called. How this is
realized in narrative is best demonstrated by looking at one episode of the
German *vita* (2, 15. 248–50) which has some relevance to the subject-
matter of *Der Butt*.

*How she was often caught up in ecstasy in Danzig, and had to suffer much
from her husband on account of it.*

And then the Lord was even more gracious towards her on shipboard on the high seas on the way to Danzig, and in Danzig by day and by night, and she was miraculously full of love, devotion, and inwardness; and so that she might be alone with the Lord her bridegroom and apart from other people, and in order to moisten the bed of her conscience with her tears, she sought out corners and hiding-places wherever she could. She did not spare her body, but prevailed against it with much kneeling, praying, self-mortification, and wounding.

Near St Catherine's in Danzig a little house was built for her and her husband, to which she was often sent by him to perform some task, and to which she often went and came back again three times before she had finished doing what she had been told, for she was so greatly troubled with the Lord that she was forgetful and thoughtless about outward things, and therefore she was rarely able to carry out what she was told to do.

Sometimes when she entered the aforementioned little house, or some other room, she sat down behind the door or in a corner and was immediately caught up in ecstasy. When her husband found her sitting there like that, he sometimes struck her, sometimes pushed her, and sometimes he complained about her to many people, and said that she was lazy and sleepy, and wanted her to work hard at outward things and to be active, which she would often have done gladly at his bidding, if she had been able to.

Sometimes she cooked fish without scaling or gutting it, or in some other unsuitable way, and did not notice that that was not right. Once it happened that she was drawn up into sublime contemplation, and had continued in it for so long, that she failed to prepare at the right time a meal of fresh fish, which take longer to prepare than the other sort; as she was going about it, and wanted to prepare them quickly, her husband became very impatient and struck her so severely on the mouth that her upper lip was wounded and almost pierced by her teeth, and her mouth swelled up horribly and she was greatly disfigured. But although she had been so humiliated and badly beaten, she nevertheless bore it with patience and smiled at her husband with affection and good humour. She was loving towards him and prayed fervently to God for him and prepared the fish quickly. And all the people who were present and saw this were amazed at the woman's patience, and that she remained cheerful, kind, and calm of temper.

At another time her husband told her to buy straw when she went to church; but then, after being told to do this, she was lifted up in great sweetness, and raised above herself in ecstasy and inflamed with great love, and so submerged in it that she was spiritually inebriated, and the time passed meanwhile, so that she was too late to buy the straw, and she came home happy and cheerful. Then her husband was enraged, and in the fury of his rage he struck her so hard in the chest that blood shot out of her mouth, and for many days after that she vomited blood and spittle. Nevertheless she did not murmur on account of it or complain to anybody, but bore it with joy like everything else that the Lord had ordained for her.

Because of this and other mishaps, two priests, the confessors of them both, came and chastised the man severely because of his unkindness and rage, and because of the great injustice he had done and the pain he had caused his wife, as they had heard from other people. Because her husband was obliged to abandon his purpose, he fell seriously ill, and lay in bed for a long time, and he was not satisfied with the nursing or service of anyone, excepting only his wife Dorothea, and both in this sickness and at other times when he was frequently bedridden with the gout she served him with love and devotion both day and night as best she could, and she put up with the long night-watches patiently, and with his impatient shouting at her whenever she did not do immediately just what he wanted as he wanted it done, whether it was by day or night.

Then, when he had recovered, he habitually scolded her for having given alms liberally and bringing him to ruin, and because of that he then took the keys away from her and left her no authority over anything at all. He went to the market himself and bought what they needed. And it was very welcome to the blessed Dorothea that she did not need to be troubled with temporal matters.

When Dorothea had dictated this to her confessor by God's command and revelation, the Lord immediately wounded her with many darts of love, and inflamed her with a piercing love, and said: 'You have indeed good cause to love me greatly, for I have often snatched you away from your husband; while he was still alive and imagined that he possessed you, I snatched you away and I possessed you. It is right that you should speak of me and magnify me, for I have helped you without your knowledge, and guided you throughout your life, which was full of pain and martyrdom. Now weep profusely and thank me greatly; my suffering and martyrdom are greater than yours. You also performed a loving service to me, in that you were willing and pleased to leave your own house, which you could well have kept for yourself; but you loved poverty and exile and rejoiced that you should do without all transient things all your days for my sake.' When Dorothea heard this from the Lord, she wept sweet tears and thanked our dear Lord, as she had been told to do.

As with many of the episodes in the German *vita*, the final paragraph clarifies the specific 'living lesson' for those who hear or read it. Dorothea has demonstrated her exemplary *conformitas Christi* to the world in the patience with which she has borne her husband's persecution, and she should now rejoice while weeping: 'Nu weyne sere und danke mir groslich; myn liden und martir ist grosir wen dyn.' Marienwerder legitimizes this teaching by attributing it to God in direct speech, uttered in the course of a vision concisely characterized by the language of erotic ecstasy which by 1400 had become conventional for texts dealing with female mysticism. Dorothea's mysticism is not the subject of the teaching itself but a means of establishing her chosen and exemplary status, thus strengthening her position against the 'world' in which she suffers, represented in this chapter by her hapless husband.

This paragraph also establishes the temporal and narrative perspective. God speaks to her after she has given Marienwerder her account of the incident (between 1392 and 1394), about six years after the events described had taken place (probably in 1387, shortly after the return from Aachen and before the pilgrimage to Rome). But the time-gap is bridged, or rather annihilated, in that the final paragraph restores Dorothea to the state of mystical experience depicted at the beginning of the chapter, and at points throughout it. This level of transcendent spiritual reality is becoming her normal mode of being at this stage of her *vita*. Encapsulated within this framework is the narrative action, which alternates between this higher level and the material world of things and people. Three incidents register the growing intensity of her experience, her increasing neglect of domestic chores such as cooking fish and buying straw, and the increasing violence and brutality of her husband in response to this. The intervention of the priests vindicates her patience, but her victory entails the breakdown of her marriage as a domestic partnership, when her husband deprives her of the keys and assumes domestic responsibility himself.

The dualistic juxtaposition of the reality of this world and a higher transcendent reality is of course ubiquitous in medieval religious literature, but saints' lives rarely accord the material details of domestic life the weight they have here. In this and many other episodes, the dualism is not just an ideological component but is also expressed in the specific narrative strategies employed by Marienwerder. Dorothea's biographer is inviting the reader to take note of these two levels of reality, and to order his or her life in imitation of a saint whose own life was an *imitatio Christi*.

The author-narrator of *Der Butt* did not accept this invitation, but he did respond to the narrative structure of those parts of the German *vita* which have such an emphatically dualist pattern. The procedure is similar to that he adopted with the folk-tale of the flounder and with the anecdote of Frederick the Great: some features of the genre are retained but are adapted to a reading in which the original intention is subverted. The two levels of Marienwerder's narrative are so clearly delineated that the text might be said to contain an implicit invitation to read it against the grain of the author's own massive commitment to the higher validity of Dorothea's spiritual experience. Such a reader has only to adopt the other perspective available in the dualistic narrative structure, which is what Grass has done. Seen from her desperate husband's point of view, Dorothea is an impossible housewife even in Marienwerder's account. In this and related chapters of the German *vita* is to be found the material which entered the author's memory and emerged 'erinnert auf dem Papier' as the passages of the second Month concerned with marital strife.

In this transposed perspective, moreover, the level of transcendental reality to which the Dorothea of the *vita* has access is also retained, but it is inverted; the husband sees his wife not as a saint but as a witch: 'ruiniert hat sie mich, die Hex' (16/13; cf. Müller, U., 1985, 128). The erotic language of mystical experience is for him evidence that she is 'des Satans Bettstück' (16/13), and the account of her visit to the flounder discussed above recalls motifs familiar from witchcraft accusations, such as that of illicit or diabolical intercourse which confers privileged knowledge but may leave disturbing traces, such as facial distortions. Dorothea implies something of the sort herself: 'Vom Satan distanzierte sie sich, indem sie ihn "valschen zungenlatz" schimpfte und auf den schiefmäuligen Ausdruck eines schmackhaften Plattfisches, "dem buttke sin fratz", reimte' (161/157). In this exploitation of the witch/saint motif Grass has touched on a relevant historical issue with remarkable perceptiveness. In the decades around 1400, as Caroline Walker Bynum observes, the prominence and influence achieved by pious and holy women in Europe was arousing the hostility of male ecclesiastical authorities, and in a climate of virulent misogyny many leading women saints, including Dorothea's near-contemporaries Catherine of Siena (d. 1380) and Joan of Arc (d. 1431), were suspected of witchcraft or demonic possession. 'By 1500, indeed, the model of the female saint . . . was in many ways the mirror-image of society's notion of the witch.'[12] The narrator's speculations about Dorothea's cooking (287–8/281–2) and the suspicions of Dr Roze and his parishioners (156–60/151–4), and of Walrabe von Scharfenberg (166/163) are not exaggerated in historical terms.

The modern reader is inclined to look for evidence of individuality in a medieval *vita*, and many of the more colourful details of Dorothea's behaviour appear to provide such evidence. One episode of the German *vita* (2, 22. 257–60) relates how Dorothea succumbed to a trivial temptation and was punished for it severely. On All Saints' Eve she is in her cell enjoying a vision of the saints in paradise, 'and because she was visited by the grace of our Lord, she was so filled with divine sweetness, delight and jubilation that all her limbs were set in motion by the superabundance of her rejoicing; she was unable to keep her feet still.' She is brought a gift of a dish of small fish, prepared exquisitely with saffron. Although she does not wish to eat, she gazes at the dish for a few moments with pleasure. This is the sin for which she is punished: 'At the fifth hour [after midnight] the Lord inflamed her intensely with his love.

---

[12] Caroline Walker Bynum, 'Religious Women in the Later Middle Ages', in J. Raitt (ed.), *Christian Spirituality: High Middle Ages and Reformation* (World Spirituality, 17; London, 1987), 121–39 (129).

She wept and broke out in such a sweat, that she was as wet as if water had been poured over her and she was sitting in a hot bath.' She is terrified and too enfeebled to dress herself, and for two hours she cannot turn the 'eyes of her soul' away from the plate of fish and is tormented by her inability to look upon God. 'She was so grievously oppressed that she was unable to stand up. She prostrated herself upon the ground in body and soul in deep humility, and wept bitterly and shrieked to the Lord that he should be pleased to send her the physician of her soul, her confessor.' At seven in the morning she is granted absolution after confession and is once again allowed to enjoy her vision of the saints: 'and she heard them openly singing their sweet song and praising our Lord thereby, and this was so sweet to her ears and resounded so loudly that she heard very little of the singing in the church.' The chapter ends with a speech from Christ in the sacrament, which contains the 'lebende lectio': if he has punished her so severely for such a venial sin, 'oh how much more severely will he punish us, who have . . . forgotten God in the pleasure of eating!'

The intense little emotional drama which takes place in Dorothea's solitary cell is an instance of a specific mode of late medieval discourse which was striving to expand the means of expressing spiritual experience (and hence of psychological states and inwardness in general) beyond those hitherto available in vernacular writing. One of the principal strategies for doing so, as here, is to contrast the sensory perceptions of the flesh with those of the spirit, and to use vivid bodily movement and gesture as a means of indicating emotional responses to both: to the sight of food, and to the sound of angels singing. That Marienwerder made use of the levels of external and internal experience in this way to help him shape a consciously constructed narrative is evident from the changes which he introduced into the successive Latin and German versions of this episode.[13] His purpose in doing so was to reinforce the didactic appeal to his reader or listener by encouraging them to identify emotionally with Dorothea's suffering and penance, which he is presenting as exemplary and recommending for general imitation. For the intended reader of the German *vita*, the didacticism and the depiction of behaviour are inseparable.

Today they are not. Unsubmissive readers, like the author of *Der Butt*, can reject the proffered interpretation and substitute one of their own. But once the medieval didactic perspective has been jettisoned and the

---

[13] For a fuller analysis of this chapter, see Timothy McFarland, 'Fisch mit Safran: Speisemotiv, Erzählstruktur und didaktische Intention in einer Episode aus der deutschen Vita der Dorothea von Montau', in K. Grubmüller, L. P. Johnson and H.-H. Steinhoff (eds.), *Kleinere Erzählformen im Mittelalter* (Paderborn, 1988), 253–69.

vita is read as an autonomous narrative, the figure of Dorothea also assumes an autonomous individuality, and her life is read as the record of an individual in a way that would scarcely have been understood by Marienwerder and his contemporaries. For them the specific details were of interest only in so far as they served the hagiographical purpose, which entailed emphasizing the universal applicability of Dorothea's experience. Once cut loose from this context, the expressive gestures and emotional language of Marienwerder's rhetorical code are free to be translated into psychological characteristics, and Dorothea's asceticism may be read as a morbid and egotistical fanaticism. In this way aspects of a general mode of discourse in a medieval text become transposed into the circumstantial details of characterization.

This is what has happened in *Der Butt*. In Grass's retelling of Marienwerder's life, the proofs of Dorothea's exemplary asceticism have become symptoms of a rather individual kind of religious neurosis. This accords well with the shift in perspective from the wife to the husband, which is also, of course, a shift from a serious and didactic to a comic narrative mode.

For our reading of *Der Butt* these questions are of greater interest, I think, than a full account of how much detail has been taken over from the earlier life and of how Grass has changed or added to it. Here there is only space for some general remarks and a few examples. The broad outlines of her life—her birth in Montau, her marriage to the swordsmith, the nine children of this marriage, the pilgrimages to Aachen, Einsiedeln, and Rome, her last year as an *inclusa*—are from Marienwerder's account, as are some of the other figures, including her confessor Nikolaus von Hohenstein. So is a good deal of the circumstantial detail, including such matters as Dorothea's desire to stay in Einsiedeln (157/153), her unseemly behaviour in church (155/151–2; 159/156), and the miracle which saved her life when crossing the river Elbe as it was thawing (157/154). In many of these and other cases there is adaptation and comic elaboration on the basis of a brief mention in the source. The visit of the two confessors to Dorothea and her husband related in the chapter given above may well be the germ from which the chapter 'Schonischer Hering' developed; the feigned death of her husband (Adalbert in the source, not Albrecht, and not Slichting either) while she is in Rome (165/161) is, of course, as much a comic invention of the author as are her recipes, her verses, and her commerce with the flounder.

Two examples of how the narrator elaborates on small details in the source are of some interest. The first relates to his description of seeing the infant Dorothea scalded with boiling water but remaining miraculously unharmed (120/117). In the German *vita* (1, 13. 209) the miraculous aspect is not that she is whole but that the episode marks the beginning of her career of suffering and of the divine visitations that are to continue until her death. This initiation in the imitation of Christ's passion takes place, as with other saints, in her seventh year. The narrator reports this incident, but then, in accordance with the threatening image of the negligent wife and mother, generates from it, somewhat sadistically, a second similar incident leading to the death of the (invented) child Kathrinchen (129/125–6), and this leads to the first incidence of wife-beating by the husband, which, as we have seen, is well attested in the source.

The second is concerned with the conventional mystical image of transparency as a sign of spirituality. In the German *vita* Dorothea attains to this state in 1387, at the age of 40:

> On the Sunday before Lent she was so greatly illuminated that she was able to see through herself as clearly as a man with good eyes can see through a crystal; and at that time she could see through herself and know herself for the first time, for she saw all her sins, no matter how small they were, and recognized some which she had not known before. (2, 2. 234)

In *Der Butt* the image of crystalline transparency becomes a principal leitmotif associated with Dorothea von Montau. After being scalded with boiling water she retains her 'blaudurchäderte Durchsichtigkeit' (120/117); Styra's etchings of her are 'offen, gläsern' (126/123); she is 'die zerbrechliche Dorothea' (477/470), 'wie aus Glas geblasen' (522/513), and 'schön wie ein Eiszapfen' (422/415). The image is extended by association to other themes related to her. A Danzig schoolgirl first matches the narrator's ideas of her: 'ich erinnere blaues Geäder in weißen Schläfen' (168/165). In 'Ein Abwasch' the Dorothean themes of fear and marital conflict are introduced with reference to the narrator's precious collection of glass: 'Vor Ilsebill fürchten sich meine Gläser' (131/128). In the latter part of the novel the leitmotif of crystalline transparency is transferred to that other great exemplar of purgation by suffering, the captive flounder in his glass case: '[er kam uns] mehr und mehr durchsichtig vor, wie gläsern' (519/510–11; cf. 527/518; 536/527). To such a pervasive degree has the narrator been 'nachhaltend geimpft ... mit dem dorotheischen Gift' (172/168).

IV. 'Verehrter Herr Doktor Stachnik'

It cannot be a common occurrence for a work of fiction to include a letter, ostensibly addressed to a living person, which after publication receives an answer—entirely outside the fiction—from its nominal addressee. It is a not-inappropriate response to a novel which accommodates specific audiences for its narratives, audiences like Ilsebill and Maria, who may interrupt and disagree with the narrator or expose his subterfuges; and it confirms that a reader innocent of the niceties of narrative theory will not hesitate to accept the narrator's invitation to treat him as Günter Grass.

Grass found in Monsignor Richard Stachnik a foeman worthy of his steel. His reply 'Zur Ehrenrettung unserer heiligen Mutter Dorothea: Das Andenken Dorotheas durch einen aus Westpreußen stammenden Schriftsteller verunglimpft' appeared within a year of the novel's publication in the last issue of *Der Dorotheenbote*, a journal which Dr Stachnik edited and very largely wrote himself between 1951 and 1978.[14] Its purpose was to publicize the cult of Dorothea and the renewed campaign for her canonization, and it ceased publication when these aims had been achieved. In January 1976, about a year and a half before the publication of *Der Butt*, Pope Paul VI proclaimed the *confirmatio cultus* for Dorothea. This was less than the full formal canonization for which her advocates had hoped, but it encouraged veneration and prayers for intercession in accordance with tradition and permitted that she be referred to and addressed as a saint. For Dr Stachnik, who had been the principal driving-force in the movement, it was the successful culmination of a lifetime's work.

Der Dorotheenbote was aimed at a popular Catholic audience and was not an academic journal, but in addition to devotional material it brought together articles by Stachnik and other scholars on Dorothea's mystical doctrines and her life, with translated extracts from Marienwerder's writings and other sources such as the record of the medieval canonization proceedings which Stachnik edited.[15] In addition it reported on the progress of the protracted negotiations with the Congregation of Rites and on other relevant matters. There was a *Festschrift* number of the journal for Stachnik's eightieth birthday in 1974, and altogether the whole enterprise bears eloquent witness to his energy and persistence into advanced old age.

The renewed campaign for Dorothea's canonization was mainly carried, in its initial stages at least, by Catholics who had lost their homes in Danzig and in West and East Prussia. The cult of a local saint appears to have acted as a focus for the specific cultural loyalties of this group

[14] *Der Dorotheenbote*, 38 (1978), 407–9. I am indebted to the Herder-Institut für Ostforschung, Marburg, for the loan of a complete run of this journal, on which I have drawn for the following paragraphs.

[15] Richard Stachnik (ed.), *Die Akten des Kanonisationsprozesses Dorotheas von Montau von 1394 bis 1521* (Cologne and Vienna, 1978).

within the Catholic Church in the Federal Republic. There is little
evidence of political activity in *Der Dorotheenbote* or of any formal contact
with the Landsmannschaften or other organizations of expellees. This
might suggest that the cult offered an alternative channel for the energies
of more devout Catholics from the area, in contrast to the strident
activities of the more political groups in the fifties and sixties. In addition
the pages of *Der Dorotheenbote* provide evidence of the increasing interest
taken by Polish Catholics in the cause. The old cathedral in Marienwerder, of which Dorothea's anchorhold is a part, had been a Protestant
church until 1945; for the new Polish population it became Catholic and
the cell became a shrine. The Polish hierarchy supported the veneration
of Dorothea as a Catholic saint of the land of Prussia, regardless of the
fact that she was German. These developments were greeted with
enthusiasm by Stachnik and others in the West, leading to the claim
being made for Dorothea as 'eine Heilige des ungeteilten Europa',
invoking her patronage for reconciliation and bridge-building between
Germans and Poles.[16] The recognition of her canonization was greeted
with extensive celebrations in Germany and Poland, for which ecclesiastical delegations exchanged fraternal visits.

The movement for canonization was approaching its climax while *Der
Butt* was being written. While these developments may not have a direct
bearing on our interpretation of the novel, they remind us that we are not
merely comparing a modern comic reading of Dorothea's life with a
medieval source-text but also dealing with the collision of two modern
readings. This has implications for how we define the readership of the
novel and generalize about the cultural assumptions of that readership.
Modern German society is pluralist, and within it there exists, alongside
the public for which Grass writes and overlapping with it, a substantial
subculture for which Stachnik's reading carries, as Grass is well aware,
the authority of the 'zeitaufhebende Kraft der alleinseligmachenden
Kirche' (170/166). This group would also accept that Stachnik's reading
of Dorothea's life is in certain respects different from Marienwerder's,
for while hagiographical scholarship is concerned to assess the validity of
sources in terms of an unchanging tradition of spiritual values, it also
acknowledges the historicity of these sources.

It is worth bearing this background in mind when considering the
more personal dimensions of the relationship between Grass and Stachnik, upon which the author has commented in interview:

Ich bin auch bis zum zwölften oder dreizehnten Lebensjahr noch religiös
gewesen. Und dann hat es für mich Prägungen gegeben, insbesondere durch

---

[16] *Der Dorotheenbote*, 38 (1978), 400.

einen Lateinlehrer, der auch im *Butt* vorkommt, Dr. Stachnik. Der wird übrigens zum erstenmal erwähnt in *Hundejahre*. Er war der Vorsitzende der Zentrumspartei, die auch längere Zeit gegen den Nationalsozialismus Widerstand geleistet hat, bis dann unter dem Prälat Kaas eine Schwenkung vollzogen wurde. Stachnik dagegen war ein Mann, der als Vorsitzender der Danziger Zentrumspartei Mut bewiesen hat und auch in Stutthof im Konzentrationslager gewesen ist und dann wieder zurückkam, seinen Unterricht fortsetzte. Ein für mich irritierender Mann mit seiner lateinischen Strenge. Und im absurden Gegensatz dazu war er als Katholik eigentlich nur an einem interessiert, an der Heiligsprechung der Dorothea von Montau, die im *Butt* eine große Rolle spielt (Casanova 1979^2, 219–20).

These remarks confirm that Stachnik was an important figure in Grass's adolescence. In his combination of admirable and irritating traits he reflects that ambiguity towards Catholicism which is a constantly recurring feature in Grass's work. Here, it is significant that his enthusiasm for Dorothea von Montau is the negative factor which stands in marked contrast to his political integrity.

School and church are what Stachnik represents in Grass's adolescent world, and it is this combination which suggests a link between the Stachnik-Dorothea sphere in *Der Butt* and an important theme in the earlier fiction with which the later novel has little direct connection. Although the Latin teacher is first brought to the attention of Grass's readers (approvingly, although with irony) in *Hundejahre* (132–3), it is in *Katz und Maus* that school and church are unmasked as the representative institutions of a corrupt society.[17] Stachnik is not mentioned directly or indirectly in the Novelle, and Grass has made a point of acknowledging his personal political heroism. Nevertheless he is firmly associated in the writer's imagination with the educational and religious institutions whose compromised moral authority makes them the target of the anger and emotional rebellion of the younger writer.

The rage of the writer, which finds potent expression in the last chapters of *Katz und Maus*, is no longer directed at the targets of adolescence in *Der Butt*. In the more complex patterning of the later novel it takes many forms and is often ironically masked. It appears directed at the issues of world hunger and the march of history towards catastrophe, but it is also present in the central theme of sexual conflict. In the direct depiction of the narrator's relationship with Ilsebill the rage is inhibited, the potential violence suppressed—but displaced into areas of the narrative which are thematically related. It emerges most explicitly in the fate inflicted on Sibylle in 'Vatertag', and in a more encoded form in the treatment of Dorothea von Montau.

---

[17] John Reddick, *The 'Danzig Trilogy' of Günter Grass* (London, 1975), 158–69.

The narrator cannot accuse Ilsebill herself of witchcraft, and he cannot suggest she should be burned or even walled up. But a simple transposition of the narrative perspective of the saint's *vita* enables him to invert the generic convention and, as her historical husband, to turn Dorothea into a witch. The reader should not be misled by the comic treatment of the whole episode which is, among other things, a rhetorical means of persuading the reader to collude with the vengeance that is being wrought on a wife who fills her husband with misery and fear.

But if he is striking at Ilsebill, he is also striking at Stachnik. His 'other truth' is an inversion of the truth of Stachnik's saint. The emotional rebellion of the adolescent against the questionable authority of church and school is being continued by other means. Because of his record of resistance to National Socialism and his stint in Stutthof, Stachnik was not to be attacked on grounds of politics or personal integrity, which were not at issue. But through his prominence in the successful campaign for Dorothea's canonization the priest had become centrally and publicly identified with the saint, and this identification had already been a major factor in the adolescent's ambiguous attitude to his teacher.

It is clear from Stachnik's riposte that the onslaught was not without effect; indeed, he clearly felt he had been hit under the belt by a former pupil whom he could not remember. Much of his article is taken up with quoting, *in extenso* and for the edification of the readers of *Der Dorotheenbote*, most of the obscene or blasphemous passages referring to Dorothea in the novel, 'Aussagen, die mich erschreckt, ja bedrückt und tief geschmerzt haben'.[18] Such a response is hardly surprising from an eighty-four-year-old priest who had devoted a great part of his life to the cult of Dorothea.

Some knowledge of these matters can sharpen our reading of the second Month, and especially of 'Verehrter Herr Doktor Stachnik' (167–72/164–8; cf. Adolph 1983, 128–30). In this letter the accurate biographical information about the author and Dr Stachnik leads on to the narrator's defensive personal memory of his marriage with Dorothea (169–70/165–6), which is toned down in comparison with his primary account. In due course it becomes clear that this is because the narrator is about to make a disingenuous compromise-suggestion that both he and Stachnik should abandon their readings: 'Ich sage nie wieder—obgleich ich Beweise hätte—Dorothea ist eine Hexe gewesen; Sie bestehen nicht mehr—obgleich sie das Zeug zur Heiligen hatte—auf der bevorstehenden Kanonisierung' (171/167). Here, speaking as one story-teller to another, he is admitting that his negative reading of Dorothea's life is the

---

[18] *Der Dorotheenbote*, 38 (1978), 408.

direct inversion of Stachnik's hagiographical work, and the biographical information just supplied makes it clear that it is, in part at least, a response and reaction to it. The narrator's proposal (on his principle that the stories provided by history are open-ended, fluid, and capable of infinite retellings) is that they should agree on a new reading which abandons ideological or emotional positions and rests upon the love of Dorothea which they share. (Dr Stachnik notes this declaration with interest, but not surprisingly ignores the proposal: not all story-tellers can abandon their adopted positions as easily as the novelist.)

But even this opportunistic example of the narrator's penchant for 'third way' solutions is not quite as open-ended as it would like to appear. It is at best a proposal for compromise between the various male readings of a female life that have been the subject of this essay. The narrator is driven into suggesting a defensive male alliance with Stachnik because a fourth version of the history of Dorothea von Montau has begun to emerge—a female version this time.

At the trial of the flounder Sieglinde Huntscha avoids discussing Dorothea's case, but her allusions to Bloch and the principle of hope are taken up by the presiding judge Dr Schönherr, a figure treated with respect by the narrator and usually permitted to express a responsible and intelligent feminist point of view. It is she who suggests, with the tacit agreement of the flounder, that Dorothea should be seen as a forerunner of feminist aspirations who had chosen the only form of freedom open to women in her age (148–9/145). It is a reading that is in accordance with a good deal of critical writing, both feminist and traditional, that has appeared on medieval women mystics since the publication of *Der Butt*.[19] But because it is a secularized reading the narrator thinks he can use it to frighten Dr Stachnik into a reactionary male alliance. It is typical of the pervasive narrative irony in this novel that a passage which appears to be written from an authorial rather than a fictive point of view should unmask the stratagems of the narrator so clearly. For it is Günter Grass, who sees Bloch as the purveyor of

[19] For the perspective of a cultural historian on a subject that should interest readers of *Der Butt*, see Caroline Walker Bynum (as in n. 12), 'Fast, Feast and Flesh: the Religious Significance of Food to Medieval Women', *Representations*, 11 (1985), 1–25, and the same author's *Holy Feast and Holy Fast: The Religious Significance of Food to Medieval Women* (Berkeley, 1986). For literary history, see Müller, U., 1985, 126–31, and also Siegfried Ringler, 'Die Rezeption mittelalterlicher Frauenmystik als wissenschaftliches Problem, dargestellt am Werk der Christine Ebner', in Peter Dinzelbacher and Dieter R. Bauer (eds.), *Frauenmystik im Mittelalter* (Wissenschaftliche Studientagung der Akademie der Diözese Rottenburg-Stuttgart, 22–5 Feb. 1984 in Weingarten; Ostfildern bei Stuttgart, 1985), 178–200, esp. 196–8. The radical feminist approach suggested by Luce Irigaray, *Speculum de l'autre femme* (Paris, 1974) remains a theoretical challenge awaiting systematic application to the texts.

necessary utopias (Raddatz 1977[1], 30), who has allowed this interpretation to surface, and he clearly favours it over the readings of Dorothea's (and Ilsebill's) husband and of Stachnik—even if he has left it untold himself, as a potential alternative version for a future, less beleagured narrator.

5
Grass and the Appropriation of the Fairy-Tale in the Seventies

HANNE CASTEIN

Since *Der Butt* appeared in 1977, a great deal has been written about Günter Grass's appropriation of a well-known fairy-tale as a referential framework for the book. Critical attention has focused on the important issue of what function the 'Buttmärchen' serves within the novel and on Grass's intriguing invention of a 'lost' second version of the fairy-tale in question: the Grimm Brothers' 'Von dem Fischer un syner Fru'.[1] What has so far been left out of the discussion is the fact that when *Der Butt* was published the 'Märchenwelle' in West Germany and the GDR was a widespread literary phenomenon, and that in basing his latest novel on a Grimm fairy-tale Grass was participating in a firmly established trend.

From at least the sixteenth century onwards writers have responded to the fairy-tale's increasing loss of relevance to contemporary reality—once frozen in a specific version—and have frequently attempted to restore some of the lost validity of these stories by modernizing their plots or by exploiting their formal and thematic richness to furnish up-to-date social commentary. The most seminal of all collections, the Grimms' *Kinder- und Hausmärchen* (1812–14), has undergone more adaptations and metamorphoses of this kind than any other. Since their first appearance in print, these fairy-tales have been rewritten and turned into plays and poems, and never with more enthusiasm than in the late sixties, when this trend gathered unprecedented momentum in both Germanies. A large number of new, and often critical, versions, travesties, and parodies of the best-known fairy-tales appeared, prompted in many cases by a profound change in attitude to the value-system implied by the tales. The *Kinder- und Hausmärchen* were attacked by Jack Zipes as '"the secret agents" of an education establishment which indoctrinates children to learn fixed roles and functions within bourgeois society'.[2] The editors'

[1] Heinz Rölleke (ed.), Brüder Grimm, *Kinder- und Hausmärchen*, i (Stuttgart, 1980), 19. Subsequent references to this volume use the abbreviation *KHM*.
[2] Jack Zipes, *Fairy Tales and the Art of Subversion* (London, 1983), 46.

value-system had in fact been superimposed upon the collection: 'Generell hat Grimm alle Märchen auf diese Weise "rund gemacht", d.h. tendenziös verändert und mit Schlüssen versehen, die der etablierten Moral entsprechen und keinerlei alternatives Denken zulassen.'[3] Jacob Grimm, who was responsible for most of the changes, made the intentions underlying the considerable modification of the tales explicit when he expressed the hope that the *Kinder- und Hausmärchen* would become 'ein Volks- und Erziehungsbuch, namentlich auch in der feineren Welt'.[4] Although previously recognized and acknowledged, the lasting impression of the *KHM*, particularly on the young, and their role in a repressive and conformist process of socialization had not been collectively challenged until this decade, when parents, sociologists, psychologists, and above all writers questioned the conventional 'Märchenweisheit' and condemned a great many of the tales as authoritarian and sexist.

Among the first and most amusing of the many collections of new readings of traditional fairy-tales was Iring Fetscher's enormously successful 'Märchen-Verwirrbuch' *Wer hat Dornröschen wachgeküßt?* (1972). Fetscher attacked the notion of the Grimms' tales as 'sacred texts', encouraging a thoroughly irreverent attitude towards them as he satirized a variety of scholarly approaches to the genre in chapters such as 'Rumpelstilzchen und die Frankfurter Schule' and 'Dornröschen oder Die Überwindung der Deflorationsphobie'. The latter is a parody of the many Freudian readings of this fairy-tale, in that it discusses the 'erotische Befreiungstat des Prinzen' from a psychoanalytical point of view and unmasks the fairy-tale as an expression of the bourgeoisie's neurotically repressed sexual taboos. After decoding the spindle's phallic symbolism, Fetscher has a footnote on it, his satire reading very much like the real thing:

Diese Deutung der 'Spindel' wird nicht nur durch ihre Form nahegelegt, sondern auch durch die Worte, mit denen die Prinzessin nach ihr fragt: 'Was ist das für ein Ding, das so lustig herumspringt?' Bekanntlich wird das männliche Geschlechtsorgan im Volksmund oft als 'das Ding' oder 'mein Ding' bezeichnet, worin sich zweifellos ein entfremdetes Verhältnis zur eigenen Geschlechtseigenschaft ausdrückt (zur Verdinglichung vgl. G. Lukács' Abhandlung über 'die Verdinglichung und das Bewußtsein des Proletariats' in *Geschichte und Klassenbewußtsein* 1923).[5]

[3] Otto F. Gmelin, *Böses kommt aus Kinderbüchern: Die verpaßten Möglichkeiten kindlicher Bewußtseinsbildung* (Munich, 1972), 44.

[4] Jacob Grimm to F. J. Bertuch, 8 Dec. 1812. Quoted in G. Ginschel, *Der junge Jacob Grimm: 1805–1819* (Berlin, GDR, 1967), 245.

[5] Iring Fetscher, *Wer hat Dornröschen wachgeküßt?* (Frankfurt, 1972), 145.

At the end of the decade *Das große deutsche Märchenbuch*,[6] with fairy-tales from Grimmelshausen to Wondratschek, confirmed that the fairy-tale was one of the most seminal genres of post-war German literature. In the GDR the anthology *Die Rettung des Saragossameeres*[7] documented the fairy-tale's considerable contribution to the establishment of a new literature and its attraction for most major writers:

Gerade auch auf der formalen Ebene dürfte für viele DDR-Schriftsteller das Interesse an diesem Medium liegen. Denn das Märchen ist eine kurze Prosaform, die durch verschiedenartige Erzähl- und Verschlüsselungsmöglichkeiten literarische Freiheiten gewährt und literarische Experimente gestattet, für die die Grenzen in den realistischen Erzählgattungen in der DDR viel enger sind. Witziges und Tragisches, Groteskes, Absurdes und Realistisches lassen sich im Märchen leicht verbinden.[8]

But in both Germanies the new fairy-tales were printed not only in anthologies, or indeed as independent works, they were also embedded in the context of a number of major novels. Among these are Ingeborg Bachmann's *Malina* (1971), Hans Erich Nossack's *Die gestohlene Melodie* (1972), Irmtraud Morgner's *Leben und Abenteuer der Trobadora Beatriz nach Zeugnissen ihrer Spielfrau Laura* (1974), and, of course, Grass's *Der Butt*. The fairy-tales in these works are mostly the free inventions of their authors, inserted into the novels as complete and separate, though obviously relevant, texts. This is how 'Die Geheimnisse der Prinzessin von Kagran' functions in *Malina*, and 'Der König geht ins Kino' in *Die gestohlene Melodie*. In other cases individual motifs, characters, or indeed the entire plot of a particularly apposite existing fairy-tale may be utilized, as in the case of both Morgner and Grass. The 'Märchenwelle' has not yet exhausted itself, but there has been a trend away from the reutilization of traditional fairy-tales to the invention of new texts. Joachim Walther, himself an author of this new kind of modern fairy-tale, comments on this development:

Die Märchen der Vergangenheit finden heute nicht mehr die gesellschaftlichen Bedingungen ihrer Entstehung vor und also neue Rezipienten: gewalttätigen Aktualisierungsversuchen verschließen sie sich—es müssen neue her, denn das Bedürfnis nach Märchen besteht.[9]

---

[6] Helmut Brackert (ed.), *Das große deutsche Märchenbuch* (Königstein im Taunus, 1979).
[7] Joachim Walther and Manfred Wolter (eds.), *Die Rettung des Saragossameeres* (Berlin, GDR, 1976).
[8] Horst Heidtmann, *Die Verbesserung des Menschen* (Darmstadt and Neuwied, 1982), 187.
[9] Joachim Walther, 'Metamorphose des Märchens', in Heide Hess and Peter Liebers (eds.), *Arbeiten mit der Romantik heute* (Berlin, GDR, 1978), 131.

Major publications in this spirit in the eighties were Peter Rühmkorf's *Der Hüter des Misthaufens*. *Aufgeklärte Märchen* (1983) and Stefan Heym's *Märchen für kluge Kinder* (1984), and a continuing widespread critical attention was focused on the fairy-tale. In 1985 Volker Klotz published *Das europäische Kunstmärchen*, the most valuable book on the subject to date, and commented: 'Mich wurmt, mit diesem Buch womöglich in eine fast schon Dauermodewelle zu geraten: von Märchensucht und Fantasy-Verzückung.'[10]

When Grass turned to fairy-tale material, as so many of his contemporaries had done before him, he made an unusual choice with 'Von dem Fischer un syner Fru'. While most writers who work with traditional fairy-tales reject and rewrite their almost obligatory miraculous happy endings, Grass found one of the few tales with a quite *un*happy end, supporting his view of the fairy-tale as a specifically realistic genre, its realism all too often buried under 'viel Lieblichkeit und Anheimelndem' (Raddatz 1977¹, 30):

> Ich meine, daß man erst jetzt das Märchen zu entdecken beginnt. Keine Verstellung von Wirklichkeit, keine Denunzierung des Märchenerzählers als eines Menschen, der—'na, der erzählt nur Märchen'—vor der Realität flüchtet, sondern die um sich greifende Erkenntnis, daß im Märchen in bündiger Form oft mehr Realität eingefangen ist als zum Beispiel im angeblich so tiefschürfenden psychologischen Roman.

This view—that the fairy-tale represented reality rather than an impossible and perhaps dangerous dream—was unusual in the seventies, when the prevailing tendency was to fight its pernicious influence. But Grass was not the only writer in this decade to defend the Grimms' tales. In 1972 Anna Seghers had initiated the 'Märchenwelle' in the GDR virtually single-handedly when she paved the way for the genre's acceptance within the theoretical limitations of Socialist Realism by stressing the fairy-tale's roots in historical reality—in terms very much echoed by Grass—and by illustrating her point with an example from the *Kinder- und Hausmärchen*:

> Symbolische oder phantastische Darstellungen, Märchen und Sagen wurzeln doch irgendwie in der Wirklichkeit. Genausogut wie greifbare Dinge. Ein richtiger Wald gehört zur Wirklichkeit, doch auch ein Traum von einem Wald. Entstand das Hexenhäuschen von Hänsel und Gretel vielleicht nicht aus der Wirklichkeit? Ich sage euch: aus der bittersten Wirklichkeit, als Eltern im Dreißigjährigen Krieg ihre eigenen Kinder in den wilden Wald schickten, damit sie nicht vor ihren Augen verhungern.[11]

---

[10] Volker Klotz, *Das europäische Kunstmärchen* (Stuttgart, 1985), 363.

[11] Anna Seghers, *Sonderbare Begegnungen* (Berlin, GDR, and Weimar, 1972), 142–3.

While Grass had not been the first to discover the fairy-tale's literary potential or to stress its 'Realitätsanspruch' ('Man darf es als einen Träger gleichzeitig von vergangener und gegenwärtiger Wirklichkeit bezeichnen', writes Max Lüthi in 1962)[12], he was to put his particular chosen tale to strikingly original use. There appears to be no precedent for the way in which Grass makes 'Von dem Fischer un syner Fru' an 'Integrationsgeschichte des Buches ... die die verschiedenen Zeit- und Handlungsebenen des Romans verbindet' (Durzak 1979, 79). Durrani elaborates on the integrating function of the fairy-tale. He sees it as:

the substratum that holds Grass's novel together by uniting the principal ideological strands, which, viewed together, provide information about the author's attitude to history:

1. The idea of progress. The fisherman's wife with her incessant demands brings about the creation of increasingly sophisticated material goods, as has happened over the past centuries. . . .
2. The idea of futility. The endless chain of demand, consumption, demand is a process which, once started, cannot be stopped. . . .
3. The idea of history as a cyclical process. . . . The level of consumption becomes so outrageous that the whole process is terminated by a 'big bang'.
4. The interaction of the sexes as part of this historical process. Their apparent polarity (the reluctant husband versus the appetitive wife) provides the battleground on which the issue of social progress is fought out (Durrani 1980, 817–18).

Other post-war authors before Grass had, however, been attracted to this particular fairy-tale. In 1976 Uwe Johnson had drawn attention to 'Von dem Fischer un syner Fru' with his rendering of the tale into modern German, and he had already pointed out one of the dimensions which Grass was to explore so thoroughly—that it is 'die Geschichte einer unglücklichen Ehe'.[13] Some ten years before Johnson, Helmut Heißenbüttel had written two versions giving a conventional reading of the text as a 'Warnmärchen' against greed. His two adaptations of the fairy-tale give expression to the antimaterialism of the sixties. In the 'Märchen vom Bürosammler' the hero works and cheats his way out of great poverty until he owns a whole city of offices, but his deceptions are discovered and he is stripped of all his riches. Heißenbüttel's 'Der Fischer und seine Frau als Stille im Lande' satirizes a couple who, though living in luxury, are discontented and unhappy:

sie trachten was trachten sie denn nach ihrem Glück das heißt sie wollens wollen sies anders haben was trachten sie denn wenn sie trachten nach mehr es soll mehr

---

[12] Max Lüthi, *Märchen* (Stuttgart, 1962), 117.
[13] Uwe Johnson, *Von dem Fischer un syner Fru* (Frankfurt, 1976), 49.

sein sonst ist es egal und wenn nur der Schein sie trachten nach Anschein
trachten sie nach dem mehr von Anschein des Glückes.[14]

There is a more light-hearted example from the GDR which uses the
fairy-tale's basic plot and comes closer to Grass's interpretation: Stefan
Heym's 'Der kleine König, der ein Kind kriegen mußte'.[15] This work is
also a variant on the 'Geschlechtertausch' theme, a variant of the fairy-
tale's central transformation motif (as in 'Der Froschkönig', *KHM* 1 and
'Sneewittchen', *KHM* 53). In Heym's story, the little king is married to
Adelheid, whose emancipated ideas force him to delegate more and more
of the women's work at his court to men. Her demands become
increasingly difficult to meet, until she complains: 'es ist doch nicht
gerecht, daß immer die Frauen die Kinder kriegen, und nicht die
Männer, oder?' (51)—and she challenges him to set an example to the
kingdom by producing the first child. This he does with the compliance
of an attractive shepherdess, who finally supplants the queen: 'Frau
Adelheid aber gründete einen Verein, und wenn sie nicht gestorben ist,
redet sie noch heute' (54).

Adelheid reads like a prototype for the members of the Feminal, and,
like Grass, Heym suggests a misogynistic interpretation of his fairy-tale.
Its chief concern is not an unhappy marriage, nor the punishment of
material greed, but the exposure of woman's rejection of her allocated
role, her presumptuous attempts at usurping the bastions of male power,
and her efforts to reduce man to a mere adjunct of her own heightened
social position (thus reversing the traditional pattern): 'ik bün König, un
du büst man myn Mann' ('I am king and you are only my husband')
(*KHM* 123).

In *Der Butt* the relative roles of women and men in the shaping of
world history are explicitly debated for the first time in a work of German
fiction, and for Grass the early nineteenth century, when the 'Buttmärchen' was first printed, was a kind of watershed in this power struggle
between the sexes:

Der absolute Machtverlust der Frauen setzt erst mit der Industrialisierung ein.
Solange es noch eine Haus- und Schlüsselgewalt gab—das ganze Mittelalter
hindurch, bis ins 19. Jahrhundert hinein, dort beginnt es umzukippen—
Haushalte auch noch ein Stück Selbstversorgung bewahrten, hatten die Frauen
einen restlichen und gleichzeitig erheblichen Machtbereich, von dem sie auch
Gebrauch gemacht haben. Damit hatten sie aber prinzipiell nicht das Heft in der
Hand. ... sie hatten aber immerhin die Möglichkeit, 'Gegenpositionen' zu
entwickeln ... Diese Gegenpositionen sind mittlerweile auch verloren gegangen
(Arnold 1978, 36–7).

---

[14] Helmut Heißenbüttel, *Textbuch* (Neuwied and Berlin, 1970), 143.
[15] Stefan Heym, *Märchen für kluge Kinder* (Munich, 1984), 49–54.

'Von dem Fischer un syner Fru' attributes this 'Machtverlust der Frauen' to their immoderate ambition. Such an interpretation does not, however, account for all of human history: the role men played in its shaping needs to be added to give us the entire truth, and *Der Butt* represents this attempt.

The section of the sixth Month entitled 'Die andere Wahrheit' describes an unhistorical gathering of a group of Romantic writers in the Olivaer Wald in 1807. Runge has brought two versions of the 'Buttmärchen' along: one in which Ilsebill is the central figure, extravagantly claiming one male power-preserve after another, and a second in which it is the fisherman who is 'maßlos in seinen Wünschen' (355/349), an attitude that ultimately leads to the destruction of life on earth. Only the solitary woman present at the gathering protests against the printing of the first version: 'Wenn man das Märchen so rausgebe, hätten die Männer leicht sagen: So sind die Weiber, zänkisch und raffgierig, die eine wie die andere. "Dabei sind die Frauen arm dran!" rief sie' (356–7/350). The speaker is Bettina Brentano, later Bettina von Arnim, herself an author with an active interest in social questions and in the emancipation of women in particular. 'Die verspielte Bettina' (359/352) is introduced to us as 'die Schwester des Clemens Brentano' and a naïvely gushing admirer of Goethe—'sie hatte im Frühjahr leibhaftig Goethe gesehn' (353/346); and in her attempts to settle the quarrel among the dissenting men she is presented as a spineless 'Kompromißler'. While the men would like to suppress the second, apocalyptic fairy-tale, Bettina is joined by Sophie Rotzoll and her daughter in her plea against the first version: 'solche Märchen seien auch ihnen bekannt. Aber nur die eine Wahrheit stimme. Nur der Mann wolle mehr, immer mehr. "Die machen doch all das Unglück!" rief Sophie und schlug mit der Faust auf das Brot' (361/354). The dispute is settled moments later, when Runge, whilst his fellow-artists admire the moon, burns the manuscript of the second fairy-tale: 'So wollten die Herren die patriarchalische Ordnung schützen' (23/20).

But which of the two versions gave the true account? Runge's Pomeranian source had suggested: 'dat een un dat anner tosamen' (356/349), and this is the narrator's understanding too. His efforts are directed at reconstructing the lost half of mankind's history: 'Wahrhaftig werde ich, was Philipp Otto Runge als andere Wahrheit mitschrieb, auf meinem Papier erinnern; und müßte ich Wort für Wort aus der Asche lesen' (23/20). *Der Butt* as a whole then represents the expanded reconstruction of Runge's destroyed original, an effort to set the record straight and balance the 'Schummelmärchen' (23/20) of Ilsebill's insatiability with an account of 'die andere Wahrheit'.

Uwe Johnson mentions one version of 'Von dem Fischer un syner Fru'
in which the roles are similarly reversed: 'nur im lettischen Märchen ist
der Mann der ewig Unzufriedene' (49), an obscure text to which Grass
himself once refers obliquely: 'Doch als der Butt philologisch auswu-
cherte und hessische, flämische, elsässische und schlesische Textvarian-
ten des Märchens herzusagen begann—"hochinteressant eine lettische
Variante"—wurde er von der Anklägerin unterbrochen' (47/44).

The only traceable version with a male culprit is referred to by Grass
as well and describes the rise and fall of Napoleon. It appeared in 1814
and was 'als Biographie Napoleons stark gekauft und gelesen'.[16] However, this 'Schrift gegen den Tyrannen' (360/353), as Grass refers to it,
reduces what he regards as a universally valid statement on gender roles
and behaviour to an individual, and thereby less worrying, instance.

While the whole of *Der Butt* might represent Runge's burnt version of
the 'Buttmärchen', the first version eventually printed by the Grimms is
echoed not only in the narrator–Ilsebill relationship and in Ilsebill's
characterization but equally obviously in the painful 'Vatertag' episode,
where both Ilsebill's hubris and her punishment are paralleled by Billy's
story. Within that chapter yet another, viciously comic, variant of the
fairy-tale is given—one which Mäxchen tells the sleepless Billy—again
on the theme of female greed, this time sexual. Ilsebill is a nymphoma-
niac who desires ever more socially distinguished partners, overreaching
herself when she asks for Beethoven and being promptly returned to her
fisherman husband.

All versions of the 'Buttmärchen', including *Der Butt* as a whole,
express a truth about women and men which Grass presents as immut-
able, for he promises no break in the see-saw of matriarchy and
patriarchy. In spite of an allusion at the beginning of the novel to the
possibility that there might be an alternative—'Vielleicht haben wir nur
vergessen, daß es noch mehr gibt. Was Drittes. Auch sonst, auch
politisch, als Möglichkeit' (10/7)—this possibility is not elaborated.
Grass cannot see beyond a continuation of matriarchal and patriarchal
patterns and appears to be stuck with a view of the feminist movement as
a struggle to replace 'Männerherrschaft' with 'Frauenherrschaft' (48/45).

According to Grass, all feminists are Ilsebills, and the Feminal is made
up of them: 'Wie der Butt von den Ilsebills angeklagt wurde' (46/42).
Grass mocks the divisiveness of the women's movement, tellingly
referred to by him as 'Feminismus' rather than 'Frauenbewegung'. From
the very beginning the Feminal is unable to agree on a joint programme

---

[16] F. K. von Savigny to Wilhelm Grimm, 29 Apr. 1814, in Adolf Stoll, *Friedrich Karl
von Savigny. Professorenjahre in Berlin 1810–1842. Mit 317 Briefen aus den Jahren
1810–1841* (Berlin, 1929), 104.

and breaks up into many splinter groups—'Lesbische Aktion', 'Brot & Rosen', 'Frauenkollektiv Ilsebill', etc. The women are no better at being in charge than the men, and no less aggressive—'die üblichen Fraktions- kämpfe fanden statt' (53/50). Although it expresses a view actually held by members of the 'Frauenbewegung', the women's assertion that under a matriarchal system life today would be 'friedfertiger, sensibler, ohne Individualanspruch dennoch kreativer, allgemein zärtlicher, trotz Über- fluß dennoch gerechter' (52/48) sounds particularly unconvincing, com- ing as it does immediately after Grass's highly ironical description of the Feminal's infighting.

Nevertheless, Grass shares the women's movement's central distrust of the rationalist 'männlicher Erkenntnisprozeß', and this leads both of them—though with very different results—to a keen interest in 'Mythen und Märchen, an vorgeschichtlichen Matriarchaten und Göttinnen- kulten mit ihren Ritualen'.[17] It was in Irmtraud Morgner's *Trobadora Beatriz* that these preoccupations of the early phase of the 'Frauen- bewegung' undoubtedly found their most articulate expression, with the result that the novel has been marketed as 'So etwas wie eine Bibel aktueller Frauenemanzipation'[18] in West Germany. While not boasting anything as singularly articulate as Grass's flounder, *Trobadora Beatriz* does make sardonic use of the Sleeping Beauty story ('Dornröschen', *KHM* 50), and the novel opens and closes with a satirical adaptation of the fairy-tale that comments on the state of male–female relations in the seventies. Morgner's Beatriz is a twelfth-century poetess who awakens from a magic sleep into the twentieth century, where she finds to her vast disappointment that men and women still conform to predetermined sex- roles. By rejecting the engineer who inadvertently wakes her up she rejects the acting-out of a behavioural stereotype—that of the passive female woken by the male's sexual touch:

Als sie sich die Schlafkrumen aus den Augen gerieben hatte, verliebte sie sich infolge übermäßiger Enthaltsamkeit in den Ingenieur und dichtete auf ihn viele gute und schöne Lieder. Anfangs verbat er sich lautes Singen, weil er verheiratet war, später, weil er sich scheiden und Beatriz ehelichen wollte. Da glaubte sich die Dame vom Regen in die Traufe geraten und wandte sich gen Osten. Sie durchquerte ein Land, in dem Frauen, wenn sie die gleiche Arbeit wie die Männer verrichten, schlechter bezahlt wurden, und eins, in dem sie für gleiche Arbeit gleichen Lohn erhielten. Dort ließ sie sich nieder und nahm Arbeit beim VEB Hochbau Berlin (447).

[17] Herrad Schenk, *Die feministische Herausforderung* (Munich, 1980), 161.
[18] This sentence (from a review in the *Frankfurter Rundschau*) is printed on the back cover of the West German paperback edition: Irmtraud Morgner, *Leben und Abenteuer der Trobadora Beatriz nach Zeugnissen ihrer Spielfrau Laura* (Darmstadt and Neuwied, 1974), which is the edition quoted in this essay.

Morgner shares Grass's views as he stated them when asked whether *Der Butt* was an anti-emancipatory book:

Es ist die Skepsis einer Emanzipation der Frau gegenüber, die sich an männlichen Leitbildern orientiert, die eigentlich nur gleichziehen will. Ich glaube, es wäre weder den Frauen noch den Männern, noch ihrem Verhältnis zueinander geholfen, wenn sich das männliche Macht- und Moralverhältnis durch eine—in diesem Sinn erfolgreiche—weibliche Emanzipation noch verstärken würde. . . . Solche Emanzipation würde das Spannungsverhältnis zwischen den Geschlechtern aufheben, nivellieren, ohne etwas Neues an dessen Stelle zu setzen (Raddatz 1977¹, 30).

With regard to this last point, the two writers diverge radically: *Der Butt* implies that nothing new is conceivable, given unalterable human nature; Morgner's novel was written to make precisely the opposite point. Early on in *Trobadora Beatriz*, Persephone and Demeter enlist women from many centuries—including the Trobadora—in a bid to re-establish matriarchy. Beatriz rejects this move as a 'reaktionäre Bestrebung' and opts for an alternative 'dritte Ordnung': 'Die weder patriarchalisch noch matriarchalisch sein sollte, sondern menschlich' (20). The prerequisite for the attainment of this humanist third order is the abolition of the sex-role differentiation, but this is something not registered by Grass. In the mid-seventies Jo Freeman summed up the women's movement's view on this point:

To seek for equality alone, given the current male bias of the social values, is to assume that women want to be like men or that men are worth emulating. It is to demand that women be allowed to participate in society as we know it, to get their piece of the pie, without questioning whether that society is worth participating in. Most feminists today find this view inadequate. Those women who are personally more comfortable in what is considered the male role must realize that that role is made possible only by the existence of the female sex role; in other words, only by the subjection of women. Therefore women cannot become equal to men without the destruction of those two interdependent, mutually parasitic roles.[19]

For Morgner, as for many of her contemporaries, the 'Dornröschen' plot was a marvellously appropriate vehicle for comment on the women's question. The qualities of passivity and obedience, which lead Bruno Bettelheim to applaud Dornröschen as 'the very incarnation of perfect feminity',[20] have prompted others to proclaim:

---

[19] Jo Freeman, 'The Women's Liberation Movement: Its Origins, Organizations, Activities, and Ideas', in *Women: A Feminist Perspective* (Palo Alto, 1975), 572–3.

[20] Bruno Bettelheim, *The Uses of Enchantment. The Meaning and Importance of Fairy Tales* (Harmondsworth, 1978), 236.

> Es kommt kein Prinz mit einem Kuß,
> macht nicht mit deinen Sorgen Schluß;
> es bringt dich auch kein Königssohn
> vom Kochtopf auf den Herrscherthron.
>
> Du kannst dir selbst dein Leben bauen,
> mußt allen deinen Kräften trauen.
> Mach noch heute den Versuch
> und pfeif auf den Prinzen im Märchenbuch.[21]

In spite of the fact that the Trobadora's encounters with men are disheartening ones for most of the novel (early on in the book she is brutally raped), she retains her faith in the possible realization of a 'third-order' relationship between men and women. Although one of the subjects of Morgner's novel, as of Grass's, is 'die ungeschriebene Geschichte, die nicht von Männern gemacht wurde' (181), her chief concern is with the present and the future. In the absence of a fairy-tale which would express her vision, she invents one of her own, a 'Wunsch-dichtung' like most of the traditional fairy-tales. This is the 'Gute Botschaft der Valeska', a manuscript left behind by the Trobadora after her sudden death towards the end of the novel. It tells of Valeska Kantus who, in Berlin in 1972, found a miraculous way of changing herself into a man and just as effortlessly back into a woman. The transformation is achieved by repeating the phrase 'man müßte ein Mann sein' three times. Valeska's experiences as a male reveal to her 'daß die physischen Unterschiede zwischen Mann und Frau gegenüber den kulturellen gering waren' (429). Moreover, her partner does not feel threatened by her ability to switch roles, and he loves her in either incarnation, just as she is able to love him when she is male. Both realize 'daß sie notfalls die Bilder entbehren konnten, die sie sich voneinander und die andere für sie gemacht hatten' (443).

On the 'real' level of the novel, one of its protagonists, Benno Pakulat, looks forward to the 'dritte Ordnung' in terms which explicitly reject a 'macho' male role. The liberation of women will also liberate men from the burden of outgrown conventions:

Uns steht kein langweiliges Leben bevor, wenn die Weiber erst tun wollen, was sie tun wollen, nicht, was sie tun sollen. Was werden sie als Menschen sagen über die Männer, nicht als Bilder, die sich die Männer von ihnen gemacht haben? Was wird geschehen, wenn sie äußern, was sie fühlen, nicht, was zu fühlen wir von ihnen erwarten? Neulich sagte die Gattin eines Dichters, von Frauen wären keine Liebesgedichte zu lesen. Die Gattin hat recht, nur wenige Damen möchten ihren Ruf dem Geruch der Abnormalität preisgeben. Frauen ohne unterdrücktes

---

[21] Josef Reding, 'Mädchen, pfeif auf den Prinzen!', in Wolfgang Mieder (ed.), *Grimms Märchen—modern* (Stuttgart, 1979), 70.

Liebesleben gelten als krank (nymphoman). Männer solcher Art gelten als gesund (kerngesund). Kann sein, wir werden eines Sommertags nicht mehr unsere Nacktheit auf dem Bauplatz verschleudern, kann sein, wir gestatten uns eines Tages nicht nur beim Zwiebelschneiden eine Träne. Ach, einmal den Hof gemacht kriegen, öffentlich, wenn die Emanzipation der Weiber dazu führt, bin ich ihr Mann (273–4).

But Benno Pakulat is looking forward to a *future* state of affairs. Even in the GDR, for Morgner 'ein Land des Wunderbaren' (447), the reality of women's lives is far removed from the one envisaged by the young man. By the mid-seventies, a time of liberal politics in both Germanies, Grass and Morgner seem disenchanted with the recent developments in the women's movement. They share a more global pessimism, and in this their novels are representative of the thematic preoccupations of their time. Both novels include indictments of extremes such as surfeit and hunger, the threat of nuclear war, and the destruction of nature through technology. At the height of the 'Märchenwelle', both authors make use of a traditional fairy-tale—albeit in very different ways—to express their fundamental views on the subject of women's liberation, supplementing that fairy-tale with their own 'andere Wahrheit'. Grass's 'Weltuntergangsmärchen' and the 'Vatertag' chapter reveal his deep pessimism. The violent end of the world and the violent crushing of a grotesquely ill-conceived female take-over bid correspond to a utopian vision in *Trobadora Beatriz*, a vision of ideal companionship where sex change has become effortless for the woman and is accepted as natural and desirable. Although many of Morgner's protagonists carry the seed of the 'dritte Ordnung' within them, the fact remains that without miraculous intervention Valeska would have no more realized her dream than Billy and her friends do.

In their choice of fairy-tales both authors express a view of actual female conduct: the aggressive Ilsebill and the passive Dornröschen, existing at the extreme ends of a behavioural spectrum, are deplored for what they are by both writers. While still providing a convenient code for the discussion of a very wide range of topical issues, the traditional fairy-tale has rarely been cited in the last two decades without an awareness of its questionable utopian promise, its sexism, and its authoritarianism. It continues to serve as a very rich source of literary inspiration, as an undiminished pool of shared reference and remembrance. However, it is not the traditional fairy-tales but the new 'Kunstmärchen' of the seventies and eighties, which have encouraged the modern reader 'mit Phantasie und Witz zu gewohnten Vorstellungen und mächtigen Konventionen den Widerspruch zu entdecken und einen anderen Weg einzuschlagen'.[22]

[22] Jens Tismar, *Kunstmärchen* (Stuttgart, 1977), 75.

6

'Wir hängen nicht vom Gehänge ab': The Body as Battleground in *Der Butt*

JOHN J. WHITE

Bodies and their appendages have always loomed large (or small) in Günter Grass's fiction. Oskar Matzerath's diminutive stature plays as vital a role in the satirical strategy of *Die Blechtrommel* as his aggressive drumming and glass-shattering abilities. Joachim Mahlke's protruding Adam's apple and his equally pronounced sexual organ feature prominently in the imagery of *Katz und Maus*. Likewise, the state of Eberhard Starusch's teeth is of crucial importance in *örtlich betäubt*, both at plot level and on the novel's ingenious symbolic plane. Usually, however, Grass's narratives are not concerned with the entire body—Oskar is an exception—but with specific parts of it, such as the navel (with or without sherbet garnishing) or an arm traversed by an emblematic snail. In this respect, Aua's three breasts, 'der Arsch der dicken Gret', the various male figures' obsession with the part of their anatomy they apologetically refer to as their 'Stinkmorchel', and the phallic surrogates that play such an important role in the 'Vatertag' episode of *Der Butt* are little more than variations on a recurrent, frequently grotesque, synecdochic concern with the body that has run through most of the author's preceding fiction and much of his poetry. As many a reader knows to his or her cost, Grass's narrators seldom spare one the minutiae of their characters' bodily functions, from the basic and perfunctory to the eccentric and often calculatingly nauseous. In this, *Der Butt*, a novel where it has been claimed that Grass 'even more than in his other works ... emphasized human physicality, sex, food, digestion, defecation, physical needs and physical deprivations' (Angress 1982, 43),[1] can be seen to be merely taking further the material concerns of his earlier

---

[1] 'Given the heavy emphasis on women and their physiology', Ruth Angress complains, 'one might have expected [the author] to make at least an attempt at describing female

novels. What is new, however, is the way in which the body has now become the battleground for the rival male chauvinist–feminist positions, and specifically—because of the male narrator's ambivalent responses to Ilsebill's particular (pregnant) female body and its characteristics— the extent to which both male and female bodies are ultimately 'psychologized' and instrumentalized in the central conflict between the sexes.

The pattern of sexual rivalry, where even intercourse becomes a key factor in the struggle for equality or superiority, is already established on the very first page of the novel. How much less problematical our introduction to the couple's ritualistic act of love-making would have been, if only *Der Butt* had begun with its second sentence: 'Bevor gezeugt wurde, gab es Hammelschulter zu Bohnen und Birnen' (7/3). The festive meal might then have suggested itself as a fitting preamble to the momentous act of procreation which sets so much of the action in motion. But to be told right at the outset that 'Ilsebill salzte nach', suggesting a pointed flaunting of dissatisfaction with the husband's efforts at cooking, or, more probable still, a desire to put him in his place using this gesture as a mere pretext, sounds more like rubbing salt into old marital wounds than the prelude to a fulfilling physical encounter.[2] Cooking is, after all, a more emotionally fraught subject in *Der Butt* than it may be in real life. And Ilsebill's question, 'Beim Essen noch, mit vollem Mund', 'Wolln wir [the dropped 'e' here is as snide a comment on her as the reference to her talking with her mouth full] nun gleich ins Bett oder willst du mir vorher erzählen, wie unsre Geschichte wann wo begann?', comes through more as an act of marital provocation than an innocuous inquiry or than sheer impatience to get down to the real business of the evening. Shall *we* . . . or do *you*? Are *we* going to proceed

bodies as they are experienced by their owners. Instead, Grass describes women in the traditional manner, as objects, the offensiveness aggravated by the current license in such matters. It's all tits and cunts, business as usual in current male fiction' (Angress 1982, 43). But such a reaction represents a bypassing—in Angress's case a no doubt consciously provocative one—of the fundamental fact that we are dealing with females *as seen by males*—and in particular by one reactionary male narrator, with, as we shall see, various axes to grind. Grass's *Der Butt* is only by that token reminiscent of 'business as usual in current male fiction'. And one wonders from whose perspective the males, with their 'Stinkmorcheln' and various complexes, are reminiscent of the products of a business-as-usual stereotype novel.

  [2] Leonard Forster sees in Ilsebill's adding of salt evidence of the fact that 'nothing is ever good enough for Ilsebill' (Forster 1980, 60). In fact, the first section (before 'Worüber ich schreibe') ends with a generalization that makes it very clear that cooking is not the real issue at stake: 'Was immer ich vorgekocht habe; die Köchin in mir salzte nach' (11/8).

with the serious business of making me pregnant—one feels that the husband's role in all this is merely functional, and perhaps just tolerated as his cooking is tolerated—or are *you* going to take all the skeletons of 'unsre Geschichte' out of the cupboard of history first? One wonders just what the love-making would have been like, or whether it would still have occurred, if it had had to take place after the story-telling. Not just because the story is long but because it is hardly calculated to bring the couple any closer together. Both its substance and the spirit in which it is narrated are riddled with sexual antagonism.

For a paragraph, though, despite his wife's obvious wishes to the contrary, the narrator does start telling his story—to us, at least, even if he is not yet permitted to rehearse it for Ilsebill's ears. 'Ich, das bin ich jederzeit. Und auch Ilsebill war von Anfang an da' (7/3). This hardly sounds as if it is yet addressed to Ilsebill; but just as the narrator is getting into his stride with his story, his version of history, we hear that 'Ilsebill will nicht Aua gewesen sein'. Unless she has heard the story before, or is even listening to it now, it is as if the narrator has built her response fictively into his own dummy run at the chronicle, suggesting that he already has misgivings about this first of many attempts at setting out his version of things that occur in the first part of *Der Butt*. In any case, Ilsebill, still described hostilely as talking with her mouth full, indicates that her question about the order of items on the evening's agenda was really hardly more than rhetorical: 'hörte ich ... dennoch, daß das Bett zuerst recht haben sollte'. (For 'das Bett' read: 'Ilsebill'!) Even before they make love, or rather engage in an activity that can at best be termed a premeditated act of procreation, apparently all-too familiar clouds gather on the marital horizon. Certainly the description of the sexual act itself, the first of many in this novel, is hardly likely to lend any great credibility to the phrase 'weil wir in Liebe zeugten':

Also legten wir uns, wie wir uns jederzeit umarmt umbeint haben. Mal ich, mal sie oben. Gleichberechtigt, auch wenn Ilsebill meint, das Vorrecht der Männer, einzudringen, werde kaum ausgeglichen durch das weibliche Kümmerrecht, Einlaß zu verweigern (7/4).

Whether such thoughts, including references, during the description of copulation, to the woman's prerogative of refusing the man entry, are in the narrator's mind during the act or are simply introduced during the subsequent process of narration, they inevitably serve to degrade the love-making, making it into an arena for sexual politics and mental sniping between the two participants. The act is no more, on one level, than a familiar mechanical routine, made stale by theories and remembered bickering about the small print of equality. But, on another level, the ensuing description of the actual encounter lives up to the mental foreplay:

Doch weil wir in Liebe zeugten, waren unsere Gefühle so allumfassend, daß ihnen im erweiterten Raum, außer der Zeit und ihrem Ticktack, also aller irdischen Bettschwere enthoben, eine ätherische Nebenzeugung gelang; wie zum Ausgleich drängte ihr Gefühl stößig in mein Gefühl: doppelt waren wir tüchtig (7–8/4).

The parodied mysticism of this parallel 'ätherische Nebenzeugung' reads like little more than a magnanimous sop to the woman's assumed penis-envy: a vicarious form of penetration is allowed to her as compensation for an assumed sense of inferiority during the sexual act. Moreover, the final 'doppelt waren wir tüchtig' satirically presents them both, in their separate ways, duplicating a mechanical enactment of the male function, the one self-consciously, the other symbolically. Moreover, if to be 'tüchtig' sounds bad enough at the physical level, at that of symbolic compensation it has a ring of frenetic perversion to it. This may ostensibly be 'love-making', but the wilful 'Zeugung' it is programmed to culminate in is little more than veiled aggression, not the coming together in a genuine act of love. As soon as it is over, Ilsebill tellingly rejects the male and appropriates the fruits of the act for herself: 'Kaum war ich— wie ausgestoßen—wieder draußen, sagte Ilsebill ohne grundsätzlichen Zweifel: "Na, diesmal wird es ein Junge"' (8/4). That this is not to be the case simply amounts to a further round in the conflict.

Significantly, it is at this juncture that the narrator first deploys his story-telling as a weapon against his wife: 'Bevor sie über umgekehrte Rollenverteilung weitere Spekulationen anstellen konnte—"Ich möchte dich mal schwanger erleben!"—erzählte ich ihr von Aua und ihren drei Brüsten' (8/5). If Ilsebill is already prepared to exploit her hoped-for pregnancy as something with which she can belittle her husband (at the same time toying theoretically with equality in other respects), then he in turn can use story-telling as a form of retreat and even counter-offensive. He is unable to bear children, but he can at least bring forth a rich progeny of fictive figures.

As this contrast between a body-dominated Ilsebill and a story-oriented husband already suggests, the contrast in *Der Butt* is not essentially between male and female bodies, but between female bodies and male minds. When asked by Dr Schönherr 'nach dem Unterschied zwischen den Geschlechtern' (403–4/396–7), the flounder launches on an extended account of how 'dürftig ausgestattet' men are in comparison with women:

Was sie [i.e. men] empfangen, sind absurde Befehle. Was sie austragen, bleibt

Spekulation. Ihre Ausgeburten heißen: das Straßburger Münster, der Diesel-
motor, die Relativitätstheorie, Knorrs Suppenwürfel, die Gasmaske, der Schlief-
fenplan. ... Denn weil die Männer nicht auf natürliche Weise empfangen,
austragen, gebären können und selbst ihr blindwütiges Kinderzeugen als lau-
nischer Einzweck fragwürdig bleibt, müssen sie geistreiche Faxen machen. ...
Kalkutta. Der Assuandamm. Die Pille. Watergate. So heißen die Ersatzgeburten
der Männer. Irgendein Prinzip hat sie trächtig gemacht. Mit dem Kategorischen
Imperativ gehen sie schwanger. ... Doch was sie gebären—ob Kreation, ob
Spottgeburt—wird nie laufen lernen, nicht Mama sagen können. Ungestillt wird
es wegkümmern oder sich nur papieren fortzeugen.

Clearly the flounder is pandering, with 'Das alte Lied, meine Damen!'
(402/396), to his Feminal audience; he is endeavouring to offer them
exactly what he assumes they want to hear. Nevertheless, even if he is not
the novel's mouthpiece in this respect, his remarks have relevance to the
treatment of bodies in much of *Der Butt*—or to the corollary, an absence
of body-interest at some points. And the narrator is presented, as far as
the above passage is concerned, as a typical male.

Hingegen bleiben die Frauen—selbst wenn sie studiert, sich emanzipiert haben
... —immer ... hübsch frisierte Natur. Sie haben den Ausfluß monatlich. Sie
geben Leben selbst dann, wenn sie namenlosen Samen aus Konserven abrufen.
Ihnen, nur ihnen schießt pünktlich die Milch ein. Ja, aus Prinzip sind sie Mütter,
auch wenn sie es nicht, noch nicht sind oder unter Umständen nie sein werden
und sozusagen jungfräulich bleiben wie Fräulein Rotzoll.
Ich sag es: Frauen müssen nicht fürs Nachleben sorgen, weil sie Leben
verkörpern; Männer hingegen können nur außer sich Nachleben beweisen,
indem sie das Haus bauen, den Baum pflanzen, die Tat vollbringen, ruhmreich
im Krieg fallen, doch vorher noch Kinderchen zeugen. Wer nicht gebären kann,
ist allenfalls mutmaßlich Vater und vor der Natur arm daran (404/397).

In case this simply sounds like the flounder over-reacting to his particular
confined predicament at this moment, one can match these thoughts with
a corroborating stanza from the poem 'Gestillt':

> Männer nähren nicht.
> Männer schielen heimwärts, wenn Kühe
> mit schwerem Euter die Straße
> und den Berufsverkehr sperren.
> Männer träumen die dritte Brust.
> Männer neiden dem Säugling
> und immer fehlt ihnen.
>
> (71/67)

Grass's male, with his 'Mutterkomplex', his 'extreme Mutterbindung', is
'ein Brustkind auf ewig geblieben', according to the accusing womenfolk
in 'Wir aßen zu dritt' (395–6/388). Yet while he has in one sense, as they

gleefully diagnose, remained at the anal-dependent stage, or (even worse) is 'nicht abgenabelt', he at the same time genuinely envies woman her maternal capabilities and seeks to find some symbolic way of competing with her on her own ground, rather than just remaining the dependent child-figure. And the area where he feels able to compete is in the act of fabulation.

The crucial biological contrast in *Der Butt* is not primarily part of some familiar Teutonic 'Geist/Natur' dichotomy, as has been suggested (Hunt 1983, 175); for whole stretches of the novel it is not even a matter of a general gender-contrast between all men and all women. Rather, it is largely played out on the more specific level of Ilsebill and the narrator, with childbearing and artistic creation (especially story-telling) being the decisive activities.[3] 'Mit der Vaterschaft bist du am Pflock. . . . Nur Schriftliches sei gleichstarke Gegennatur,' the tempting voice of the flounder once whispers in the husband's ear (107/103). According to this argument, Ilsebill is graced with what both the flounder and the male narrator appear to consider a woman's 'natural' function, whereas the narrator (like most of his historical counterparts) is allowed the privilege of a more rarefied contrast-activity. Clearly this is a loaded, unfair juxtaposition, as well as a token of reactionary thinking on the part of both man and fish. (The masculine definite article of '*der* Butt' nicely reflects such entrenched chauvinist attitudes.) In real life, on the other hand—and that is presumably what *Der Butt* purports to be about—not all males are story-tellers, they do not each produce such impressive 'Kopfgeburten' as a novel entitled *Der Butt*, the Theory of Relativity, the diesel engine, or even Knorr's stock-cubes. The novel's fundamental contrast is thus an impure one; it levels the majority of women, and certainly the archetypal Ilsebill to whom the stories are primarily addressed, to a physical reproductive function.[4] On the other hand, it presents men in a most favourable light by emphasizing the unique intellectual achievements of *some*, where it would be impossible to argue that they were 'aus Prinzip' all capable of such achievements, even if they

---

[3] The force of this distinction is not negated by the fact that many of the womenfolk in Grass's novel also tell stories. Aua tells the tale of how she brought the fire down from the heavens (28–9/25–6), 'Die kochende Nonne, Margarete Rusch erzählte beim Gänserüpfen unter der Buche . . . Mestwina wußte Auageschichten' (297/291). But although these stories undoubtedly play their respective part in keeping the menfolk in their places, they are not highlighted and certainly do not play the vital role in the act of sexual self-assertion that they do for the modern Ilsebill's husband.

[4] I am choosing to ignore here (as the novel also conveniently tends to) the fact that childbearing is not the prerogative of all women but only—and then only hypothetically—of women within a certain age-group. No doubt the narrator's generalizations, as well as those of the flounder, who may be no more than his own creation, are dictated largely by the home circumstances to which he is reacting.

do not actually carry them out—which is the line that the flounder takes on women and childbearing. Yet if this makes it look in theory as if the flounder is stacking the cards exclusively in favour of the males, or at least reintroducing some notion of parity, much of Grass's novel betrays to what extent there remains an inevitable imbalance—resulting from a sense of male inferiority—on the narrator's part. It is not just that many of the male's 'Kopfgeburten' (Calcutta, Watergate, the ICBM, the pill) are of dubious value; the males' cerebrality renders all such compensatory activity by definition inferior, a counterbalance, to woman's much-vaunted oneness with nature.

In fact, the very structure of Grass's novel is directly related to this issue of male–female differences. For the nine parts of *Der Butt*—though they might at first seem to be an example of strict formal parallelism, with the nine months of Ilsebill's pregnancy coinciding with the duration of the fish's trial and the series of nine historical periods about which stories are told, ranging from Aua's matriarchy to the present—represent a complex sublimating strategy. Various features of a more recalcitrant nature suggest, in fact, a contrived pattern of deliberate compensation on the male narrator's part, rather than some innocuous, manneristic parallelism at authorial level. As the narrator's imagery at times readily reveals, his 'Kopfgeburten' are being displayed as a deliberate counterbalance to Ilsebill's feat of gestation. In 'Neun und mehr Köchinnen' the narrator sets the tone for this extended analogy between artistic and biological creativity by referring to the 'Köchinnen . . . die in mir hocken und raus wollen' (13/9). Later, when introducing Amanda Woyke, for instance, he talks of the creative 'Nabelschnur, die aufgewickelt zu ihr führt' (296/290). Elsewhere he refers, using similarly competitive biological imagery, to the fact that 'Die neunte Köchin in mir wurde geboren, als Sophie Rotzoll . . . im Herbst neunundvierzig starb' (20/17). And, although some of the imagery at the same time carries overtones of defecation rather than of giving birth,[5] there is enough specifically birth-related detail to suggest that this is the analogy paramount in the narrator's mind.

[5] In Ronald Speirs's reading of the initial copulation in the novel, 'Ilsebill fertilizes the narrator's imagination with the story being told . . . [The novel begins]—parthenogenetically, one might say—with the narrator's being impregnated by one of his female characters (Ilsebill) with the very novel in which they will act out their roles' (see above, p. 20). This might explain the fact that in the second paragraph of the entire novel the narrator refers to Aua without yet using the 'in-mir-hocken' leitmotif of later parts in this section (since it can come logically only after the double impregnation). After this initial suggestion of her role, however, it hardly suits the narrator's competitive purposes ever to remind himself of Ilsebill's putative fathering role in all the subsequent births. And in any case, as I have tried to show above, the dual impregnation serves a satirical function as well.

Just like its extension—viewing all male activity as a matter of 'Kopfgeburten', 'Ausgeburten', or 'Ersatzgeburten' (403/396)—the narrator-husband's imagery is above all intended to offset the triumphs of literal childbearing with some figurative notion of creation, understood in a variety of ways and presented with an almost self-defeating insistence as 'giving birth'. If childbearing is simplistically equated with nature, then the narrator appears to be echoing the flounder's seductive assertion that 'Männer überleben nur schriftlich' (107/103), tellingly a remark made just after we have been reminded that Ilsebill is now 'bald im zweiten Monat. Nur ihre Zeit, die sie streng macht, zählt.'

In fact, the stories about the nine or more cooks, i.e. the narrator's metaphorical (creative) 'births', look like over-compensation rather than the evidence of any satisfactory balance having been achieved between the two forms of giving birth. Ilsebill is literally pregnant with one child (although the husband does at one point entertain, without exploring it, the idea that she too may be pregnant in a figurative sense, just as he considers himself to be)[6]. In contrast to her one literal child, he produces a child every month. Or, as the heading 'Neun und mehr Köchinnen' implies, he can even outdo the figure nine. This is a significant number, of course. Ilsebill, we learn very near the beginning of the novel, confident that she is pregnant, 'gab ... mir neun Monate Zeit, meine Köchinnen auszutragen. Gleichberechtigt sind uns Fristen gesetzt' (11/8). That is to say, Ilsebill imposes her biological number, governed by the nine months of gestation, on the narrator. But he, in fact, refuses to be constrained by the number nine, an equivalent to the number three that for a long time held sway over the males during Aua's reign. No doubt as an act of defiance, the narrator has in reality managed to give birth to his nine promised cooks by the end of Ilsebill's seventh month of pregnancy, so this time he is really 'tüchtig': desperately working overtime to show he can compete in a metaphorical (for him, though, equally important) sense with his wife's actual childbearing.

The narrator stays away during the period immediately before the baby's birth and is absent again fairly soon after it, as if unwilling to concede Ilsebill's superiority in this realm. As he witnesses the birth by Caesarian operation (dwelt on in some detail, as if to savour a specifically less natural form of childbirth which consequently devalues Ilsebill's achievement in her moment of potential glory as a mother), he struggles to divert attention from Ilsebill's triumph to cooking, one of his fortes: 'Außerdem sah ich noch, wie gelb, ähnlich Hühnerfett, Ilsebills Bauch-

---

[6] 'Zum Beispiel hat Ilsebill einen Koch in sich—der werde wohl ich sein—den sie bekämpft' (346/339). The change of formulation here is significant: if there is a cook in Ilsebill, then it will seem more like an alien body than a baby waiting to be born.

fett ist. Ich hätte mir damit, weil ein Stück abfiel, zwei Spiegeleier[7] braten können' (545/536). Now, it is conceivable that this lack of joy at the moment of birth, and the malicious concentration on one of the more disgusting features of Ilsebill's anatomy, could be less a matter of biological jealousy—after all, the same fat is praised when it is on Margarete Rusch—than simply a token of the sad possibility that the narrator and Ilsebill no longer love one another,[8] or at best exist in some kind of love–hate relationship. Indeed, Ilsebill's own apparent lack of maternalism could well be attributed to the same root cause. But the narrator's general imagery and narrative strategems when it comes to giving birth to his cooks makes it seem nevertheless more likely that these details are all part of an attempt on his part to offset Ilsebill's 'Natur' by various surrogate activities and forms of psychological displacement. Even the fact that the narrator's stories are supposed to be organized according to the nine months of Ilsebill's pregnancy, for this was her stipulation, but actually have a narrated time of twelve months (extending, as they do, three months beyond the birth of the baby daughter) in all probability represents a deliberate refusal on the husband's part to be bound by the female, biological number nine. Yet this remains, for all that, little more than a Pyrrhic victory. That 'ihre Natur' is 'stärker und immer im Recht' is something that this particular male has had to face up to from the second month of the pregnancy onwards (cf. 107/103).

Although the section-titles—'Im dritten Monat' etc. rather than 'Der dritte Monat'—can be read specifically as descriptions of the woman's bodily state during the various phases of pregnancy, the narrator actually displays little interest, on the physical plane, in what is happening to her. There are few references to his wife's change of state, and even these are mainly there in order to emphasize her fads and moodiness. This is, admittedly, not the first birth in the family; two children already exist, so it might be that the miracle of birth has lost some of its earlier wonder for the male in the wings. In any case, the other children play virtually no role in Grass's novel. As has been argued,[9] being motherly in almost all of the historical relationships from Aua and Edek onwards is more a matter of satisfying the needs of the adult males with their mother-complexes

---

[7] Here, frying eggs looks like an image deliberately chosen to suggest *destroying* nature, in contrast to Ilsebill's giving birth to life.

[8] Cf. 'unsere Liebe, die nie aufhören wollte, ist nicht mehr' (371/364). Yet despite this declaration, the narrator appears to find it still important for Ilsebill to listen to his stories, indeed important for both of them.

[9] See Hunt (1983, 202) on this issue. Hunt also explores Ilsebill's attitude towards motherhood (200–1) and comes to the conclusion that she is 'nicht mütterlich'. This does not, however, prevent the narrator from envying her the biological ability to bear children.

than looking after any actual progeny resulting from the various mar-
riages and couplings.

Very near the end of *Der Butt* one finds a revealing footnote to these
pathetic compensatory activities on the narrator's part. He discovers to
his dismay that he does not feel all that close to his new baby daughter,
not primarily because of her sex but because of his own body ('weil er
keine Gebärmutter hat', 546/537). Nevertheless, he reasons that he will
eventually be able to make up for this biologically interpreted lack of
bonding by telling her stories: the same strategy that he had adopted all
the way along with Ilsebill, thus making his daughter into a second-
generation Ilsebill. 'Dein Vater ... kommt immer wieder und erzählt dir
Geschichten ... auch vom Butt will ich dir erzählen' (547/537). This is a
remark which shows just how out of tune with the changing times he is,
since by then it should be his daughter who is able to tell *him* about the
flounder.

Nowhere is the sense of deficiency that the male narrator perpetually
feels and which explains so many of the nuances of his story-telling
behaviour made clearer than when he confesses, near the end of the
novel, to a dream that he has had:

So träumte ich kürzlich: ich bin eine hochschwangere Frau, die vor dem
Hauptportal des Kölner Doms ... mit einem Mädchen niederkommt, das
gleichfalls schwanger ist—meine Ilsebill—und knapp nach mir aus schwieriger
Steißlage einen Knaben gebiert, der jedoch buttköpfig ist ... (494/485).

Not only do we here have the latent desire to give birth explicitly enacted
in a dream-sequence—with his uncomplicated, while hers is a breech-
birth (i.e. even in such details their conflict dominates the dream)—the
miraculous double birth also produces the only male offspring in the
entire novel, and the overtones are decidedly Messianic, albeit with
strongly parodistic overtones.[10] For the real Maria of the novel, who
really comes into her own near the end of *Der Butt*, love-making is not
presented as an act of deliberate 'Zeugung' and is therefore devoid of
the false hopes that surround both Ilsebill's wish for a son and the
copulations of the 'Vatertag' episode. While the female figures dream of
giving birth to Emmanuel, a male saviour, the narrator raises birth to the
level of a fetishized biological achievement symbolizing oneness with
nature.

More enigmatic than the dream of giving birth is the detail that the

---

[10] In his detailed reading of the penultimate part of the novel John Reddick (Reddick
1983, 143–58) makes much of the Messianic imagery in the work, but he is inclined, I feel,
to underestimate the extent to which the imagery is attached to false Messianic hopes. This
may explain why, at the end of *Der Butt*, we are left with the contrast image of a Maria now
released from the role of bearer of the saviour-to-come.

result will be a 'buttköpfig' son.[11] Since the flounder often appears to represent the principle of historical progress, one can only assume that this amounts to a more positive equivalent to the women's dreams of bearing the new Messiah.

If all the male narrator needed, in his story-telling, was some intellectual counterbalance to Ilsebill's childbearing *qua* nature, then he could simply have been allowed the privilege of writing successful novels; indeed, he might even have been permitted (to compensate for the value set on childbearing) to receive the Nobel Prize for Literature that had eluded his own author some years before. But clearly he not only needs to 'give birth' to the characters that are inside him struggling to get out, he feels the urge to relate history/his stories to his wife, despite her apparently dismissive attitude to much that he has to say.[12] As well as being his equivalents to children, they are also his dialogue with Ilsebill. Indeed, if one reads an episode like 'Vatertag' in the light of such an intention, then it achieves a further significance as a subtext to their marriage. 'Vatertag' too, like the stories of Aua, Mestwina, Gret, and the others, is one of the narrator's stories; in other words, he gives birth to its main protagonist. 'Billy (die eigentlich Sibylle hieß)' is referred to repeatedly as 'die zehnte Köchin in mir'. And this Sibylle, whose name is a near-anagram of 'Ilsebill', the actual wife who is the real target of these tales, is here subjected by the husband-fabulator to a fictional death which comes as close to a symbolic murder of his wife as any of the subjects of the previous stories. The leitmotif 'Billy, die mal meine Sibylle gewesen ist' (e.g. 468/461) is readily decodable, under these circumstances, as 'Billy, die meine Ilsebill auch sein könnte', or words to that effect. Tellingly, this tenth cook is closer to Ilsebill, the pregnant wife, than most of the others. She has previously lived with the narrator and borne him a child, as the male idiom has it, and they had at one stage intended to marry (462/455). In fact, she is virtually Ilsebill's double. Thus, while it is possible to see 'Vatertag' as Grass's attack on the mores of a caricatured radical feminism, within the novel's multilayered

---

[11] According to Hunt's interpretation, 'der Traum deutet ... außer dem Wunsch des Mannes nach Frausein und Gebären auch gewisse Befürchtungen darüber an, was der Butt als "fischige" Überinstanz mit seiner Beratung in der Zukunft hervorbringen könnte: etwas Monströses, oder eine Aufhebung der weiblich-männlichen Polarität des Menschen' (1983, 174). Yet the notion of a monstrosity seems misplaced. Nowhere has the flounder been described in such terms, and even when Dorothea von Montau returns from her encounter with the fish with a mouth now resembling his, this is not presented in terms which would suggest that even she is anything of a monstrosity.

[12] '"Du mit deinen historischen Ausflüchten und Lügengeschichten!" schimpft sie täglich. (Ilsebill glaubt nur, was in der Zeitung steht)' (172/168). '"Deine ewigen Geschichten", sagt Ilsebill. "Das lenkt doch nur ab vom eigentlichen Prozeß"' (346/339).

fictiveness it is at the same time the particular narrator-husband's tenth story, and hence as much directed at his wife as the other ones were. The story of Sibylle who then becomes 'Billy' ('anders geartet ... anders geworden' (463/456)) and gets her come-uppance, coming to a literally sticky end, is meant as a cautionary tale and as the next round in the month-by-month marital boxing match. In other words, Grass's narrator is a figurative mother giving birth to metaphorical children (or cooks) who are then used in the sexual conflict with the real mother-figure of the novel.

Of course, this is not the only respect in which the body is the battleground for the sexual infighting that goes on throughout the novel. Attitudes to the body and bodily functions in general also become pretexts for attacks.

When asked recently 'welche Funktion ... die Schilderung sexueller Dinge, die für soviel Aufregung gesorgt haben, im Gesamtrahmen Ihrer Romane, Ihres Schreibens haben', Grass came out with what might be reckoned a characteristically enlightened, progressive reply:

Ich glaube, daß der sexuelle Umgang der Menschen miteinander nicht nur als ein Anhängsel zum Leben gehört, sondern eine Grundlage unserer Existenz ist. Sonst säßen wir hier nicht. Für mich ist der Begriff 'sexuell' zu einengend, es ist bei mir doch sehr erweitert ein erotischer Begriff, also nicht eine Auffassung vom Leben, in dem der erotische Umgang der Menschen miteinander zumeist auf bloßen sexuellen Verkehr reduziert ist. Dagegen schreibe ich an, dagegen setze ich eine Flut von sinnlichen Eindrücken, von riechbaren, von betastbaren, von körperlichen Möglichkeiten, die in uns stecken, die natürlich alle nicht dem katholischen Katechismus entsprechen (Müller, H.-J., 1985, 144).

Such an answer may sum up the emancipatory function of sexual and other physical descriptions in Grass's early fiction—he does in fact refer to the masturbating passages in *Katz und Maus* in just such terms: 'ich wollte die Dinge beim Namen nennen, um sie zu entschärfen und ihnen diesen dämonischen Charakter zu nehmen' (ibid.). But this comment was made eight years after the publication of *Der Butt*, where the role of the physical is more complex and devious than this would suggest.[13]

A key incident in this respect comes at the beginning of 'Im vierten Monat', when Ilsebill swallows a gold filling while indulging in her manic, pregnancy-inspired appetite for hazel-nuts. We learn that she would rather pronounce the filling lost for ever than search for it next day among her own faeces or let her husband do so on her behalf. The episode—over in half a dozen lines—seems only to serve as a pretext for

---

[13] See Rollfinke (1986, 179) for a dissenting reading, which sees these issues as a sign of Grass's enlightened position rather than of any vindictive tactic on the husband's part.

his three-page diatribe against modern sanitized attitudes to the body and
its by-products:

'Das ist deine zu gute falsche Erziehung', sagte ich; denn unser Kot sollte uns
wichtig sein und nicht widerlich. Ist doch nichts Fremdes. Hat unsere Wärme.
... alle Köchinnen (in mir) haben ihren Kot und—wann immer ich zeitweilte—
auch meinen beschaut (241/235 f.).

The catalogue of detailed illustrations that follows is intended to make
Ilsebill's modern prudishness appear the historical exception, although it
is really no more than the typical 'Vorrücken der Scham- und Peinlich-
keitsschwelle', to use Norbert Elias's terminology,[14] during the modern
process of civilization. Excrement, the scatological, according to the
narrator's stories, was once a matter of healthy communal rites, and in
prehistoric times was a source of prophetic information. Like the ritual
'Kotbeschau' and the primeval 'Hordenschiß', 'das beiläufige Furzen war
auch ein gesellschaftlicher Vorgang', binding, joyous, and acknowledging
the body's right to our attentions. 'Was man heute Gestank nennt . . . war
uns natürlich, weil wir mit unserem Kot identisch waren. . . . Wir
schieden ja keine Fremdkörper aus. Wenn uns Essen notwendig war
und Geschmack brachte, konnte uns das Ausscheiden der verwerteten
Nahrung nur Lust bringen' (243/237).
  The idea is taken up in a later poem, 'Kot gereimt':

Dämpft, wird beschaut.
Riecht nicht fremd, will gesehen werden,
namentlich sein.
Exkremente. Der Stoffwechsel oder Stuhlgang.
Die Kacke: was sich ringförmig legt.

Mach Würstchen! Mach Würstchen! rufen die Mütter.
Frühe Knetmasse, Schamknoten
und Angstbleibsel: was in die Hose ging.

Erkennen wir wieder: unverdaut Erbsen, Kirschkerne
und den verschluckten Zahn.
Wir staunen uns an.
Wir haben uns was zu sagen.
Mein Abfall, mir näher als Gott oder du oder du.

Warum trennen wir uns hinter verriegelter Tür
und lassen Gäste nicht zu,
mit denen wir vortags an einem Tisch lärmend
Bohnen und Speck vorbestimmt haben?

---

[14] *Über den Prozeß der Zivilisation. Soziogenetische und psychogenetische Untersuchungen*
(Berne, 1969²), ii, 397.

> Wir wollen jetzt (laut Beschluß) jeder vereinzelt essen
> und in Gesellschaft scheißen;
> steinzeitlich wird Erkenntnis möglicher sein.
> Alle Gedichte, die wahrsagen und den Tod reimen,
> sind Kot, der aus hartem Leib fiel,
> in dem Blut rinnselt, Gewürm überlebt;
> so sah Opitz, der Dichter,
> den sich die Pest als Allegorie verschrieb,
> seinen letzten Dünnpfiff.   (286/280)

However, the main function of the narrator's would-be ethnological ruminations at this stage in his wife's pregnancy is, I would suggest, far from merely elegiac; and its context differs from that of the same ideas in 'Kot gereimt'. (In any case, he seems to have forgotten that in his version of Aua's time the 'Hordenschiß' and 'Kotbeschau' were both matriarchally ordained rituals and thus part of the females' regimented ways of repressively controlling the males.)

On the surface, all this seems to be leading up to an attack on 'unsere humanistische Neuzeit', where only babies still retain a supposedly natural relationship to the by-products of their bodies' metabolism, a world where the appropriate nouns have (as the poem suggests) been displaced by coy euphemisms or else been changed into terms of abuse. But what begins looking like a general, heartfelt desire to put the clock back eventually gets down to its true target, which is, of course, Ilsebill, not the modern age in its entirety:

> (Ach, hätten wir doch das Doppelklo, wenn nicht das großfamiliäre.) Sei ehrlich, Ilsebill, auch wenn du deinen Goldzahn nicht aus den Exkrementen klauben wolltest und das Wort Scheiße (wie allgemein üblich) nur und sinnwidrig als Schimpfwort benutzt. Gib es zu, Ilsebill, und schütze nicht Schwangerschaft vor: auch du blickst hinter dich, wenn auch scheu und zu gut erzogen. Wie ich riechst du dich gerne. Und gerne würde ich dich riechen, wie ich von dir gerne gerochen wäre. Liebe? Das ist sie (244/239).

The reason why the narrator is thus browbeating Ilsebill in particular has little to do with demonstrably modern habits of defecation.[15] He is so insistently concerned with body-related issues here not in order to win her over, install a double loo, and engage in consciousness-raising sniff-ins, but because he knows he can even score ego-boosting points off her here, and do so on what he takes to be axiomatically her own territory: the body. After all, there is little historical evidence for the detailed rituals he describes with such manifest enthusiasm. Essentially what he has done is

---

[15] Cf. Peter Reinhart Gleichmann, 'Die Verhäuslichung körperlicher Verrichtungen', in *Materialien zu Norbert Elias' Zivilisationstheorie*, ed. P. R. Gleichmann, Johan Goudsblom, and Hermann Korte (Frankfurt, 1977), 254–78.

to construct a series of early historical tableaux which stress behaviour that is by its very nature a tacit condemnation of Ilsebill's prudery. He may be coincidentally ruminating at a time vastly influenced (indirectly, as well as directly) by the large-scale cultural diagnoses of books like Norman O. Brown's *Life against Death*, but the narrator's stance is invariably *ad feminam*, his target is specifically his wife, not the modern world in general.

One can see this very clearly in 'Der Arsch der dicken Gret', one of the most important parts of the novel as far as the body is concerned. The section's position is significant: it comes in the Month immediately preceding the more direct outburst against Ilsebill's prudishness in 'Den Kot beschauen'. That is to say: what was already an indictment in the description of Gret becomes even more barbed, overt criticism in the next section.

The narrator's imaginative performances with 'dicke Gret' are recounted in salacious detail, essentially in order to put Ilsebill ('die am Donnerstag manchmal kühn ist', 208/204) in a poor light. This 'Urform der Nächstenliebe, unsere partnerbezogene Inbrunst' becomes crucial ammunition in the modern husband's feuding with his wife:

meine Ilsebill . . . hat mir noch nie . . . den Arsch geleckt, weil sie befürchtet, es könne ihr mit dem Wegfall der letzten Scheu die Zunge abfallen.
Sie ist viel zu gut erzogen worden. . . . ich werde ihr auch diese spatbürgerliche Verweigerungsmechanismen . . . austreiben (ibid.).

Yet despite all pretences to the contrary, 'Der Arsch der dicken Gret' is little more than a Grass version of sex-in-the-head. For even when the narrator appears to be pontificating on behalf of enriched experience ('Der [Geschmack] ist nicht klassenbedingt. Von dem wußte Olle Marx nichts. Der ist der Schönheit Vorgeschmack. Jeder Mund weiß das. Sich beschnuppern, lecken, schmecken, sich riechen können'), all that he succeeds in conjuring up is his 'fiction' of a life of physical fulfilment with 'dicke Gret'. When he, offering to take a thorough bath (hardly consistent with what he has just been claiming) and be ready for the great encounter, finds himself put down by Ilsebill, he complains: 'wir sind entwöhnt. Weil wir darüber immer nur lesen' (209/204). He is practically passing judgement on his own predicament. For his sole panacea is merely to tell (rather than read) stories about what things could be like. He can do no more than invent a compensatory past and then use it as a stick with which to beat Ilsebill. Even if the narrator would really like it to be so (and this remains open to doubt, given the kind of person we are dealing with), the body—and especially the partner's body—is not some neutral phenomenon to be explored and enjoyed. It is psychologized and colonized as part of the all-pervading sexual conflict we find in *Der Butt*.

In the section 'Der Arsch der dicken Gret' (a title which marks a deliberate attempt to rescue the word 'Arsch' from its debased status as a term of opprobium)[16], the body is often described with the vocabulary of *play* and *nature*: 'unsere Spielwiesen', 'Mein Grund und Boden, dein Hügelland. Unsere Äcker' (209/204). Yet despite the way in which this imagery is manipulated to imply that this is a region free from the property speculation of ideology, it is by no means free from the land-grabbing of sexual politics. How could it be? The seemingly innocuous 'An Feldwegen Rast. Sanft abgeweidet wollen die Hügel sein' is immediately followed by modern male recriminations. 'Ach Ilsebill, jetzt, wo du schwanger bist und überall aufgehst, solltest du, solltest du . . .' — such thoughts are hardly worth the bother of completing, given that it is to Ilsebill that they are vainly addressed.

Ilsebill is duly ridiculed for finding all this talk of arses and farts 'vulgär' (210/205). But then surely the narrator's extended hymn in praise of the body of 'dicke Gret' and its potential has been calculated to set her up. An aphorism such as 'Wer den Furz seiner Liebsten nicht riechen kann, der soll nicht von Liebe reden' (210/205) is likewise tantamount to being a matrimonial provocation, not some disinterested apodictic pronouncement on the subject. Constantly aware that the pregnant Ilsebill has, existentially speaking, scored one over him with her pregnancy, the narrator in turn tries to beat her on her own territory in other ways. Indeed, he even tries to minimize the importance of her present state by telling her not to use her pregnant condition as an excuse when it comes to the 'Kotbeschau', as if other aspects of the body were more important than the one (her own) which dominates so much of the novel.

At various junctures the narrator-husband links writing not only with childbirth but with another form of physical expulsion: excreting. 'Alle Gedichte, die wahrsagen und den Tod reimen, | sind Kot, der aus hartem Leib fiel' (in the words of the final part of 'Kot gereimt', 286/280). Here, the connection between excrement and prophecy, on the one hand, and the divining power of writing, on the other, is re-established, as if the poet/writer were Aua's successor. 'Wer von so viel Vergangenheit verstopft ist und endlich zu Stuhl kommen möchte, den drängt es, von Mestwinas Bernsteinkette zu erzählen' (22/19), to cite another example of the rhetorical analogy, this time putting the stress more on the difficulty of creative ex-pression. It is as if the narrator is trying to compete on more even terms with Ilsebill's childbearing ability by at times equating

---

[16] On the implications of this predilection for the scatological in German (as opposed to English) terms of abuse, see Jakov Lind, *Counting My Steps: An Autobiography* (London, 1969), 126–8.

writing with a bodily function that he does at least possess; and, as we have seen, this is one which he feels he can exploit to suggest his superiority to her in some respects. Added to which, the parallel between the ex-pression of the body in labour and the efforts of excretion (already referred to by Gottfried Benn in his 'Saal der kreißenden Frauen') bring a further similarity to his busy attempts at equating writing/excreting with Ilsebill's childbearing.

This may not account for all the associations of the excreting metaphor in the narrator's mind,[17] but it is one further ingredient in his sexual-cum-biological sparring with Ilsebill. Moreover, the analogy between story-telling and excreting (one of the male's versions of being 'natural' in the face of much modern prudery, for it is attitude that is important rather than the sheer act itself) is given a further twist within the novel's scheme of values: it may not be the contemporary equivalent of the prehistoric 'Hordenschiß', but story-telling—in contrast to the lone act of writing—does demand a listener, a kind of partner, even if it is one as reluctant as Ilsebill. So it is, in this respect, a metaphorical equivalent to the introduction of the 'Doppelklo' into the modern household.

The narrator's exploitation of all this body-talk and imagery in his conflict with Ilsebill finds its earliest and most tangible expression in the symbolic image of Aua's third breast. This 'männliche Wunschprojektion', the focus, in its most obvious physical terms (no matter what it may also come to symbolize), of a male 'Schrei nach der Ur-Super-Nährmutter' is again a means of deflating Ilsebill. 'Oft fehlt heute die dritte. Ich meine, es fehlt irgendwas' (9/5). Which is, not least, another, and very pointed, way of saying that *Ilsebill* lacks something. In fact, the narrator's disingenuous assurances that it does not matter ('Natürlich sind zwei genug ... wo du schwanger bist und deine zwei bald mehr als Auas drei wiegen werden, bin ich zufrieden') can only be calculated to add fuel to the flames, especially since he cannot resist going on to declare: 'wenn ich ins Leere greife, meine ich immer die dritte Brust' (10/6). If one ever required evidence to suggest that Grass and the novel's reactionary male narrator need to be carefully distinguished from one another, then surely such a passage provides it. Here, we find the chauvinist narrator callously

---

[17] Rollfinke (1986, 175–9) has much to say about the link between defecating and the narrator's account of history. As Ronald Speirs has reminded me, the act of defecating is in any case not presented in *Der Butt* as the unambiguously happy, anal-phase achievement that it might have been in a more conventionally Freudian—or at least equivocating— novel. The 'Dünnpfiff' and 'schwarte Schiet' that haunt many of the novel's pages, particularly in conjunction with the plague, have sinister overtones. Here, a fear of one's body is often translated into darker, apocalyptic terms. And if defecation is also a form of waste-production, then this must ultimately have pejorative repercussions for the image of both birth and writing conveyed by such analogies.

rubbing his wife's nose in her imputed inadequacies, both literal and figurative, physical and non-specified, while at the same time pretending not to be a prey to the very 'typisch männliche Tittomanie' (9/5) that is symptomatic of his pronounced mother-complex.

Timing is very important in this context. The narrator tells Ilsebill of Aua's third breast immediately after what they take to be the conception of their third child, so certain are they both that their copulation will bear fruit. That is to say: at the very moment when he fears that Ilsebill is bound to upstage him in physical terms, he launches into a fabrication to suggest a fundamental inadequacy in her, when compared with the triply endowed Aua. And the title of this section—'Die dritte Brust', not just historically 'Auas dritte Brust'—emphasizes the still-missing element, as if to deflect attention from the beginning of the wife's childbearing triumph. Similarly, 'Der Arsch der dicken Gret' and 'Kotbeschau' were, as we saw, brought into play at the very point where Ilsebill's pregnancy was beginning to loom large as a physical fact. One of the paradoxes of the narrator's position, on this score, is that he puts a high value on what he deems to be 'nature'—this, after all, explains many of the strategies looked at so far—and yet he is jealous of its manifestations in Ilsebill and tries to find some way in which he can compete with her.

Attributing penis-envy to the females in his stories is, of course, one respect in which he can exact a token revenge. This tactic finds its most obvious form in some of the early stories in outright acts of aggression against the males' organs, or surrogates thereof.

Und wie aus allem, das in seiner Form Vergleiche zuließ, machte Aua auch aus dem Wurzelbeißen einen Kult. Anzüglich hielten die Weiber, wenn Opfermond war, die Urrüben vor sich. Bevor sie krachend zubissen, stießen sie kurze wütige Schreie aus, uns Edeks zur Warnung. . . . Doch das Rübenbeißen blieb weiterhin Spaß und treibt uns Männern bis heutzutage Urängste ein (75–6/71–2).

Margarete Rusch, in various ways Aua's obvious successor in a later phase of history, bites off one of the testicles of a male. And the phallic imagery is linked with male aggression so often in the novel that the females' hostility to male sexual parts seems at least symbolically justifiable. At a very early stage there is a reference to 'zeugungswütige Männer, die ihre Stinkmorcheln zu Geschlechtertürmen, Torpedos, Weltraumraketen umdachten' (36/33); and phallic images of aggression occur at a number of points from here on, not only on the literal level of the penis as a weapon in acts of rape but in the piece of wood used to batter Lena Stubbe to death and in the phallic motor bikes that destroy Billy on 'Vatertag'. It is, as is suggested at one point in the final section of the novel, 'als sei das Töten die Fortsetzung der Sexualität mit anderen Mitteln' (529/520). Or, one might add: *vice versa*.

Penis-envy and aggression against the sexual organs of the opposite sex have their equivalent in the male's creation of the third-breast myth. But it is really in the 'Vatertag' episode that this imagery reveals itself in all its brutality. Even before the 'Kunstfick' perpetrated on Billy, Mäxchen takes part in another artificial act of copulation. In her androgynous role as mock representative of 'das neue Geschlecht', she 'nahm sich die Freiheit, eine der preußisch gewachsenen Kiefern zu besteigen' (479/ 472). As if giving her sisters a practical demonstration of the new symbolic freedom ('Klemm dir son Bäumchen zwischen die Schenkel', 480/473), she mounts the tree aggressively and is female rapist to its parodied maleness:

auch halfen die Zurufe der Freunde Fränki und Siggi, deren rhythmischer Triebvers 'Steht kerzengrade wie zur Parade' das Mäxchen nicht nur anfeuerte, sondern vorerst nur hintersinnig, doch kurz vorm knorrig gezausten Wipfel der phallischen Kiefer regelrecht Lust brachte, weshalb das himmelhoch verstiegene Mäxchen abermals eine Pause einlegen mußte: eng an den vibrierenden Stamm gegossen, bis es ihm ganz natürlich und geradezu weiblich kam: Achachachachach (480/472).

This is clearly an inversion of the second 'Kunstfick', with Mäxchen here playing female to the tree, whereas in the act with Billy she plays male to Billy's femaleness. 'Das neue Geschlecht', in other words, is not displayed in the act with Billy alone but in the combination of the two acts. In both, males are absent and the enterprise involves a surrogate phallus. In the case of the rape of Billy this is often referred to by commentators as a 'dildo', for want of a more accurate noun, but it is worth recalling that this was not actually the primary function of the device in this episode. It is above all a mechanism for allowing Fränki to urinate like a male. The elaborate description of the contraption which allows Fränki to pee while standing upright is followed by the triumphant exclamation 'Kein Neid auf die Stinkmorchel mehr. Nie wieder erniedrigendes Weibergestrull. Wie die tausend und abertausend Männer im Verhältnis zu hunderttausend anderen Kiefern pißte Fränki aufrecht in leicht schrägem Winkel gegen aufrechte preußische Bäume: Jawoll!' (472/465). If nothing else, this sequence gives a new twist to the dubious concept of female penis-envy. For the root cause is jealousy of the organ not as a sexual organ but as some 'butch' attribute that allows the male the convenience of being able to urinate while in a standing position. That the device later assumes the more conventional role in the sex act (what Gide would call its 'disponibilité' is truly remarkable, though not without biological precedent) comes almost as an afterthought. But the notion that urinating can be sexual aggression is there even in the first use. For it is images of male militarism, 'Prussian' trees, that are urinated against.

Mäxchen, however, is not acknowledged as the undisputed leader of the women because of this act. Indeed, Siggi is quite dismissive of the charade, and presumably attributes just as little symbolic significance to the later 'Kunstfick' with Billy:

'Ihr mit eurer symbolistischen Kacke!' sagte Siggi und spuckte ihren zerkauten Brasilstumpen aus. 'Und was hat das zu bedeuten? Hier, ein Hosenknopf. Da, Nadel und Zwirn. Etwa die fleißige Hausfrau? Irgendwo Schräubchen locker? Knöpfchen auf Suche nach passendem Knopfloch? Abwarten, sag ich. Nix Hokuspokus. Zeig ich euch' (481/473–4).

Her subsequent gratuitous act of sewing a button to her left cheek is clearly intended as a far more radical questioning of the role-allocations that Mäxchen is also opposed to than either of the episode's provocative 'Kunstficke'. With her phallic trees and penis substitutes, Mäxchen is made to look a pathetic victim of false consciousness. For the needle-buttonhole image deliberately lampoons both the busy-housewife mentality and the conventional sexual assignment of penetrating and penetrated roles which Mäxchen also seems unable to transcend.

The central problem which is touched on at a number of points in *Der Butt* is that in the twentieth century both sexes seem to have a critical relationship to their own bodies in terms of their sexuality. This comes out, in a variation on the 'spittoon theory', near the end of the novel, when Ilsebill gives birth to a daughter instead of the hoped-for son. Her dismay is presented in very physical terms:

Als Ilsebill niederkam, enttäuschte die Tochter sie. Da war nur die Muschel, die Möse nur, das Ziel aller Männer, die unterwegs unbehaust sind und sich loswerden wollen, immer wieder und nochmal (Mich zischte die Mutter an: 'Du Sparbüchsenmacher!') (544/534–5).

Using some phallic surrogate is not a solution to such a problem, it merely compounds it. And the males, with their ambivalent, if not downright disgusted, relationship to their so-called 'Stinkmorchel',[18] are certainly in no more enviable a situation. As far as attitudes to one's own body are concerned, Grass appears to have been fairly even-handed in *Der Butt*. Although one has to allow for the further complicating factor that the body is historicized as a phenomenon during the course of the novel and different responses to it, different body-fashions even, are

---

[18] As Ralph Manheim's translation 'stinkhorn' suggests, the fungus in question is probably the *Phallus impudicus* of the *Phallaceae* family, although the mushrooms depicted in *Ach Butt* (29, 65, 71), if 'Stinkmorcheln' they be, look more like surreal versions of the male sexual organ than even the stinkhorn does.

encountered at various stages of history. This point is brought out very emphatically in a résumé entitled 'Einige Kleidersorgen, weibliche Ausmaße und letzte Visionen', which the male narrator delivers just before the baby itself is finally born.

After a thumb-nail sketch of the physical characteristics and attire of each member of the Feminal (520–1/511–2), each of whom has a clearly discernible counterpart in the earlier historical periods described in the narrator's stories, the narrator moves on to a critical contrast between Ursula Schönherr and her historical double, Aua. 'Doch Aua war dick, nein: fett, geradezu unförmig. ... Ein über die Ufer tretendes Fleisch. Überall schwellend gepolsterte Geniste, Kuhlen und Kühlchen' (521–2/ 513), a shape conforming to, or rather even dictating, the contemporary concept of beauty and such aesthetic issues as the ideal shape of vases. Of all the historical cooks it is Margarete Rusch ('dicke Gret') who is the closest to Aua's lovingly presented endowments, although Ilsebill too is presented as getting more like Aua, largely due to her pregnancy. (Though such a short-lived condition is hardly going to solve the problem of the missing breast for ever.) One suspects that part of the narrator's increasing frustration with his wife lies in the fact that she has, physically, the makings of an Aua or a Gret—after all, he did, with his pronounced mother-fixation, decide to marry her in the first place—but does not realize her potential. In any case, he is probably aware that this aspect of her is largely coterminous with the nine months of her pregnancy. As the archetypal woman, Ilsebill is contrasted with the 'Strichmänner' of politics; of her it is claimed: 'In ihren Ausmaßen widerlegt sie die männlich verwaltete Macht' (524/515).

In terms of sheer physical presence, one of the novel's most striking contrasts is between Margarete Rusch ('die ihren Fettmantel pflegte') and Dorothea von Montau ('Fleischlich ... so knapp ausgestattet, daß sie den Stallziegen glich, die im März, sobald die Futterspreu ausgeht, nur noch Phantom sind und Kinderschreck', 522/514). This is more than just the obvious contrast between High Gothic asceticism and a later (Gargantuan) worldliness. For if size also ostensibly refutes male attempts at domination, as we see with Aua and Gret, then the proportions of the various female characters offer some form of correlative to their power, or lack of it. For all her frailty, Dorothea may have exerted some hold over her contemporaries, yet one suspects she means less to the modern male narrator than either Aua or Ilsebill. Aua remains the prime, and significantly mythical, example of the equation of physicality with domination, although in Margarete Rusch we have an instance of the body being used, quite literally, as a weapon in the power struggle between males and females. But these are pathetically biased images, and in many senses merely tokens of the male's sense of helplessness. In projecting his ideal woman back into history and equating physical proportion with domination, he allows his mother-fixation to obscure the fact that nearly all the females have exercised power of some sort over the males and that his stories have in no way been simple illustrations of the gradual shift from matriarchy to patriarchy.

After speculating in seemingly disinterested fashion about the historical significance of such 'weibliche Ausmaße', the narrator eventually reveals his true colours with the words 'Laß mich rein! In dich hineinkriechen will ich. Verschwinden ganz und meinen Verstand einbringen. Ich will es warm haben und die Flucht aufgeben' (524/515).

The flounder's earlier expatiations on 'dicke Gret' and her Rabelaisian qualities (223–4/218–9) need to be reassessed in the light of these remarks. For Margarete Rusch, 'eine herzhaft lustige, weil durch niemand zu bedrückende Frau' (223/218), is not only a physical image of what the narrator would like to propose as the (male's version of) emancipated woman, she at the same time embodies what we have just seen to be his regressive thoughts about ideal maternal proportions. No wonder the argument at this point centres on the lack of 'weibliche Literaturpersonen in komischer Hauptrolle'.[19] 'Dicke Gret' is, after all, *only* a 'Literaturperson', even for the protagonist of Grass's novel (like the majority of other women, and many of the men, who people the narrator's fictions). Not only is the husband indirectly congratulating himself for having created her (having 'given birth' to her); she is also, and more importantly, created in his own counter-image, as an expression of the projected wishes (physical gratification, motherly protection, return to the womb, physical expansiveness) *and* (castration-)anxieties of her progenitor. Even when he is pretending to cite historical illustrations as theses and establish connections between the characters' bodies and their personalities and powers, the narrator is not infrequently engaged in the manipulation of self-justifying, self-promoting, or self-gratifying fictions, no matter what precarious basis these may have in historical reality. He projects aspects of his own conflict with Ilsebill during the dying phase of their relationship, and this is true of his treatment of all of the cooks. And yet, surprisingly for someone with his proclaimed interest in the body, he tells us virtually nothing about his own body. (We know more about the flounder's body, in fact, than we do about the narrator's!) And, despite his boasts of having slept with the entire Feminal, he is

---

[19] For much useful, and certainly less biased material on the same subject, see U. Montigel, *Der Körper im humoristischen Roman: Zur Verlustgeschichte des Sinnlichen. François Rabelais—Laurence Sterne—Jean Paul—Friedrich Vischer* (Hochschulschriften Literaturwissenschaft, 76; Königstein im Taunus, 1986).

hardly ever seen engaged in any bodily activity except the ingestion of food. Body matters, when they do not relate directly or indirectly to Ilsebill, are merely verbalized, a matter of claims related to the past of his 'stories'. Tellingly, in the first section of the novel, the act of copulation itself is glossed over in half a dozen lines, whereas twenty times that space is taken up with unfolding his fiction of the world of Aua with her third breast and her ability repressively to satisfy the tribal males in one way or another. Where the body occurs elsewhere, it is largely presented in voyeuristic terms, as befits the degree of fantasizing in the novel and the child–mother relationship that largely underlies the male narrator's attitude to women.

The exception to all this is the encounter with Maria right at the end of *Der Butt*. Here, the physical act of love-making plays a very perfunctory role:

Maria ließ sich in eine Mulde fallen und zog die Jeans und den Schlüpfer aus. Ich ließ die Hosen fallen. Sie half mir, bis mein Glied stand. Ich weiß nicht, wie lange ich gebraucht habe und ob sie fertig wurde. Küssen wollte sie nicht, nur schnell das. Gleich nachdem es bei mir gekommen war, kippte sie mich raus und zog sich den Schlüpfer, die Jeans an (555/546).

It is hardly an unequivocally positive description, to be sure. The male still seems to need (maternal?) help; he is not quite sure exactly what happened in the case of his partner, and little affection seems to be involved. (Which, given that 'love' has been presented elsewhere in the novel as a form of subjugation, may not be a totally bad thing.) However, when compared with the encounters of 'Vatertag', or with the narrator–Ilsebill relationship and its various historical analogues, this does at least look healthily free of complexes and conflict. Maria certainly does not come through as a 'männliche Wunschprojektion', either physically or in her behaviour. And that must be a sign that times are changing for the narrator and his entire sex.

In a critical survey of responses to *Der Butt*, Manfred Durzak pointed out that while the obscene and the pornographic were frequently issues in the reception of Grass's early work, such is no longer the case with this novel (Durzak 1985, 95). But of course this is not because taboo subject-matter, potentially distasteful aspects of bodily functions, and other deliberately provocative physical material are not present in *Der Butt*. As we have seen, such material is there in great abundance. But it tends largely to be used specifically against Ilsebill by the husband-narrator, rather than becoming part of a familiar strategy of reader-provocation, as it was in many of Grass's earlier works.

7

Rabelais's Sister: Food, Writing, and Power

ANTHONY PHELAN

A great deal of Grass's *Der Butt* is explicitly about food and cookery. The section of the third Month entitled 'Wer ihr nachkochen will' (228/223) substantiates the apocryphal theory—perhaps merely a PR ploy—that any educated household would need two copies of the novel, one for the library and the other for the kitchen. Grass has recorded his own surprise in discovering that the various reading strategies promoted by the novel had in some cases made it a 'Hausbuch', a kind of domestic vade-mecum, to which at least some of his readers were drawn by what he called the 'Trivial-Anlaß des Kochens' (Arnold 1978, 27). The complaint is perhaps a little disingenuous, given the fact that Grass could also define his most general conception of the work as 'stichwortartig "ein erzäh-lendes Kochbuch"' (ibid., 30). Indeed, this very prospect is dramatized in the enterprise of 'Ilsebills Schuppen'. It is clear, however, that Grass's novel recognizes a specialized discourse of cooking and food which in itself raises a recurrent question of coherence. A culinary reading of *Der Butt* gives a particular turn to the problem. Why, after all, do we need so much *detail* in the narrator's accounts of the varying achievements of his cooks? There is a pleasure in such writing, certainly, both in the history of the cookery book and in the largest literary traditions of which Grass reminds us. Thus Christoph Perels recognizes 'die seit der Antike lebendige Koch- und Küchenkomik' seen in contrast to 'eine Geschichte der Ernährung—und des Hungers—des vierten Standes' (Perels 1978, 89). Heinrich Vormweg prefers a subsequent model: 'der Gegenstand des "Butt" ist mit all seinen Aspekten zunächst das Fressen, das vor der Moral kommt' (Vormweg 1978, 95), invoking Brecht and thereby, as he says, the relations obtaining between the sexes. To these culinary discourses I shall add that of Rabelais, as indicated by the text of *Der Butt* itself, when the nun Margarete Rusch is called 'eine Schwester des Pfarrers zu Meudon' 'der aufgeklärten Lebensart wegen' (223/218).

It is in the difficulty of a recapitulation and modernization of the humanist discourse of food that the central problem of Grass's writing about food can be seen. For in Rabelais (and in Grimmelshausen) the sensuous particular is presented as something actually to be eaten, as it were in its comestible immediacy; and it is this physical reality which gives rise to what Mikhail Bakhtin identifies as revolutionary 'prandial' gaiety.[1] These are innocent if anarchic pleasures. But Lena Stubbe's *Proletarisches Kochbuch* sees that writing about food is not an innocent activity:

> denn Lena war gegen die bürgerliche Küche und deren 'Man-nehme-zwölf-Eier-Ideologie'. Einleitend schrieb sie 'Soviel protziger Aufwand macht die kochenden Arbeiterfrauen unsicher, verführt sie, über ihre Verhältnisse zu leben, und entfremdet sie ihrer Klasse' (431/425).

Her claim is that such writing about food is always already ideologically determined. This can be identified in two senses of her phrase 'protziger Aufwand', for it entails both the economic ostentation of sheer quantity and the implied excess of a style. If the implicit suggestion that cooking and writing exist in close parallel seems too large or strong a claim, then a weaker version of it may stand which usefully locates Grass's writing in an extensive tradition. In one of her essays on 'Food as a system of communication' the anthropologist Mary Douglas writes, 'From Culpeper to Beeton and Elizabeth David, from Brillat-Savarin to the *Larousse Gastronomique*, the recipe is seldom left to speak for itself.'[2] In this respect culinary *texts* are traditionally set in other contexts—often narrative or historical—and so can take on meanings beyond any straightforward sense of their use in the kitchen.

In the course of an increasingly drunken conversation with Sieglinde Huntscha ('Wir tranken im "Bundeseck" paar Bier, paar Korn', 'Darüber sprachen wir bei Bier und Korn', 'Wir tranken dann noch paar Bier und paar Korn', 149–50/146–7), the narrator gives some account of his current project:

> Auf Sieglindes Frage 'Und was haste momentan in der Mache?' gab ich vorsichtig Auskunft: Das Tribunal an sich, das ganze Thema überhaupt interessiere mich. Ich sei nicht nur als Autor, sondern auch als Mann betroffen. Und zwar irgendwie schuldhaft. Das alles komme mir sehr entgegen. Anfangs hätte ich nur über neun oder elf Köchinnen eine Art Ernährungsgeschichte schreiben wollen: vom Schwadengras über die Hirse zur Kartoffel. Aber der Butt sei gegengewichtig geworden. Und der Prozeß gegen ihn (150/147).

[1] Mikhail Bakhtin, *Rabelais and His World*, tr. Helene Iswolsky (Cambridge, Mass. and London, 1968); esp. ch. 4, 'Banquet imagery in Rabelais'.
[2] Mary Douglas, *In the Active Voice* (London, 1982), 117.

By any normal standards the narrator must be in a considerable state of inebriation by this stage—such that we might be entitled to expect *in vino veritatem*. On the other hand, he claims to be 'vorsichtig' in releasing the information he does provide, as if it were a strategic leak designed, presumably, to ease his way into the deliberations of the Feminal. It is important to see the 'Ernährungsgeschichte' as at issue, at least by implication, in the movement of the Feminal's arguments and evidence, as well as in the writing itself. For it is here that the continued intrication of the matriarchal past and the patriarchal present can still be seen. There remains an unresolved anthropological paradox: the discovery of fire inaugurates culture through the conversion of raw to cooked and so installs woman as cook, but the notion of plenitude is itself posited as a *transition* (from 'nature' to 'culture') within the historical logic of 'male' progress. In Grass's writing, as Edward Diller discerns, a *history* of cooking is designed to rob the mythical moment in the relation of raw to cooked of its power, because history and myth are opposed categories of thought (Diller 1983, 102). The very project of an 'Ernährungs-geschichte' puts Grass himself securely on the rational path of male progress. But even if these remarks to Sieglinde need to be taken in a (locally) political or diplomatic sense, the subsequent gloss on the preoccupations of the novel seems generally appropriate. Three import-ant elements are distinguished: a history of nutrition, the counterweight of the flounder's role in history, and the trial of the flounder at the hands of the women. This threefold division gives a useful outline of the dynamics of the novel, and in fact of its largest historical movement—from 'mere' naïve 'Ernährung' into a patriarchal history which must then confront the challenge of feminism. This displacement and survival of the 'original' project will concern us first.

The notion of a history of nutrition is interestingly ambiguous. For an 'Ernährungsgeschichte' is a history not simply of 'human foodstuffs' (Manheim) but of human foodstuffs within the processes of production, distribution, and cooking (domestic or other). At the very inception of the project, therefore, the 'neun oder elf Köchinnen' are of central importance. However, the original outline of a history of foodstuffs survives in the novel in a more than rudimentary way. The earliest parts of Grass's narrative are organized around the basic transition from the life of hunter-gatherer to herding and agriculture:

Mit [Wigga] wurde der Ackerbau zur Fron. Solange Aua in ihrer Nachfolge fürsorgte, blieben Gerste-, Emmer- und Haferanbau in Grenzen, hielten wir uns als Fischer und Jäger beruflich autonom ... (74/70).

While Aua is the patroness of cereals, Wigga develops root vegetables in extraordinary variety—charlock, mangel, radish, salsify—and her successors can add 'Rüben, die unseren Karotten, dem Sellerie, den Teltower Rüben verwandt waren' (75/71), to be joined later by rutabaga, the 'Wruke' or 'Kohlrübe'.

Together with mutton, the local fish—pike, perch, bass, cod—and the real 'poverty staple' 'Schwadengras'[3], these are the elements of 'pomorsch' diet which Saint Adalbert finds before his martyrdom. Amusingly, these early indications are extended in the very last episode of the novel 'Dreimal Schweinekohl', where that dish provokes a number of questions and a meditation on the historical importance of the brassicas.

Was ist das, Geschichte? Genau kann man nicht sagen, wann unser Weißkohl (Brasica [*sic*] oleracea), der als Neuerung wichtig war wie der Buchweizen, die Hirse, die Kartoffeln, und Wruken, zum ersten Mal großflächig angebaut wurde ... (551/542).

What we (and, in principle, the narrator) mean by history is at least disturbed by these relatively unanswerable questions. But even (or especially) here history remains in one important sense unchallenged and unchanged—'und doch verlief die Geschichte nicht anders, sondern wie immer und überall böse.' For if 'eine Art Ernährungsgeschichte' is unlike other more familiar kinds of history, it cannot be independent of them, 'immer und überall böse'; but, perhaps more importantly, the reverse is also true. When the narrator speaks of 'ziemlich mit uns zur Suppe verrührte gepidische Goten und eingewanderte Sachsen' (111/107), he aligns the largest developments of history with the processes of combination and transformation which define cooking itself; and the moments of culinary time may be as good a guide as any: 'als meine Frage: welches| Jahrhundert spielen wir jetzt? küchengerecht|beantwortet wurde: Als der Pfefferpreis fiel ...' ('Aufschub', 216/212). In this last instance the history of cooking can be seen to include what is a merely metaphorical cooking(-up) of history in the preceding one.[4] This metaphorical move is important in its own right, however; for the intractable immediacy and individuality of food history takes on a concrete significance beyond culinary rhetoric.

The 'Küchengerechtigkeit' of the historiography suggested by the poem lies somewhere between the uncertainties adumbrated in the food-stuff history of buckwheat, millet, or the cabbage family, and the dated history rejected by the novel. Of course, the fall in the pepper price after

---

[3] I am grateful to Elizabeth Dowler of the London School of Hygiene and Tropical Medicine for helping me to understand some fundamentals of human nutrition.

[4] Diller (1983, 97) observes, 'Man had to consume what he had cooked up.'

Vasco's navigational achievement *could* be dated, and yet such history seems rather short on historical meaning. Or, more precisely, it yields a compelling narrative of a different kind, though one which is itself undermined, as we shall see, by the problem of world hunger. The narrator's attempt 'den kaschubischen Legendensumpf statistisch trocken[zu]legen' entailed an account of Prussian feudalism designed to concentrate on agrarian and economic development. This attempt is frustrated—'es will mir kein rückwirkendes Bild geraten'—and the failure becomes part of the narrator's resistance to Ilsebill, who wants to know 'Deputat wieviel? Spanndienst wie oft? Wie war die preußische Domänenkammer organisiert?' (299/293).

Such material is beyond narrative; and so historical reconstruction derived from statistics will always fail by comparison with the story-telling generated in the preparation of food—'Doch nicht das Gezählte, das Erzählte hängt an. Mundgerecht überkommt es' (299/293). Grass's word-play highlights the coincidence of food and language (often but not uniquely *about* food) which recurs in the novel. The possibility of coherence, and therefore of meaning, is focused on food and the shared or communal food-events of preparation, cooking, and eating. It is this prospect of meaning which is present in the contiguity of the poem 'Hasenpfeffer' and the narrator's last attempt at a stabilization of his relationship with Ilsebill in 'Wer ihr nachkochen will' in the third Month. The 'Ich' of 'Hasenpfeffer' moves backwards through history, overturning all rules of necessity, determination, and chronological sequence:

> Zerstückelte fügten sich,
> von den Pestkarren sprangen, vom Rad geflochten,
> aus Feuern, die in sich sanken,
> hüpften Hexen mit mir ein Stück Wegs.
>
> (228/223)

The larger determinant forces of military campaigns (the 'Wiedergekäute Kriege' (227/222), whose epithet already equates the experience of history with eating), of civil and ecclesiastical authority, and even of mortality itself are displaced as the 'Ich' traverses history 'Keinem Faden nach, nur dem Gefälle': the only sense of direction is that provided by the actual point of arrival, 'Hasenpfeffer, was sonst.' The goal of this historical retrospect is, however arbitrarily, Gret's cooking, and indeed this specific dish. In this way the journey achieves some sort of sense, even though intentions and goals are relatively unclear—'Ahnte ich doch, daß du kommst.' The specificity of the dish, its sensuous particularity, is the very opposite of an historical 'goal' and so belies the trajectory it has been able to create. As Erhard Friedrichsmeyer notes, 'food and its history, cooking and recipes . . . are overshadowed by much more private concerns' (Friedrichsmeyer 1983, 151).

Food and the cooking process are deployed to create just such a displacement in the prose which follows this poem. The narrator announces 'Mein letzter Versuch, Sinn zu geben: ein Rinderherz mit Backpflaumen gefüllt in Biersoße'. The guests on this occasion—two architects and a vicar—are not satisfied with his attempt. They 'suchen bei allem, was anfällt, den immer tieferen Sinn', until the narrator ironically offers a figural or allegorical meaning to satisfy their (and the reader's) demands:

'Aber es muß ihn [den Sinn] doch geben', sagt aufgeschlossen der Pfarrer, 'und sei er auch negativ, denn wie sollten wir ohne Sinn nur von der Hand in den Mund leben?'

Auf starker Flamme wird das gefüllte und mit hellem Faden geschnürte Rinderherz allseits angebraten, dann mit braunem Bier gelöscht. ('Das sollte— Herr Pfarrer—auch theologisch sinnfällig sein') (229/223–4).

The parson's unintended pun on living from hand to mouth (and it is the narrator's and perhaps even Günter Grass's point that that is precisely what we do) unwittingly extends Ilsebill's trope ('Unser Streit . . . liegt mürbe in seinem Saft auf den Tellern. Es schmeckt uns') at the opening of this section and its kitchen talk. But the figural meaning, of hell-fire 'extinguished' with beer, is hardly the kind of thing the theologian had in mind, whether it is conceived as a kind of epicureanism or as an atheistic demythologization. This uneasy exchange, and the slips and slippage of metaphoricity within language ('von der Hand in den Mund') and in constructed figuration, illustrate the arbitrary ease with which food history or cooking can be exploited as discourse, as moments of meaning. When this is achieved, however, the real food—the, as it were, *'merely physical'*—seems abandoned in mute objectivity.

However, elsewhere in the novel, this sort of 'Sinnfälligkeit' is exploited by the historical cooks themselves. In varying ways food itself can be made to take on meanings. Thus Dorothea von Montau only ever cooks Lenten fare ('Fastenküche') and introduces unusual ingredients ('Asche von verbranntem Sargmoderholz') in order to transform the very food which sustains the body into an evangelical sign of human mortality. This is the most obvious kind of meaning which food can take on; and the specific sense of 'die Hinfälligkeit der Menschen' (158/154) is echoed by another symbolic additive in Lena Stubbe's restorative 'Nagel und Strick'—though clearly the sympathetic magic by which they take effect introduces a further dimension.

While there exist institutional meanings for food within the terms of the liturgical calendar, of the kind observed by Gret, for instance, ('bevor sie Fisch, Makrelen auf Lauch, weil Freitag war, tischte', 197/193), Dorothea's cookery exaggerates the normal rules for Lent so that all her cooking becomes a sign of her piety and of the need for universal penitence; but her 'Fastenküche' has other consequences. The 'schonische Heringe' served by Dorothea to her inquisitors, even though they visit her out of Lent and on a Thursday, gives the dish connotations (the inquisitors are themselves in need of penitence, at the very least) to which they remain oblivious. When the same 'Fastenküche', with its concentration on the sour (quark and sorrel, used both as ingredient and decoration), appears on the table at her own wedding, it begins to acquire social meanings concerning her relationship to the guilds, and their relationship to the patricians she has also invited, along with her confessor. The wedding celebration ends in a rough house, provoked again by a culinary symbol, when one of the Teutonic knights 'dem geputzten Töchterchen des Patriziers Schönbart einen Gartenrettich roh in den Schoß geworfen hatte' (135/131). No doubt it is one of the 'rohe Rübchen' (134/131) used in this way that is thrown by the knight, so that 'roh in den Schoß geworfen' retains in a marginal way the culinary sense of 'raw' as well as the social one of 'coarsely'. Aua's matriarchs would have known what to do with such a provocative root, and Dicke Gret and her nuns had their own way with carrots (75–6/72–3 and cf. 288/282); but its phallic suggestion here also alerts us to the significance of Dorothea's table-decorations, which combine root vegetables with sorrel: for Slichting the pleasures of the bed rather than the table are certain to be soured too.[5]

Dorothea's cooking uses food within ceremonial, including liturgical and quasi-sacramental contexts, to generate meaning by transgressing conventional rules. This is generally her way; in the broadest terms, so the argument in the Feminal runs, she bends the standards of 'Kinder, Küche, Kirche' to her own need for freedom. Margarete Rusch's approach is similar but nevertheless distinctive. She too succeeds in revising the liturgical categories by persuading the bishop that the heart and lungs of an Easter lamb should not count as meat and therefore may

---

[5] The figuration of cornucopian productivity as phallus, as in the description of Gargantua's codpiece in Bk. I, ch. 8 (François Rabelais, *Gargantua and Pantagruel*, tr. J. M. Cohen (Harmondsworth, 1955), 55) encounters a powerful matriarchal challenge in *Der Butt* (75–6/72–3): in 'copious' writing the semic replaces the seminal—and both are challenged by the matriarch's root vegetable. Here as elsewhere I am indebted to Terence Cave's *The Cornucopian Text: Problems of Writing in the French Renaissance* (Oxford, 1979). On *Gargantua*, I, 8, see 183–93.

be consumed on Good Friday (230/225); and her intervention in the Reformation debate about the kind of meaning to be attributed to the Eucharistic elements is more radical than Dorothea's emblematic exercises (213/209). Her ceremonial cooking, such as the 'Henkersmahl', and particularly the narrator's glosses on it, introduce a new principle: for her tripe dishes (tripe itself emblematically recalling Rabelais's *Gargantua* via Gargamelle's extraordinary diet before his birth) are appropriate to a specific mood or humour—

Wenn es dich inwendig friert: Kutteln vom vierten Magen der Kuh. Wenn du traurig, bodenlos aller Natur entfallen, todtraurig bist: Kuttelfleck, die uns lustig machen und dem Leben Sinn geben. Oder mit Freunden, die Witz haben und gottlos genug sind, um auf der Spötterbank zu sitzen: aus tiefen Tellern Kutteln löffeln, die mit Kümmel abgeschmeckt worden sind (197/193).

The *meaning* of life can be restored by tripe but its pleasures are reserved for the godless, we should note, recalling the Pfarrer who was unhappy about living 'von der Hand in den Mund'. Such cookery for the emotions or for the intellect (of 'Gäste ... mit Sinn für Lügengeschichten' (235/ 230), for instance), but also for the needs of the body, as in the case of her recipe to counteract impotence ('Man nehme zwölf bis siebzehn Hahnenkämme...' (236/231), which of course also smacks of sympathetic magic), establishes culinary meanings by reference to individual needs and in the context of social celebration. In this respect, Gret anticipates the anti-suicidal but also, in the largest sense, socialist cookery of Lena Stubbe (429–30/422–3).

Gret adds extraculinary and non-nutritional meanings and intentions to her cookery, both by way of witchcraft and by commentary. When the narrator claims 'Nichts kochte sie um des reinen Geschmackes willen' (288/282), he has the former in mind. But as a successful 'society cook' she spices her service with table-talk and 'subliminal blather': 'Für wen sie auch abkochte, ihr Reden bei Tisch war inbegriffen: ein unterschwelliges Gebrabbel' (198/194). In an important sense, the meanings attaching to food considered so far are all subliminal, but they are derived from the food and its particular context. With Gret the food event becomes an essentially political forum: 'Immer teilte sie mit dem Kellenschlag auch ihr fein abgeschmecktes Interesse aus' (198/194). What is initiated here as a politicization of the food *context* will reach different kinds of fulfilment in the cookery of Sophie Rotzoll and of Lena Stubbe. In Sophie's case, the social or historical meaning is inscribed on the dish, via the menu, as it were. In this way the revolutionary sentiments which accompany the preparation of food in song (as incantation) find appropriate culinary expression in names such as 'Weißkohl zu Gänseklein à la Marengo' (369/361).

By the time of Lena Stubbe the ingredients and mode of preparation of food, as well as the discourse in which these are described, have become totally political, so that meaning is no longer in any sense additional to the culinary: everything can and must be seen within its class-defined context. (It is perhaps also worth noting that Sibylle's cooking in our own time has lost this politicized 'geschichtliches Bewußtsein' (442/436), both by virtue of its international preferences—'Ihr rheinischer Sauerbraten, ihr ungarisches Paprikagulasch, ihre Saltimbocca, ihr Coq au vin . . .', 471/464—and because cooking in the context of 'Vatertag' is uniquely a marker of gender-role.)

The reference to Gret's 'fein abgeschmecktes Interesse' suggests that the food she provides has become an instrument of policy, and general claims of that kind are made in the novel, of course; but before the relations of cooking and power are considered there remains a further aspect of the location of cooking and food in the context of other kinds of language and discourse. Gret 'konnte mehrere Handlungen (aber auch lehrreiche Abhandlungen) gleichzeitig abspulen, ohne einen Faden fallen zu lassen' (197–8/193), and this is another of the ways in which she 'mengte ja alles mit jedem' (288-282). Several plots or disquisitions can occupy her table-talk, as an accompaniment to food, simultaneously. But this relation of food and discourse is most extensively dealt with in *Der Butt* as what might be called kitchen-talk. 'Beim Eichelstoßen Gänserupfen Kartoffelschälen erzählt' (295/290) provides the largest single account of this coincidence of the labour of food-preparation with the activity of narrative. The stories told in this way vary considerably. Mestwina narrates mythical material, while Gret tells tales which are 'irdisch gedüngt' (297/292); Amanda Woyke's story ('Ihren Schalen las, lese ich ab, was gelockt über den Daumen glitt und sich zum dünngeschälten Bericht legte', 296/290) is a history of food, of hunger, and of invasion, always ending with the triumph of the potato and so opening a prospect of utopian narrative—'Aus der Praxis der Gesindeküche schöpfte sie die Utopie' (306/300).

As in other respects, Agnes Kurbiella is an exception. No narrative commentary accompanies her preparation of 'Schonkost' for Opitz and Möller, for her role as muse to the two artists requires on her part what the flounder calls 'ihr episches Schweigen' (262/256), such that 'selbst ein Rubens, ein Hölderlin hätten ihr Angebot nicht erschöpfen können.' Agnes's emptiness is the ground of an increasingly guilty aesthetic fullness. More importantly perhaps, her food commentary is supplied by Opitz's lost poem, a fragment of which is quoted by the flounder in what is a miserably weak pastiche (275/269). In a different division of labour, as it were, the proximity of the two processes can be seen again—of the preparation of food, and of writing, more particularly of the writing of narrative. The figures of the potato peelings falling from Amanda's knife can themselves be read, and the plucking of the goose produces both the instrument of writing and the figure of the narrator's creativity, and indeed of Grass's (see 'Geteert und gefedert' (207/203) and the accompanying drawing).[6] And it is further asserted that each of these modes of food-preparation establishes its own narrative rhythm—in the case of Mestwina's acorn-pounding 'knappe Reportersätze' 'auf geradezu motorische Weise' (305/299), while Gret has 'einen luftigen, federleichten Stil' from plucking geese, and Amanda's narratives are extended but interrupted by exclamations, corresponding to breaks in her ribbon of peel. It seems unlikely that any correspondence to the narrator's or Grass's own narrative style could be empirically established. What is clear is the importance of the parallel between writing and the manual gesture of certain kinds of culinary activity. Yet these parallels, and the aestheticization they imply, are not so much contested by Ilsebill as rejected out of hand.

The narrator and his (no doubt male) guests conclude that the production line excludes the possibility of narrative rhythms; and Ilsebill agrees:

'Stimmt!' sagte Ilsebill. 'Aber Eicheln im Mörser zu Mehl stoßen: das wollen wir Frauen nie wieder. Gänse kauf ich lieber gerupft. Die paar Kartoffeln für uns schäl ich wie nix und rauch noch dabei. Willst wohl, daß wir am Spinnrad hocken. Hast wohl Sehnsucht nach Singers Nähmaschine mit Fußantrieb.' (307/301)

This is one of a number of feminist rejections of anything suggesting the homespun or the idyllic (including Simon Dach's 'Kürbishütte'). In particular it echoes the Feminal's response to the flounder's remarks on child malnutrition and infant mortality, when a boycott of all Nestlé products is rejected in favour of 'Trockenmilch' and 'Fertignahrung in Gläsern mit Vakuumverschluß' (281/275). Given the importance attached by professional nutritionists—and by Erasmus (279/273) and the narrator ('die dritte Brust')—to breast-feeding, this may seem an unlikely argument from a feminist audience; perhaps it is no more than historically accurate. What is certain is that this context, of malnutrition and famine in the Third World, presents the strongest empirical challenge to the narrator's attempts to establish a narrative of food, but also one anticipated by Grass's relation to a Rabelaisian vision of plenitude.

Vasco's encounter with Calcutta already presents the fundamental problem:

[6] See Grass, *Ach Butt*, 42–3.

Wohlgenährt leidet Vasco am Welthungerproblem. Wieder- und wiedergeboren ist Vasco jetzt Schriftsteller. Er schreibt ein Buch, in dem es ihn zu jeder Zeit gegeben hat ...
   Gleich nach dem Start zitiert er sich: Man müßte einen Hungerreport schreiben. Man müßte historischen, gegenwärtigen, zukünftigen Hunger ins Verhältnis setzen (179/175).

Against the presence of the narrator everywhere and at all times, *his* plenitude as it were ('Ich, das bin ich jederzeit'), another history is envisaged here which would be the constant shadow of his achievement. Indeed, as a shadow it is already perceptible in the text, both on the historical plane and in the consciousness of the narrator. Amanda's children and some of Dorothea's, as well as Agnes's first child, suffer and die from malnutrition; on the other hand, there is a sense in which the narrator's recognition that 'nicht das Gezählte, das Erzählte hängt an' (299/293) *must* be set aside. Vasco's question, challenging his own rhetoric and the metaphorical function of nutritional language, 'Was heißt das, am Hungertuch nagen?' (179/175: Manheim's 'what it really means to be starving' misses this linguistic point) can only be answered— in the first instance—by a recourse to the statistical:

Aus Statistiken kann man neben anderen papiergewordenen Schrecknissen herauslesen, daß die europäischen Säuglinge mit ihrer Spezialkost neunmal soviel Eiweiß, Kohlehydrate und Kalorien verschlingen (oder angefressen verkommen lassen), wie den indischen Säuglingen bleibt (279/273).

Yet this 'statistical reading' does not generate narrative: the preamble to the Feminal's discussion of Western baby-foods, women's emancipation, and the Third World (they refer to Africa rather than India) in fact resorts to a nutritional analysis of foods currently available for infants. Similarly, though the narrator parodies the flounder's speech on the popularity of his 'These von der Rumford-Woykeschen Weltverköstigung', at the general level the flounder's essential questions—'Wie stellen wir uns dem Eiweißmangel und damit dem Sojabohnproblem?' (338/332)—are unavoidable. What provokes Ilsebill's irritated response, 'Sind Küchenschürzen wieder gefragt? Will man sich nun—Ohgott!—mit Hilfe des Kochlöffels emanzipieren?' (339/332), is the short circuit in the flounder's logic, which sees the first step in the Great Leap Forward as the experimental transformation of Therese Osslieb's restaurant into a 'Woykesch' soup-kitchen.
   If starvation resists narrative (even though the ironic treatment of 'tourists of starvation' in *Kopfgeburten* represents an honourable attempt to place world hunger within the innovative form of the narrative essay) but *can* be represented statistically, the poems 'Am Hungertuch nagen'

(335/329) and 'Lena teilt Suppe aus' (411/405) offer a different approach. Both begin with the food receptacle (for want of a better word)—'Immer schon sprach aus hohlem Bauch | die Mehlschütte Trost', 'Aus Kessel tief, | . . . schöpfte Lena'—and end with a social and political context. In reality the empty belly is a human one, just as Lena's almost infinite provision is humanly achieved at great cost. In these images the two aspects of a cornucopian vessel are articulated. It does not need to have been a deliberate reminiscence of the prologue to Rabelais's *Tiers Livre* for the parallel to be present.[7] For the cornucopia figures as 'cup of Tantalus', as 'Pandora's jug', and as the 'Danaids' tub'[8]—the image of fullness must always threaten exhaustion, which the Third World makes only too real.

The sight of Lena, and her constant attempt to provide (in this respect she is closely related to Gret and Amanda), makes the bourgeoisie fearful:

> Deshalb beschlossen sie,
> der Armut einen verklärenden Sinn zu geben:
> als Antwort auf die soziale Frage.
> ('Lena teilt Suppe aus', 412/406)

Faced with such a strategy of mystification, Lena has every reason to see discourse associated with food as ideological, in the pejorative sense of promoting false consciousness. The poem 'for' Amanda—'Am Hungertuch nagen'—which explicitly confronts the question of starvation treats such ideology with heavier irony:

> Gegen den Hunger ist viel geschrieben worden.
> Wie schön er macht.
> Wie frei von Schlacke seine Idee ist.
> Wie dumm die Made im Speck bleibt.
> (336/329)

The first line here defeats Manheim's 'in defense of hunger'; what follows is not 'against' hunger in the sense of an attack but is more an ideological defence put up against those who suffer from it. Whether we take 'Wie schön er macht' etc. as directed against misplaced Western ideas about slimming or against the Rilke of the *Stundenbuch*, 'die Made im Speck' is simply natural and idiomatic because it is proverbial. The transfiguring meaning attributed to poverty in Lena's poem is far more influential than the ideological decision of some historical bourgeoisie ever could be. This recognition perhaps gives some point to the studied

---

[7] Siegfried Mews notes that Rabelais is also 'one of Grass's favourite authors' (Mews 1983¹, 168).

[8] See *Gargantua and Pantagruel*, ed. cit., Prologue of the Author to Bk. 3, 286; and Terence Cave, op. cit., 171–2.

use of metaphors derived from food, its preparation and consumption, which so extensively characterizes Grass's vocabulary in *Der Butt*: where elementary material necessities have been expunged from memory and history, in the metaphorical discourse of food in *Der Butt* they can be reinscribed. However, 'Am Hungertuch nagen' does not remain in this moral context for long. There is not just a material and ideological dimension to hunger; ultimately, it must be understood by reference to the economic. The second stanza had continued to rework 'dead' metaphors by recording that while the belly of the flour-bin ('Mehlschütte') was hollow, other stores ('Speicher') had been cunning, other markets were 'gesättigt'—at once saturated and replete. The agencies here, as ever, must be human, and they are finally revealed:

Aber als endlich genug war
und Amanda Woyke mit Korb, Hacke und ihren Töchtern
in die Kartoffeln ging, saßen woanders Herren am Tisch
und sorgten sich um den fallenden Preis der Hirse.

Es ist die Nachfrage, sagte Professor Bürlimann,
die immer alles am Ende regelt—
und lächelte liberal.

(336/329)

Just as the novel includes two versions of the original tale of the fisherman and his wife, so too there exists another story about hunger elsewhere ('woanders Herren am Tisch'), and this testifies to the resistance of 'das Gezählte' to narrative.[9]

In one of his moments of sympathy for the ecological movement, the flounder recognizes the failure of the 'Männersache' in the symptom of world hunger, whether in the capitalist or the communist world:

Die Natur wurde euch anvertraut, worauf ihr sie ausgelaugt, verschmutzt, unkenntlich gemacht und zerstört habt. Bei all dem Überfluß, den ich euch eröffnet habe, könnt ihr dennoch die Welt nicht satt machen. Der Hunger nimmt zu. Eure Ära klingt mißtönend aus. Kurzum: der Mann ist am Ende (459/453).

Perhaps there is one point at which this failure is formulated in the language of economics, when the flounder declares that 'Es hat das Prinzip der Freien Marktwirtschaft die permanente Unterernährung von Millionen zur Folge: auch Hunger ist Krieg!' (530/521), thus formalizing what the narrator's reflections on baby-food had hinted at earlier. By and large, however, the narrative is cagey about the nutritional consequences

---

[9] In the light of this narrative tendency, it is possible to understand the absence of *economic* history, noted by David Jenkinson, in a stronger sense as an avoidance, and perhaps a rejection, of political economy.

of the (capitalist? merely male?)[10] exploitation of nature—even when it
admits to its own reticence:

Wofür ich nichts kann: Dürre, Frostschäden, Regenperioden, Viehseuchen,
Hungerzeiten, in denen nur Schwadengrütze vorrätig war: immer zu knapp.
Womit ich ablenken möchte ... (104/100).

It is appropriate enough, of course, that this narrator (from the age of
Wigga) should be helpless in the face of natural disasters. He seeks to
distract from the guilt he has incurred in betrayals and derelictions of
duty. Yet that sad history will also displace the political economy of food
production with a narrative of cooks which itself is in need of forgetful-
ness: '*Woran ich mich nicht erinnern will* ... An das Fett und den Stein,
an das Fleisch und den Griff, an dumme Geschichten wie diese...'
(99–100/96). If there is a guilt in narrative or in writing itself, it lies in the
false fullness of meaning mimed and promised by it. Where there is in
writing 'ein Wort zuviel', practical life needs another supplement: as
ever, 'Ilsebill salzte nach' (7/3).

Cooks and their work both are and are not 'part of' history. The poem
'Fleisch' records this ambiguity when, with the 'triumph of fire over the
Raw', 'verriet uns der Rauch, | träumten wir von Metall, | begann (als
Ahnung) Geschichte' (55/51–2). History proper begins away from the
cooking-fire and ends, provisionally, in Wigga's 'Zeitweil', in anal
intercourse with an ageing Goth. 'So wurde ich durch die Geschichte
überfordert' (105/102)—the return to Wigga's cooking is a withdrawal
into harmonious domestic intimacy, well away from the upsets of this
public world. This is the pattern repeated by Gret's fugitive monk, by
Amanda Woyke's August Romeike, and by Stobbe/Stubbe, even though
in his case reincarnation is necessary for a brief respite between a death in
the Franco-Prussian War and another at Tannenberg.

The densest, and in some respects fullest, account of this tension
between history and nourishment is provided in the poem 'Esau sagt'
(194/190). Esau's sentence has been commuted to lentils (Manheim), and
in his penultimate utterance he claims that once paid off (in the lentil
currency of the mess of pottage) he lives in lentil-probity and under (a
new) lentil law. His escape from another law ('begnadigt') admits him to
a realm of ease and superabundance; not faith like a grain of mustard seed
but hope the size of a lentil encourages (nutritionist or perhaps agro-
nomist) prophets to seek a miraculous abundance of the pulse. The
'wunderbare Linsenvermehrung' substitutes Esau's lentils (Gen. 25: 34)

---

[10] The uneasiness of the novel's economic critique is apparent in a comparison of these
remarks with the hopeless 'ob im Kapitalismus oder im Kommunismus' of the conversation
with Jan (459/453).

for the fish of John 6, and so transposes the story from the Old Testament to the New, where the deferment *sine die* of the eschatological banquet leaves the younger brother to face a new problem.

At the same time, the poem slides into a Brechtian tone (identified by the 'Und als', the ellipsis and syntax of the first line of the couplet, and the dactylic elements in its second line) with

> Und als er auferstanden am dritten Tag,
> war sein Verlangen nach Linsen groß.

The mood here is the ironic blasphemy of the *Hauspostille*, and the appetite is Baal's.[11] After a paragraph of present and past lentil meals, the poem concludes with a concentrated account of the fundamental security brought by a simple freedom from hunger. To have enough lentils is to be free from fear; but the consequence is an abandonment of the principle of primogeniture ('Seit mir sind Erstgeburten zu haben') and its central role within patriarchal structures, and hence a flight from the 'Männersache' and the course of history (cf. 50/46, where the flounder identifies 'die verantwortliche Disziplin des Vaterrechts' as guaranteeing 'die apollinische Vernunft'). On this reading, and within the context of 'Drei Fragen' and 'Zuviel', the last line of 'Esau sagt' suggests that the younger brother is left to cope deprived of lentils; the mess of pottage was in reality Jacob's loss, and living at the forefront of the patriarchal progress has become a torment. History, if history there be, has moved to Calcutta.

On the other side of the ambiguous position of food in relation to history, the novel outlines another development according to which the culinary is increasingly engaged with politics and so with power. While the meanings of Dorothea's 'Fastenküche' are essentially a means of self-assertion by a woman within a patriarchal society, Mestwina's aphrodisiac soup is already a political instrument; and this theme is developed more fully in the case of Margarete Rusch. What begins as a means of personal power in enabling Gret to become abbess becomes an occasion for 'das demokratische Murren und aufrührerische Reden' 'zwischen gedünsteter Dorschleber, Hasenpfeffer und Krammetsvögeln' (214/210): Gret's 'unterschwelliges Gebrabbel' (198/194), her food commentary, can articulate the political interests of a class and actually realize them ('Ich darf an die "Statuta Karnkowiana" erinnern' 219/214–5), as is recognized by the 'third affidavit's' reference to 'die Klosterküche als

---

[11] The Brechtian tone acknowledges another master of the culinary—in the narrow sense—though also one who was inclined to leave the 'Herren' 'woanders' when it came to food prices, as in *Die heilige Johanna der Schlachthöfe*.

Machtzentrum' (222/217). The flounder, of course, sees this development as a policy of containment (270/264–5, cf. 49/46).

Sophie Rotzoll is the next practitioner of political cookery (as in other ways, Agnes Kurbiella remains enigmatically unyielding). Sophie repeats Dorothea's instrumental perversion of food, but for explicitly political ends. The political gloss spoken over Gret's dishes is now literally embodied in Sophie's 'Honigkuchen, in den sie, neben einer besonderen Zutat, aufmunternde Zettelchen, ihre gereimten Barrikadenlieder eingebacken hatte' (367/361). Ultimately, her hallucinogenic or toxic mushrooms become the direct agents in what is still a personal struggle— to this extent she is aligned with Gret and Dorothea—but which encompasses ends that render her cooking potentially and poisonously 'politisch wirksam' (372/366). Her case can throw further light on the relationship between food understood within discourses of different kinds and food as an inarticulate social event. What Fredric Jameson writes of the 'autonomization' of sexuality, which makes possible its function as an independent sign-system in psychoanalysis, also applies to the bodily dimension of eating and food:

as long as sexuality remains as integrated into social life in general as, say, eating, its possibilities of symbolic extension are to that degree limited.[12]

As the symbolic possibilities of the food event are developed, so that its meanings are written across it or inserted within it, the 'merely' sensuous matriarchal plenitude of the food object is exhausted in its acquired meaning. And so the political cook appears in contradiction with her maternal 'instinct', her essential being; and Sophie Rotzoll remains childless.

In Lena Stubbe and her *Proletarisches Kochbuch* cooking becomes explicitly political because of its class orientation: here, food preparation and political discourse, which are in varying degrees separated in her predecessors, converge in a single political activity. In a marvellous vision of Lena addressing the 'Gewerkschaft Nahrung-Genuß-Gaststätten' (441/435), Grass describes her attack on 'das Fertiggericht', whose espousal by a trade union is close to the feminists' preference for 'Fertignahrung in Gläsern mit Vakuumverschluß'. Like Sibylle's international cuisine in 'Vatertag', the industrialization involved in these food processes emphasizes the existence of food as mere commodity, stripped of all articulation—a newly mute, dehistoricized object, without meaning *or* flavour. Lena's claim that her modern colleagues cook 'ohne geschichtliches Bewußtsein' introduces a recapitulation of the history of female cooking seen now as a sustained and sustaining commitment to the

---

[12] Fredric Jameson, *The Political Unconscious* (London, 1981), 64.

oppressed class in its struggle. The ground of class politics and class struggle is and always has been Büchner's 'Brotfrage'—despite its absence in Marx and despite Bebel's merely aesthetic understanding of the question for socialism:

Der Ruf nach Gerechtigkeit hafte zu platt am Papier. Das Sinnliche fehle. Der Bauch wolle nicht nur voll sein. Deshalb gehe dem Sozialismus, so scharf witzig er treffen könne, der lustvolle Humor ab (443/437).[13]

Curiously, it is Jan and not Maria who concludes this line of argument in *Der Butt* (though not the line of culinary-political activity) by relating the price increases instituted by the Polish state to a history of food in politics, determined by economics. What remains of Lena in Maria is her maternal 'Nu komm mal' (515/506) and her willingness to support and encourage trade-union resistance to price increases—in consequence of which 'lief vom nächsten Tag an in Gdańsk und Gdynia ... der Streik der Hafen- und Werftarbeiter' (513/505); so it is left to Jan to hint at the economics of food production in a final retrospect which raises questions that the novel has mostly disposed of 'woanders'. Finally, the narrator takes up Jan's speculation in more general terms which bleakly see history as repetition without progress: 'Das hört nie auf. Auch nicht im Kommunismus. Immer die Niederen gegen die Oberen' (515/506).

I have been suggesting that there is a moment of avoidance or absence in *Der Butt*, expressed by the phrase 'woanders Herren am Tisch'. It is accompanied by (or is the obverse of) another absence of which the narrator, and Günter Grass, are well aware. As Philip Brady says of the poems of the third Month (p. 212), the 'physical exuberance' of Gret becomes the starting-point of the writer's self-doubt when faced with the world's hunger. I think this is systematically so and that it accounts in part for the mystery of Agnes Kurbiella.

The obverse of 'woanders' (the incompletion of a novel which is also *in extenso* 'das Wort zuviel', 99/96) is that world hunger itself. Within the novel's own conceptions it remains possible that some other writing activity might be, if not adequate to the problem, at least not inappropriate either: 'Man müßte einen Hungerreport schreiben' (179/175). The writing of *Der Butt* itself, however, in its irrepressible fabulation, is most clearly figured in Gret:

Ach hätte er [Rabelais] sie gekannt! Ich bin gewiß daß ihm zu Gargantua ein genauso gewichtiges Gegenstück in Gestalt unserer dicken Gret eingefallen und zum platzvollen Buch geraten wäre (223/218).

---

[13] Manheim's translation excludes Bebel's remark that 'Der Bauch wolle nicht nur voll sein' ('It wasn't just that the belly needed to be filled').

Der Butt is such a book, elaborating many variations on 'die große Köchin', who is the archetypal source of the historical cooks and of the narrator himself (512/503). In reinventing something like a Rabelaisian narrative, Grass exposes both the innate alarms of 'the cornucopian text' and the impasses to which his own writing is subject.

Erhard Friedrichsmeyer has praised the novel for the honesty Grass brings to his own 'male chauvinism' (Friedrichsmeyer, 1983). It might be argued that within the novel, in the very texture of its writing and metaphors, Grass's deference to Rabelais enables him to undertake a similar self-analysis. For in a number of respects the 'erzählendes Kochbuch' unmasks the richness of its writing as risking mere repetition:

Wer aber Gäste kennt mit Sinn für Lügengeschichten, der brate Hasenklein — die Läufe, die Köpfe halbiert, die Rippchen, Lappen, die Leber — mit durchwachsenem Speck an, wie es die dicke Gret getan hat . . . (235/230).

Gret's cooking, in this description, is not structurally or stylistically distinct from Billy's preparing 'zuvor mit gestoßenem Pfeffer, mit Thymian und Öl eingeriebene Steaks vom Rind' in 'Vatertag', because the form of the recipe *is* the list. In a kind of historical pun on the Renaissance form, then, *Der Butt* recognizes one element of its own text as the list, extendible *ad libitum* but always in danger of falling short, or of possible exhaustion, or — and this is particularly true of the recipe — of being incomplete for want of practical realization. Underlying the form of the novel as a history, the list is seen again as repeated realizations of the same — of the narrator as 'Ich', of Ilsebill, of the Luds, and, of course, of 'die große Köchin'. In these sequences and networks, as Terence Cave notes of Rabelais himself, 'the cornucopia always presages a fall: its dynamic productivity will sooner or later begin to appear, in the post-lapsarian world, as emptying out, or mere flux and repetition.'[14]

If this is true formally, it is also true of the Rabelaisian project undertaken in the figure of Gret. Far from engendering something as original as 'weibliche Literaturpersonen in komischer Hauptrolle' (223/218), she is an elaboration of pre-existent material which the richness of Grass's own writing does not conceal. Gret remains, as Friedrichsmeyer notes, a cross between Falstaff and Gargantua (Friedrichsmeyer 1983, 153). It is characteristic of the 'copious' writing of Grass's novel that it must repeat its models ('Don Quichotte oder Tristram Shandy, Falstaff oder Oskar Matzerath' (223/218)), just as it successively rewrites the texts of Dorothea, of Opitz, of the Grimms, or of Grimmelshausen and of Rabelais. The list, or the repetitions of successive metamorphoses, all

[14] Cave, op. cit., 193.

threaten the exhaustion to which the text testifies in tragic parallel to the real world's inability to feed itself.

Der Butt, as a cornucopian text, is a metaphorically culinary work as well as one that literally displays the kitchen arts through its meticulous representation of the recipe (which, we have noted, is also one of its basic narrative forms). In a parallel and inverse way the actual culinary work of the cooks becomes progressively textualized, loaded with meanings in the form of gloss and commentary and political ideology. The fullness of this textual artefact is best represented by Gret, the historical cook most likely to restore Aua's primal matriarchy; the uneasiness recognized and acknowledged by Grass's writing when faced by the actual demands of world hunger uncovers the extent to which rhetorical richness is implicated in its own inversion—real impoverishment. Gret must therefore be complemented by a figure of emptiness and, as it were, meaninglessness, in Agnes Kurbiella. This is the structural position she takes up in the pattern which matches Dorothea and the virginal, unmarried Sophie as perverters of the role of woman as mother and nurturer; and Lena and Amanda as the class-conscious fighters against hunger and poverty. Gret and Agnes are dialectical opposites and so are their respective cuisines, the one copious, the other diet-conscious. The narrator speaks of Agnes's 'nicht auszufüllende Leere' (264/258) and thus recalls another image of emptiness which undermines his writing:

> Wie will ich,
> wo die Hand auf dem Foto
> bis zum Schluß ohne Reis bleibt,
> über die Köchin schreiben:
> wie sie Mastgänse füllt?
> ('Drei Fragen', 193/189)

Agnes and the hand in the photograph remain unfilled to the end—in their case an end represented by death, although the same 'nicht auszufüllende Leere' haunts both the narrator and the novel itself until its end. In the face of this image of need, cornucopian writing amounts to Opitz's bad faith—'des Menschen ganze Erbärmlichkeit mit Wortplunder verhängt'. Agnes continues to present a challenge: to a poet and to an artist (and hence significantly for Grass also) she represents the muse, and so offers the empty space which Grass's *writing* fills up—the muse is the condition of its possibility; historically 'Agnes, die ja genug hatte, wollte nicht haben, nur geben' (282/276), and she presents a tantalizing sense of possible sufficiency. In our own time the void is unfillable: Calcutta's challenge is as terrible as it is radical, and discourses adequate to these—Agnes or India—remain, it seems, for Grass 'woanders'. Yet in a remarkable way *Der Butt* allows this inadequacy to be seen. It is only in the extended meditation on hunger, death, and culture of *Kopfgeburten* that Grass develops the problem—by abandoning historical narrative in the formal renewal of the 'erzählender Essay'. But that is another story.

8

Male and Female Violence in
Der Butt

PETER PROCHNIK

I find it ironic that the sex which cannot control its sex organ is the one that considers itself fit to control the world.

Marilyn French

The appropriation of *Der Butt* by numerous critics as a hostile statement by Grass on the feminist movement is to some extent attributable to Grass's own often quoted comments in an interview with Fritz Raddatz that 'Der "Butt" handelt von den Geschlechtern und von ihrem Verhältnis zueinander' (Raddatz 1977[1], 30). This innocuous assertion, however, is followed by some sceptical views about women's emancipation, especially that kind which is based on male principles. But then comes the significant clue to Grass's real attitude:

Solche Emanzipation würde das Spannungsverhältnis zwischen den Geschlechtern aufheben, nivellieren, ohne etwas Neues an dessen Stelle zu setzen. Damit würden dann Praktiken wirklich, wie wir sie in der theologisch-soziologischen Trivialliteratur finden: Partnerschaft. Umschreibungen eines Verhaltens zueinander, das bindungslos ist, jederzeit auflösbar, von Vorsicht diktiert. Nur nicht sich aufeinander einlassen. Das zweimal absolut gesetzte Ich, wobei die Bindungsangst der Männer, die seit Jahrhunderten anhält und zu dauerndem Fluchtverhalten geführt hat, nun auch noch von den Frauen praktiziert wird. (Raddatz 1977[1], 30)

The special chemistry that supposedly exists between men and women would disappear—to the disadvantage of men who would be repudiated and excluded.

It is the highly complex nature of this relationship between the sexes, particularly the ostensible historical power-struggle, that exercises the author. But while this is undoubtedly an important aspect of the novel, there is in fact another vital ingredient to this multi-layered work that colours everything, namely the discordant relationship between the narrator and his wife, Ilsebill, and the breakdown in communication between them in the throes of their decaying marriage.

In general terms, Grass examines the disturbance of accepted, traditional roles played in society throughout history by men and women: the struggle for domination by aggressive males and for emancipation by rebellious females; the growth of female self-awareness and aspirations and their concomitant present-day challenge to male superiority and complacency. Readers, however, who expect a coherent, rational discussion and analysis of these important issues are quickly disappointed.

It soon becomes evident that Grass has an axe to grind. The persistent male hostility towards women in the novel is perhaps the result of a far more complicated set of circumstances than plain misogyny and male chauvinism, namely the severe crisis in his own marriage at the time of writing the novel (cf. Hunt 1983, 66–7). One cannot, of course, identify Grass with the self-centred narrator of *Der Butt*; none the less the ambivalent feelings nursed by the narrator for his wife, their mutual unhappiness, and in particular their incessant feuding, with its undercurrent of violence, lead one to suspect more than just a fictional connection.

The result of this painful, emotional confusion is that Grass gives free rein to his stereotyped male fantasies and attitudes, and in the process creates grotesque, cliché caricatures of women: Ilsebills of the traditional fairy-tale, strident and insatiable in their demands, ideologically extreme and hidebound in their views, vacillating and uncertain, but above all castrating. The reference to castration as the male's profoundest fear comes early in the novel (76/72) and is closely linked to the imagined power that women have over men: 'Stimmt, Ilsebill: das ist die Angst der Männer, so gebissen zu werden. Es gibt Theorien, nach denen in allen Frauen der Wunsch zappelt, allen Männern die Klöten und auch den Pimmel abzubeißen' (301–2/296). Fear of the female is normal to the psychology of the male in early childhood, but the idea of the woman as a devouring mouth, a *vagina dentalis* which castrates, is used in this novel not as a descriptive psychological statement but as a weapon with which to disparage women. In this sense, Grass seems to share his misogyny and prejudices about women with Nietzsche and Freud, subscribing to the generally held pejorative view of women in Western philosophies and cultures which Freud enshrined in his basically patriarchal psychology.

Women, on the whole, fare badly in *Der Butt*. They are exploited and treated brutally by men, for a variety of selfish reasons but primarily for their presumption in challenging the authority and superiority of 'die Herren der Schöpfung' (263/257). This is especially evident in Grass's satirical treatment of the Feminal, where the eternal sex-war is fought out linguistically but on the author's own omniscient male terms. Superimposed on to this basic theme is an all-embracing historical framework that, according to Grass, purports to be 'über die Entwicklung oder die Geschichte unserer Ernährung' and encompasses 'den anonymen Anteil der Frauen an unserer Geschichte' (Raddatz 1977[1], 30). Within this context Grass presents the reader with a series of historical cooks, whose main function is to cater to man's sexual and nutritional needs—as 'Wärmeflasche' and 'Köchin'.

Food and culinary skills are of inordinate significance in *Der Butt*, the narrator spending a great deal of time either discussing food, preparing it, or eating it. Nor is its social significance lost on him, for the notions of provision and dependency are highly symbolic and determine hierarchical positions and power. As Rosalind Coward puts it, 'Eating meals is a hazardous activity, infused as it is with implications for sex roles and living arrangements. Small wonder that our digestive tracts have become the site of hidden warfare.'[1] The cooks' modern counterparts are to be found among the members of the Feminal and have the added purpose of haunting the narrator as reminders of Ilsebill: 'Doch alle Skizzen bestanden darauf, Ilsebill zu gleichen: drei erschreckende Schmalgesichter, vorherrschend, nicht zu löschen' (145/141–2).

The purpose of this essay is to consider Grass's perception of male–female relationships and in particular to examine his presentation of violence (emotional, verbal, and physical) within these configurations as a *sine qua non* of the novel. The roles imposed upon both men and women by society are patently key determinants of their personalities, and also contribute to the degree of violence they inflict upon one another. By extension, the role of sexual relations can be seen to be paradigmatic of social relations. In some way Grass is attempting to create a typology of the sexes, but in a very casual, stereotyped form, for nowhere does he define females and males clearly, other than through satirical clichés. John Reddick, in a highly illuminating article, explores the function and presentation of violence in *Der Butt* and especially in the 'Vatertag' chapter. He sees violence as an ever-recurring phenomenon and suggests that Grass is depicting a situation in which 'the search for emancipation turned into a permanent process of systematized violence' (Reddick 1983, 150), in which the pattern of violence is cyclical, manifesting itself in many differing forms throughout history.

Before the novel begins its great panoramic, narrative sweep, the domestic battle-lines between Ilsebill and the narrator are clearly marked out and the underlying antagonism between the sexes graphically

---

[1] Rosalind Coward, *Female Desire: Women's Sexuality Today* (London, 1984), 113.

illustrated both in the matter-of-fact way Ilsebill suggests they go to bed and in the ensuing sexual act itself.

Following this initial dubious act of love, the narrator, as if in competition with Ilsebill, produces his stories of prehistoric times. He describes a matricentric world, a benevolent tyranny exercising an authoritarian love characterized by submission and domination. In this fatherless matriarchate, women wielded complete control 'durch Informationsvorsprung' (48/45) and 'Auf allem, was hätte strittig sein können, hatten damals die Weiber den Daumen drauf' (38/34). The world was comfortable and womb-like for the men, who were deliberately kept in a state of unknowingness and innocence, a 'Stillzeit' where 'nur Mutterrecht galt' and 'das machte friedlich' (13/10). This is an early formulation of Grass's fundamental belief that women should be equated with nature, or, as the flounder later says: 'Frauen müssen nicht fürs Nachleben sorgen, weil sie Leben verkörpern; Männer hingegen können nur außer sich Nachleben beweisen' (404/397). This is the seductive role of women: that of mother—passive, close to nature, embodying life, and the source of unqualified affection. Women are seen as basically conservative by nature and as the upholders of tradition. Significantly, though, there is an ambiguity here, for the men were sexually abused and used by women, as the narrator attempts to force Ilsebill to acknowledge:

Und du, Ilsebill? Was meinst du? Angenommen, du müßtest mit jedem Kerl, der Lust oder nur halbe Lust hat? . . . Sag, daß das repressiv war, uns einfach von Horde zu Horde auszutauschen: ungefragt, wie es den Weibern grad paßte (70/66).

Yet out of this time of female supremacy there began an irreversible movement that wrested power from women and created a patriarchal society in which dynamic masculinity and its attendant aggressive, phallic symbols—designed to denote purposiveness and intent—led to the dominance of the 'harter Männersache', which 'ließ sich nicht aufhalten, doch immerhin ein wenig vertagen' (14/10). However, the beginning of liberated masculine human experience, freed from maternal control, like the beginning of all life, is not without its trauma: birth. Separation from the mother (in this case Wigga) leads directly to the experience of being buggered by a Goth. But men with their destructive rationality and ceaseless striving are seen as the precursors of violence. The 'männliche Prinzip' (329/322) embodied in the flounder is linked unequivocally to the latter's dubious advice to men to wean themselves. The narrator, however, finds this more easily said than done:

Wir, jedenfalls, brauchten noch ein sattes Jahrtausend, um männlich im Sinne des Butt zu werden. Doch dann wurden wir Männer, wie man nachlesen kann:

Männer unter Lederkappen und Helmen mit nagelndem Blick. Männer mit schweifendem, die Horizonte abtastendem Auge. Zeugungswütige Männer, die ihre Stinkmorcheln zu Geschlechtertürmen, Torpedos, Weltraumraketen umdachten. Männer mit System, in Männerorden versammelt. Wortgewaltige Wortspalter. Sich unbekannte Entdecker. Helden, die nicht, nie und auf keinen Fall im Bett sterben wollten. Männer, die mit hartem Mund Freiheit verordneten. Durchhaltende, sich selbst überwindende, standhafte, ungebeugte, immer wieder trotzdem sagende, den Feind sich erfindende, grandios verstiegene, die Ehre um der Ehre willen suchende, prinzipielle, zur Sache kommende, sich ironisch spiegelnde, tragische, kaputte, darüberhinaus weisende Endzielmänner (36/33).

This adumbrates the events of 'Vatertag', in which hordes of men, freed from conventional ties for a day, engage in the fierce pursuit of a ritualistic hedonism: '[sie wollen] die ganz große Sau loslassen, wollen herrlich, selbstherrlich und abgenabelt von Muttern sein' (462/455).

In this depiction of the triumph of the destructive nature of the male, Grass shows that this nature necessarily also finds expression in personal relationships, and particularly in marriage and domesticity. The daily internecine war—which consists of rivalry and strife, the hostile silences, the mutual contempt with which men and women come to regard each other and which is compounded by violence as they each endeavour to assert themselves—takes its toll:

> Haß bildet Sätze.
> Wie sie abrechnet, mich fertigmacht,
> aus ihrer Rolle wächst, überragt
> und zuende redet: Ausreden! Laß mich ausreden!
> und gewöhn dir endlich das Uns und das Wir ab.
>
> ('Manzi Manzi', 144/141)

The narrator wants to recreate his former idyll, the 'Kürbishütte', which is immediately rejected by Ilsebill as reducing her to the tyranny of an imprisoning domesticity so characteristic of male-dominated societies in which men wish to control women:

Aber du willst nicht mit mir einranken, zuwachsen. 'Deine Scheißidylle!' sagst du. 'Deine barocken Ausflüchte. Das könnte dir so passen. Mich wie ein Landei nach Bedarf aus dem Nest holen. Und deine ewige Nabelschau spannend finden. Dafür habe ich nicht wie verrückt studiert', sagst du, 'um hier auffem Land mit Kindern und Küche in einer Kürbishütte, auch wenn das Spaß macht manchmal, dir das Kopfkissen zu schütteln. Nein!' sagst du. Reisen willst du ... 'Und außerdem', sagst du, 'fehlt uns eine geräuscharm laufende Geschirrspülmaschine und eine städtische Zweitwohnung. Kürbishütte? Dann kannst du auch Pißpott sagen; wie es im Märchen steht. Eher treib ich das ab, und zwar in London, eh ich mich hier von dir einranken lasse. Ist doch der alte Männertrick. Goldener Käfig und so' (98/94–5).

Ilsebill repudiates this romantic male ideal with a form of dumb insolence and silent aggression: 'Schwamm drüber. Vergessen wir das' (106/102). But physical and verbal violence too are accepted weapons in this interminable struggle, forming an integral part of the foundering relationship, coloured as it is by mutual, even wilful, misunderstanding: 'Fang doch nicht immer gleich Streit an. Wird doch wohl noch erlaubt sein, ein bißchen zu träumen. Oder? Einfach lächerlich diese Eifersucht auf alles und nichts. Wo kämen wir hin, wie müßten wir verarmen ohne Entwürfe und Utopie!' (10/6), says the narrator plaintively.

The alliance between the narrator and the flounder has served to promote the 'Männersache', and this, as history has shown, has centred on a lust for power and domination that has inevitably involved violence and today has brought the world to the brink of extinction. But male hubris, the desire to transcend earthly limitations in the pursuit of supremacy, is seen as bankrupt: 'Eure Ära klingt mißtönend aus. Kurzum: der Mann ist am Ende … Euch ist nicht mehr zu raten. Die Männersache erledigt sich selbst' (459/453). Man has been the cause of wars and misery; a corrective to history is needed, and man's mentor, the flounder, decides to change sides, intending to guide and help only women in the future: 'Die Geschichte will weiblich geprägt werden' (530/521), for: 'Einzig die emanzipatorische Tat zählt! … Schließlich sind wir doch alle daran interessiert, daß das weibliche Defizit endlich, ich sage endlich, ausgeglichen wird' (225/220).

This, however, must be viewed with caution and some scepticism, for the flounder is in a predicament and pleading for his life before the Feminal. His tactical conversion to the women's cause is as spurious and self-interested as it had been earlier in the novel, after he had let himself be caught by the three lesbians and had offered them his services:

Die Männersache gebe nichts mehr her. Demnächst werde eine Krise weltweit das Ende maskuliner Herrschaft signalisieren. Die Herren seien bankrott. Machtmißbrauch habe ihre Potenz verausgabt. Keiner Impulse mehr fähig, versuche man jetzt, den Kapitalismus durch den Sozialismus zu retten. Das sei ja lachhaft. Er, der Butt, wolle sich fortan behilflich nur noch dem weiblichen Geschlecht zuwenden (42/39).

High-mindedly, the flounder signals his new convictions with the words: 'Auf dem Machtwechsel der Geschlechter beruht mein Prinzip' (42/39).

The flounder never genuinely identifies with the women's cause, and the narrator, who is perhaps very close to Grass here, maintains an ironic and satirical distance from the women's demands, which are maliciously distorted to suit his own purpose. The cunning aspect is that the women themselves will have to make the final decision about whether they want to accept the flounder's help in future:

Doch wie sollte ich, das verkörpert schuldhafte, das männliche und—nachgewiesen—kriegerische Prinzip geeignet sein, die Sache der Frauen, fortan nur noch die Frauensache zu beraten?
   Ich will. Ich könnte. Schon wüßte ich wie. Das Feminal möge urteilen (532/523).

This, however, is totally disingenuous of the flounder, for the offer to place at the disposal of women precisely those violent and aggressive qualities usually associated with men degrades women and reduces them to the same dubious condition as men. The narrator, in a moment of cynical inspiration at the 'Buttessen', acknowledges this: 'Sein Rat hieß: Töten! Sein Wort setzte Gewalt. Aus ihm wirkte das Böse ... Du Todbringer, Lebensfeind!' (536/526–7).
   Women who wish to displace men simply by becoming more like them, that is by being assimilated into the male-dominated world or by surpassing men in their own aggressive aims, will not only become emotionally impoverished but will ultimately destroy each other—which is made explicit in the 'Vatertag' episode. By complying, women merely prolong the unremitting inhumanity and violence perpetrated daily by the patriarchy towards women, but in a new guise. They will become the instruments of their own oppression. Indeed, the Feminal well illustrates Grass's scepticism towards handing over power to the feminist movement, with his caricatured portrayal of the bitter factional in-fighting of the group and their studied ideological responses to historical situations. In fact, the women's prevarication and marshmallow compromises engage Grass in none-too-subtle parody and satire:

Es ginge heute sicher friedfertiger, sensibler, ohne Individualanspruch dennoch kreativer, allgemein zärtlicher, trotz Überfluß dennoch gerechter, und weil ohne männlichen Ehrgeiz, nicht so verbissen, sondern heiterer zu; auch gäbe es keinen Staat (51–2/48).

However, these conciliatory words by Ms Schönherr, the presiding judge, are followed by the Feminal's showing its claws against the narrator by abusing him verbally and threatening the flounder with physical violence. Violence, which terrifies the narrator, is in fact never very far from the surface, especially when he is in his hallucinogenic state:

Schon nahmen die Weiber drohende Haltung ein. Schon besetzte mich Angst. Schon war jede Ausflucht versperrt. Schon fühlte ich mich gepackt, um gevierteilt zu werden. Kribbeln zwischen den Beinen. (Rief nicht die Simoneit: 'Mit dem Küchenmesser ruckzuck!'?) (400/393–4).

The curious but revealing aspect about the Feminal episode is that the narrator sometimes seems ambivalent about women's activities and ambitions, reflecting perhaps Grass's own views. Male history is condemned outright, and the episode cited above forms the climax to the verbal and physical assault on men. When the flounder, doubtfully at first, offers his services to the women's cause, he pointedly asks 'wird . . . die Forderung nach sozialer Gleichberechtigung dazu führen, daß auch der männliche Moralkanon gebrochen wird? Oder wird die Gleichberechtigung der Geschlechter nur die Potenzierung des männlichen Machtstrebens zur Folge haben?' (532/523). The answer seems to lie in compromise, for the Feminal fails to sentence the flounder to death but instead decrees that he be returned to the sea to expiate his crimes, and so he changes sides. The narrator, perplexed and in despair, has a final one-way conversation with the flounder as he carries him to the sea:

Sag doch was, Butt. Ein Sterbenswörtchen. Soll nun alles aus sein mit uns? Hast du mich wirklich abgeschrieben? Willst du nur noch die blöden Weiber beraten? Was soll ich denn machen, Butt? Sag doch was, sag! Ich versteh die Welt nicht mehr (539/530).

Ominously he reflects: 'Ach Butt! Dein Märchen geht böse aus' (552/543).

There is a bond between women which arouses the narrator's antagonism. Often feeling spurned and discomforted, he is reduced to a mocking derision which reduces women to the level of empty-headed gossips. Sisterhood is a threat to him, for it is a union that excludes him not only biologically but emotionally, that acts as if he does not exist. In a revealing passage following the flounder's ironic advocacy of the establishment of feminist convents and the collapse of male hegemony, the narrator sardonically hypothesizes about the general social, political, and sexual advantages that would accrue but ends with the pathetic plea to Ilsebill: 'dürfte ich dann—angenommen, es trüge sich alles so zu—dich einfach als Mann auf ein Stündchen besuchen?' (227/222). In 'Wir aßen zu dritt', in which past and present are inextricably mixed in the narrator's mind, the women talk impersonally about 'him', dissecting the narrator psychologically and making great play of his mother-complex and childlike dependency. 'Er ist nicht abgenabelt!' they repeat, but then more threateningly 'Der muß abgenabelt werden! Endlich abgenabelt werden! . . . Im Grunde ist er kindisch geblieben' (396/389–90). The narrator's wish not to 'grow up', to remain tied to the comfort of his 'Mutterkomplex', is a rejection of reality, as is clearly indicated later on:

Schon ist Ilsebill Landschaft geworden und jeder Deutung verschlossen. Laß mich rein! In dich hineinkriechen will ich. Verschwinden ganz und meinen Verstand einbringen. Ich will es warm haben und die Flucht aufgeben ... (524/515).

But this is also Grass speaking—the author who said: 'Da ich zum Beispiel einen ausgewachsenen Mutterkomplex habe, bin ich auch nicht bereit diesen Mutterkomplex zum Psychiater zu tragen, sondern mit ihm zu leben' (Casanova 1979², 223).

Clearly the question of feminism has concerned Grass over and above his personal problems. The flounder recognizes in Ilsebill 'soviel unverbrauchter Wille zur Macht' (153/150), and the implication is clear—women want mastery not equality. Ruth K. Angress, however, defends the feminist position, which she says calls for 'a greater democratization of society and not ... a continuation of patriarchal patterns in reverse' (Angress 1982, 47). For Grass, however, it is adherence to the so-called feminine principle—cyclical, life-creating, vital—that is of greatest value. The child-bearing female represents the natural heritage of humanity, while the male carries on with the burden of ruling and rational thinking. 'Erwärmt euch am Weiblichen. Lebt wieder auf' (256/251) recommends the flounder from his male-orientated vantage-point, praising the virtues of the female muse. The attraction of the earthmother figure is irresistible to the narrator, who devotes much of his time to lamenting the loss of the comforts of the womb and his former state of innocence and harmony. Under the influence of fly agaric his deep-rooted wish surfaces:

Zeit zahlte sich zurück. Bilder kamen freihaus. Es neigte sich Aua. Und ich, der Mann, das kostbare Einzelstück, war aufgehoben in Fürsorge. Im Schoß meiner schwangeren Ilsebill lag ich und nuckelte an ihrer großen Brust: satt, in Frieden, entkommen, glücklich, wunschlos wie nie ... (401/395).

But the dream and wish are shattered: 'Was willst du noch. Immer nur das. Das brauch ich nicht mehr. Hau ab! Hau endlich ab. Geh schon' (524/515).

Pleading with Ilsebill is done in the guise of love, the virtues of which he extols, but love for the narrator is really of an autistic, self-regarding kind, whereas for Ilsebill love is predatory, leading to marriage, which is possession and ownership. Marriage is appropriation and subservience camouflaged by the romantic notion of love: 'weil so, der ehelichen Zeitweil ans Bein gebunden, eine Abhängigkeit entstehe, welche besonders den Frauen zieme' (140/137) says the narrator, although he claims in mitigation that it was the flounder that persuaded him of this chauvinist view. Women, the flounder asserts, gained both power and

security through marriage, and in the utopian future the ideal world will
be bathed in the beneficent glow of love: 'Liebesglanz wird alles schönen.
Millionen wunschlose Ilsebills. Beschämt von so viel Sanftmut werden
die Männer ihrer Macht und Herrlichkeit entsagen. Nur noch Liebe
wird sein und überall werden' (274/268). But this is the typical male voice
subscribing to the conventional male notion of possession, which the
Feminal condemns as a 'männliches Unterdrückungswerkzeug' (140/
137) and which is focused in the novel into the torment and torture of
dishwashing, just as Sophie Rotzoll's hatred had boiled down to a recipe.
Marriage, a traditional form of possession, has often been used to secure
women's labour to the advantage of men:

Es hatte sich mittlerweile die besitzsichernde Ehe dergestalt eingeübt, daß die
Frauen, womöglich überdrüssig der himmlischen Liebesergüsse und verhärmten
Keuschheitsspiele, geradezu begierig waren, unter die Haube zu kommen; mit
der Haus-Schlüssel-Küchengewalt blieb ihnen Herrschaft genug (270/264).

The wish to purchase a dishwasher (in itself harmless enough) is,
within the narrative context, a sign of a deeper malaise in the relationship
and becomes the cause of extreme anger and violence. It is a small signal
of freedom for the woman, but one which the narrator sees only in terms
of endless dissatisfaction: 'das dumme Luder. Nie zufrieden. Immer fehlt
was. Neulich der Streit um die Geschirrspülmaschine. Jetzt eine Zweitwohnung in der Stadt. Und was sie hat, das will sie nicht. Und was sie
kriegt, das paßt ihr nicht' (152/148). Women are fighting back, challenging the men for their rights, as the narrator ruefully comments: 'Sie sind
so aggressiv geworden, die Weiber' (152/149).

However, as Ilsebill becomes further estranged from her husband, and
more aggressive, he, in a perverse but calculated ploy in the bitter marital
game, encourages her aggression by deliberately misunderstanding her or
provoking her to extremes, thus sowing the seeds of further dissension:

Als sie wegen nichts oder weil das Wetter umschlug oder weil ich ihr Essiggurkenwasser, das sie wie süchtig soff, ins Klo geschüttet hatte, als meine Ilsebill
plötzlich, weil ihr der Faden riß, in kalte gelierte Wut geriet—wie sie zitterte,
nachbebte später ... (131/128).

There is almost a grim delight in recounting this, but at the same time the
narrator is revealing his own complex feelings towards Ilsebill. Tender
feelings can emerge in an act of violence, while aggressive feelings can
appear disguised as a caress, each following their own inevitable logic.
Ilsebill, on the other hand, is in no mood for such subtleties and with one
clean, unhesitating sweep destroys the narrator's treasured collection of
glassware, after which he provocatively replaces the shattered pieces on
the shelf. 'Die sind kaputt heiler als wir' (133/129), he says, reflecting the

fragility of their marriage. But Ilsebill's pent-up bitterness and hatred increase, and as usual the narrator fails or refuses to understand their root causes, attributing them to spurious feelings of jealousy, which he encourages, or to the female's inadequate biology:

Dieses tägliche Gezänk. Ihre Lust, den geliebten Mann fixfertig zu machen. Ihre Wut, die wieder zunimmt nach kurzer Pause, nur weil sie es nicht geschafft hat, ganz aus sich (ohne männliches Zutun) schwanger zu werden. Dabei gibt es für mich immer und einzig nur: Ilsebill Ilsebill ... (389/383).

The male–female conflict and the violence it engenders is seen primarily in sexual and domestic terms as Ilsebill angrily confronts her husband not only with infidelity but also with the facts of her domestic imprisonment: 'Aber Eicheln im Mörser zu Mehl stoßen: das wollen wir Frauen nie wieder ... Willst wohl, daß wir am Spinnrad hocken. Hast wohl Sehnsucht nach Singers Nähmaschine mit Fußantrieb. Bist wohl müde und willst auf der Ofenbank sitzen' (307/301). To all this the narrator is indifferent; he trivializes and oversimplifies the situation. His sexual hypocrisy is paramount as he cynically recalls his flings and affairs in the past and present with the entire Feminal, although finally he is dismissed in an indictment of all males in the poem 'Mannomann' with the words:

> Hör schon auf.
> Machen Punkt.
> Du bist doch fertig, Mann, und nur noch läufig.
> (547/538)

This final dismissal perhaps explains, but does not excuse, his earlier behaviour: 'Ich war wohl nicht bei Trost, als ich kürzlich was Neues einfädelte oder schlimmer: eine alte Geschichte aufwärmte' (387/381). The narrator is concerned with guilt that demands global forgiveness. Like a child, locked in the anal-phallic stage of development, he wants and needs sexual and verbal analgesics. Indeed, his interest in all things excremental can be considered a sign of regression, although the sexual connotations are ever present. The perverse use of genital creativity (a form of violence) by both the narrator and Ilsebill serves only to let them score points off each other. Even though Ilsebill does become pregnant and the narrator, almost in competition, 'creates' stories, there is none the less a failure of true creative intercourse between them. It is also worth noting that psychoanalysis has often found that failure at the genital level can lead to anal regression, characterized by a preoccupation with money, power, and sadism—all three of which are elements in the novel.

Sex is of the utmost interest to the narrator, not only for its pleasurable side but also as another form of aggression towards women. The sexual act can be viewed as a power struggle, something inflicted on someone else. Sexual antagonism is violent, serving only release or self-satisfaction (cf. Friedrichsmeyer 1983), as the abbess Rusch, herself the personification of unbridled sexuality, tells her nuns:

Wie eindringlich tief er ist und wie knollig beschaffen. Wie bald er schlapp macht und kümmerlich wegsackt. Wie grob er wird, wenn er lustlos bleibt. Wie wenig das schnelle Gebumse den Frauen nützlich ist. Wie er nur Kinder will und Söhne zuallererst. Wie rasch er das Wechselspiel in fremder Bettkiste sucht. Wie aber sein Eheweib nie ausfliegen darf, auf andere Rüben scharf. Wie hart seine Hand schlägt. Wie schroff er die Gunst entzieht und wie ihm die Rübe außer Haus weichgekocht wird (200–1/196–7).

For the male, sex is seen simply as release from tension or as 'sex in the head'. Women are to be used to service men: 'die Muschel, die Möse nur, das Ziel aller Männer, die unterwegs unbehaust sind und sich loswerden wollen, immer wieder und nochmal' (544/534–5).

The sexual violation of women is unrelenting. The narrator and other males in the novel, when engaged in sexual activities, plainly act out their own fantasies and desires, reducing women to mindless objects willing to be abused. Angress, in her attack on Grass, puts it succinctly: 'It's all tits and cunts, business as usual in current male fiction' (Angress 1982, 43). The narrator, for instance, for whom all kinds of unrestrained sexual activities are welcome and evidence of total oneness with one's partner, dismisses Ilsebill's objections to arse-licking as prim and proper: 'weil sie befürchtet, es könnte ihr mit dem Wegfall der letzten Scheu die Zunge abfallen' (208/204) or because she has a 'puritanische Maulsperre' (208/ 204). He utterly rejects her objections by demeaning her as a person and accusing her of inhibitions, failing to recognize his typically male condescension. Indeed, whenever the narrator summons up sexuality with which to berate his wife, he uses either farce or irony to humiliate her, but the intention is always the same—to demean: 'doch meine Ilsebill—die am Donnerstag manchmal kühn ist—hat mir noch nie, so fromm ich vor ihr auf die Knie geh, den Arsch geleckt' (208/204). This attitude permeates *Der Butt*, ironically culminating in 'Vatertag', where the supreme violation of woman takes place, although actually initiated and carried out by women who, despite their rejection of men, none the less act like them.

Most of the violence that occurs in the novel is the result of fear, jealousy, misunderstanding, and above all the desire for power, often expressed through sexual domination. Fear and dread of women is perhaps most pronounced among men who not only fear being considered inferior but also nurse an atavistic horror of castration, the violation of their manhood: 'Doch das Rübenbeißen blieb weiterhin Spaß und treibt uns Männern bis heutzutag Urängste ein' (76/72). On the other hand, within the narrative framework, these fears are hardly products of an overheated, wild imagination. Margarete Rusch actually does bite off a testicle of the Lutheran pastor Hegge, thus making the idea a reality to be conjured with: 'Unter den Röcken habe sie das Kerlchen gepackt und ihm, als alles Drücken und Pusten nicht habe nützen wollen, das linke oder rechte Hodenei abgebissen' (200/195). The portrayal of Sophie Rotzoll on the feminist poster speaks for itself: 'Drauf sah man Sophie . . . den Butt linkshändig bei der Schwanzflosse fassen, während sie rechts ein Küchenmesser im Griff hatte' (406/399–400).

With increasing self-confidence, however, women have shifted from sullen, passive resistance to an active defence of themselves in which resorting to the extreme of killing is not alien to them. When driven to extremes, they act. The repulsive and ascetic Bishop Adalbert becomes sex-crazed and quite transformed after eating the amber-seasoned soup: 'Immer wieder und noch einmal drang der Asket mit seinem gar nicht mehr bußfertigen Werkzeug in ihr Fleisch' (88/84) until the violated and maddened Mestwina kills him with a cast-iron cooking-spoon. There is no pleasure in this union, simply male lust which cannot be denied. Sexual arousal is so strong that despite consummation it persists even after death: 'Adalbert hat nur kurz geseufzt. Sein Widersacher jedoch blieb ungebeugt, stand tapfer um seiner selbst willen und hat den Kopf nicht senken wollen, auch als der Bischof schon tot und ein Märtyrer war' (90–1/87). Margarete Rusch also kills, but in a calculated way, her plans in one case having been nursed for fifty years without any loss of conviction. The abbot Jeschke is fattened to death and the mayor Ferber is flattened: 'Es mag schon sein, daß sie dem herrischen Eberhard Ferber so überlegen den Atem verkürzt, den alten Bock unter ihrer Bettlast erstickt hat' (213/208).

The desire for revenge on men for their sexual rapacity and general oppression of women is still prominent today. The constant emotional bullying, the importuning by men, and the misogynistic view that presents women as anti-intellectual and of lower ethical ambition than men—these are all part of the deliberate violation of women, captured in the novel by Ilsebill's desire for a dishwasher, an act of symbolic importance, an assertive articulation.

Women's vengeance, however, pales into insignificance compared to the violence meted out to women by men, such as the horrors of the rapes of Lena Stubbe and of Agnes Kurbiella by the Swedish soldiers, where the act of rape is associated with male supremacy and where there is an implicit suggestion that women actually like it, or at least provoke violence. As Lena, the socialist, puts it: 'wenn er kloppen muß, soll er.

Mich trifft das nich. Auch wenn er mir Veilchen haut' (438/432). But such devotion, like that of Agnes and Sophie, remains unrequited; these women have been conditioned to suffer a romantic delusion.

Yet women are also condemned by the flounder in his final speech to the Feminal for having acquiesced in force and violence:

Kein weibliches Votum schlug durch, als—noch standen die Trümmer—die Wiederbewaffnung verordnet wurde. Ergeben nahmen die Frauen die Fortsetzung des männlich beschlossenen Wahnsinns hin. Und selbst dort, wo es Frauen gelang, politisch Einfluß zu gewinnen, haben sie—von Madame Pompadour bis zu Golda Meir und Indira Gandhi—Politik immer nur im logischen Streckbett des männlichen Geschichtsverständnisses betrieben, also—nach meiner Definition—als Krieg fortgesetzt (531–2/522–3).

The irony of this state of affairs is that women are just as capable of extreme violence and brutality as men, especially when they renounce their 'womanhood', when they become 'denatured' in the emulation of male stereotypical behaviour. This dual aspect of male–female, as we have already seen, is both positive and negative, it is productive and destructive. When the narrator is in India we are informed: 'Die Göttin Kali gilt als weiblicher Aspekt des Gottes Shiva. Ihre Kraft zerstört. Nach Laune reißt sie ein, was notdürftig steht. Wir leben in ihrem Zeitalter' (179/175), and this androgyny, this sexual ambiguity, is conveyed vividly through the lesbian figures of Billy, Franki, Siggi, and Mäxchen. Their aim is to reject the traditional role of dependence forced by men upon women, and often meekly accepted by them. They are no longer prepared to be sexually used: 'Ihr wollt doch bloß immer rein raus und fertig. Aufreißen und liegenlassen ... Bedien dich sonstwo' (463/456). But this goal cannot be achieved, for it is in the very act of imitating men that they violate Billy, one of their own number.

'Vatertag' is quite different from any other part of the novel, although we are constantly prepared for these events (cf. 22/18, 149/146, 422/415, 455/447, 459/452). It is bleak and menacing, overpowering in its violence and sexual excesses. It forms the culmination of male degradation and depravity, and, whereas violence and abuse occur in many other parts of the novel, their impact is less forceful there because of the awareness that new life is beginning inside Ilsebill or because of the distance of history. Here, though, there is only death—death as a sudden, discontinuous experience. 'Vatertag' is a chilly celebration of maleness with which the lesbians identify: 'Kesse Väter wir, wie man sagt' (465/458). This identification proceeds from a simple assertion and acknowledgement of being 'anders', through a more traditional male roughness and competitiveness—'Da begann das große, überall das ganz große, das noch nie dagewesene, wirklich sehenswerte, weil von Amateuren gebotene, den-

noch profihafte männliche Kräftemessen' (479/471)—to the physical and
sexual imitation of male role models. The crude, earthy energies of men
are appropriated by the women, who abandon themselves: they fight and
argue with each other, they urinate standing up with the aid of a device,
and in general act without restraint until inevitably 'war das Gelächter
... in männliche Trauer umgeschlagen, wie das so üblich ist: aus einem
Extrem ins andere' (488/479). Significantly, the catalysts for the final,
inevitable brutalities are cooking and the row over dishwashing, with all
its implications of subservience.

Then, as if in a dream world, Fränki, Mäxchen, and Siggi are
consumed by the greatest of all passions: the monumental desire to
procreate:

'Ich will einen Sohn zeugen!' ... auch Siggi und Fränki hatten, wie das Mäxchen,
den großen, eindeutigen, jede Nebenhandlung löschenden, nur auf sich bestehenden Zeugungstraum gehabt, der tiefer wummert als je gedacht und dessen
urdumme Kraft sich auch dort steilt, wo die Natur nichts geplant hat (494/486).

With Messianic single-mindedness, they determine that Billy is to be
raped and become their receptacle: 'In Billy wollten sie ihr Kapital
anlegen. In ihr sich fortwuchern. In ihrer Körperlichkeit gründete
dreimal Hoffnung auf einen Sohn: Jajaja!' (495/486). The horror and
sterility of this act on a sleeping companion is lost on them in their frenzy
as they 'crucify' Billy until Fränki 'meinte ... den Übersohn gezeugt zu
haben' (497/488) and Siggi, with unintended irony, says 'Das mußte sein.
Jetzt erst ist richtig Vatertag' (497/488). They have degraded themselves,
while their victim gains in stature, ironically saying 'Wenn ich das will,
nehm ich mir nen richtigen Mann. Der ist mir lieber. Das sag ich euch als
Frau. Habt ihr verstanden! Als Frau' (497/489). But the real men,
waiting their turn, violate her even more than her friends. The motor-
cycle gang see the very presence of the girls at the Grunewaldsee not only
as an insult but as an affront and threat to their very manhood: 'das
Unerhörte. Die ganz dicke Sauerei. Den Kunstfick. Die Beleidigung aller
vatertäglichen Saubermänner' (496/487). They must act as avenging
angels, and at the moment when Billy becomes aware of the abject futility
of recent events, when she redefines her 'lost' womanhood and self-
image: 'Was für ein neues Gefühl: Frau sein' (500/491) and exults: 'Ich
bin eine Frau, eine Frau, eine Frau!' (501/492), history repeats itself and
she is brutally raped by the motor-cycle gang who, as a final, dehumaniz-
ing gesture, repeatedly ride their motor cycles over her body until she is a
mutilated mass: 'War das noch ein Mensch? ... ihre Billy ... zum
Klumpen gefahren' (502/493). The ultimate humiliation has been played
out. Billy dies without dignity. The message is bleak and pessimistic:
'Danach ging das Leben weiter' (502/493), but nothing has changed.

9
Men, Women, and the 'Third Way'

JOHN SANDFORD

Less than half a dozen pages into *Der Butt* comes the observation: 'Vielleicht haben wir nur vergessen, daß es noch mehr gibt. Was Drittes. Auch sonst, auch politisch, als Möglichkeit' (10/7). It is a remarkably early point in such a long book for such an apparently sententious and programmatic statement. Yet if this is an anticipatory glimpse of a programme, of a way out of the perilous impasse that the book goes on to portray as our contemporary condition, it is a programme that singularly fails to take on concrete form. As the novel proceeds, references to, and visions of, a 'third way' recede: the theme seems to have been a red herring, a utopia that hard-nosed 'realism' is unable to sustain.

Yet, although explicit references to a 'third way' are lacking, the notion remains a potent one, and its failure to materialize may be seen as a factor that informs both the novel's more explicit references to the male–female relationship and the narratorial strategies through which those references are mediated. The distinctive waywardness, the provocative evasiveness of the novel's perspectives—in particular in its attitudes to feminism— suggest a narratorial 'third-wayism' that represents a response to the very failure to locate a tenable third position beyond 'masculinity' and 'femininity'.

The reference to 'Was Drittes. Auch sonst, auch politisch, als Möglichkeit' comes in a distinctly elegiac part of the novel: the whole opening chapter, and in particular these first few sections, is pervaded by a sense of loss. The lament at a general level is familiar enough: it is for the loss of innocence, of contentment and carefreeness, of a quasi-paradise preceding the fall that comes with the getting of knowledge— the tempter here being a flounder rather than a serpent. This blissful childhood—both of men and of humankind—evokes numerous echoes, not only in myth and religion but of an anthropological, political, and psychological kind too.

But at a more specific level, the familiar imagery of loss is given a

characteristic twist. In these opening pages, with their heading 'Die
dritte Brust', the narrator introduces the conceit of the three-breasted
mother-figure Aua. The elegy for the lost prehistorical paradise with its
'geschichtslose Weiberfürsorge' (16/12) is given substance in the form of
the recurrent lament for the loss of this third breast: the world, it is
proposed, is the poorer for the sudden appearance of two-breasted
women:

> Wer trug dich ab, ließ uns verarmen?
> Wer sagte: zwei ist genug?
> Schonkost seitdem, Rationen.
>
> ('Aua', 23/20)

The number three is made much of here—it is, apart from anything
else, the furthest men can count in their prenumerate innocence. The
third breast—'die dritte'—is subsequently experienced as an absence,
something undefined but missing in the life of the narrator's later
incarnations, and nowhere more so than today: 'es stimmt schon, oft fehlt
heute die dritte' (9/5). But the lack, concretized in 'die dritte', slips back
into the abstract in the next two sentences—into 'das Dritte', something
at once less tangible and more suggestive than the missing breast: 'Ich
meine, es fehlt irgendwas,' the narrator continues, 'Na, das Dritte.' In
the following sentence—'Ich werde bestimmt keinen Kult daraus
machen'—the 'daraus' seems initially to refer to 'die dritte' rather than
'das Dritte', but the link between the two, once established, is further
developed, with the third breast functioning now more distinctly as
something lost and dimly recalled, whilst 'das Dritte' shifts into the
future as the dimly perceived promise of 'noch mehr ... Was Drittes.
Auch sonst, auch politisch, als Möglichkeit' (10/7).

The possibility of 'was Drittes', of 'die fehlende Dimension' (10/6) is
hedged about with doubts. The number three is, after all, a notoriously
meretricious one: 'Wie überhaupt die Zahl drei mehr verspricht, als sie
hält' (9/6).[1] Yet the narrator remains defensively possessive towards it:
'Das Ganze ist mehr ein Traum. ... Wird doch wohl noch erlaubt sein,
ein bißchen zu träumen. Oder?' (10/6). It is, he concedes, a Utopia, but

---

[1] On the role of numbers in *Der Butt* see Willson 1982, 57, who talks of 'Grass's definite
affinity for the number three', basic to which is 'the tacit but allusive mode of triadic
thought, the production of a synthesis through the use of a thesis and an antithesis'. 'Grass',
he continues, 'in a mode of thought that has always been typical of him, seems to plead for
the middle way, for the resolution of extremes through a synthetic choice. ... *Der Butt* is a
novel of possible numbers that makes a singular unity out of two opposing, mutually
dependent forces' (61). However, Willson does not take this line of argument further, into
an analysis of the book's failure to concretize this 'synthesis', 'resolution of extremes', and
'singular unity'.

perhaps a necessary one: 'Wo kämen wir hin, wie müßten wir verarmen ohne Entwürfe und Utopie!' (10/6).

The sense of lack engendered by the missing third breast seems, then, to have shifted into an uneasy assertion of a much broader utopian need. Appropriately enough, the most forthright reference to utopia in this first chapter comes in the poem 'Was uns fehlt'—significantly in the only line (out of thirty-nine) in which the title-phrase of the poem is repeated. The reference is preceded by lines that indicate a consciousness of the writer's need—and failure—to go beyond the rehearsal of platitudinous invocations of a lost golden age and instead 'beweiskräftige Alternativen zu entwickeln' (51/47) for a concrete future:

> Auf Lauchblätter tippe ich: Die Steinzeit ist schön.
> Ums Feuer sitzen: gemütlich.
> Weil eine Frau das Feuer vom Himmel geholt hat,
> herrschen die Frauen erträglich.
> Was uns fehlt (einzig) ist eine griffige Utopie.
>
> (58/55)

Yet a utopia—'griffig' or otherwise—continues to be missing right through to the end of *Der Butt*, and the explicit presentiment of lack and potential—integral to the tenor of the opening chapter—recedes as the months pass. The vision of a world in which one

> ... hätte nicht zwischen die Wahl
> und müßte nie wieder entweder oder
> ('Aua', 22/19)

is shouldered aside by a reality that seems to allow only for duality and that has no room for 'was Drittes'.

What *Der Butt* does in the event explore is, then, not the possible forms that 'was Drittes' could take but the outlines of a much more unsubtle 'Machtwechsel der Geschlechter' (42/39). Its premisses thus find themselves confined to the level of a biologistic rehearsal of conventional 'male' and 'female' characteristics, and its vision extends no further than to grotesque or despairing surmises about a superficial imposition of the former on to the latter. The novel's iconography of 'maleness' and 'femaleness' is already adumbrated in the first chapter, where most attention is devoted to pinning down specifically 'male' characteristics. This viewpoint dominates the novel, which is recurrently explicit about men, whilst 'female' characteristics are more often implicit, or are to be deduced *ex negativo* from what is posited of men. Men are characterized here by being, amongst other things: exploitative; marked by a Faustian 'Unrast'; warriors; obsessed with division—with categorization, logic, dates; and goal-orientated.

Male exploitativeness is explicit above all in remarks about man's relationship to nature, rather than simply the male–female relationship: 'Die Welt beherrschen will er, die Natur bezwingen und von der Erde weg sich über sie erheben' (356/349); earlier, the woman–nature relationship has been contrasted with man's: 'Die Natur will nicht mehr weiblich erduldet, sondern männlich bezwungen werden' (36/32–3).

Male 'Unrast' is dated from the loss of the third breast: 'Wir ungestillten Männer waren ziemlich zappelig und wie von germanischer Unrast infiziert. Fernweh kam auf' (14/11). 'So verloren wir unsere Unschuld. Weg war die dritte Brust. . . . Ungestillt griffen wir fortan ins Leere. . . . Danach besetzte uns Unruhe, Ungenügen kam auf' (72–3/69). Henceforth, men striving, peering into the distance, exploring, moving on, ever dissatisfied, form a recurrent motif. Unlike Faust, Grass's ever-striving men find no salvation, only temporary amnesia in a return to the breast (and the—in German happily ambiguous—'Schoß'): 'Im Schoß meiner schwangeren Ilsebill lag ich und nuckelte an ihrer großen Brust: satt, in Frieden, entkommen, glücklich, wunschlos wie nie . . .' (401/395). The novel is given to psycho-sexual theorizing about the origins and nature of this 'Unrast': 'die Muschel, die Möse . . . das Ziel aller Männer, die unterwegs unbehaust sind und sich loswerden wollen, immer wieder und nochmal' (544/534–5); when the flounder indulges in similar speculation—'Männer . . . können nur außer sich Nachleben beweisen, indem sie das Haus bauen, den Baum pflanzen, die Tat vollbringen' (404/397)—he is rapped over the fins: 'die Beisitzerinnen des feministischen Tribunals [zensierten] seine grundsätzliche Unterscheidung der Geschlechter als "ausschließlich biologisch" und "stockkonservativ"' (404–5/398).

The equation of maleness with war becomes increasingly explicit in the later stages of the book—'der erste Weltkrieg, dieses Meisterstück europäischer Männlichkeit' (417/411); 'das zerstörende, dem Leben feindliche, das mörderische, männliche, das kriegerische Prinzip!' (527/518). The flounder's final address in 'Das Feminal' expounds these ideas at length; here too a sexual explanation is proposed: 'als sei das Töten die Fortsetzung der Sexualität mit anderen Mitteln' (529–520).

The male's associations with division and order run from the physical (the invention of metallic tools for cleaving and cutting) to the intellectual (men as 'logical'—'strenggenommen hat sie als Frau keine Logik zu haben', 136/133), the forensic (man the lawmaker—'[der Mann] überschaut . . . die Lage und handelt nach Vorschrift', 468/461), and his role as the 'maker of history'—both in the sense of the doer of 'historical' deeds and of the subsequent recorder of those deeds.

The masculine fixation with goals—'den Blick aufs Endziel genagelt' (529/520)—is the most fatal characteristic of all. The text plays at various points with reverberations and compounds of 'Ende' in association with men (cf. particularly 'Endziel', 'Endsieg', 'Endlösung' brought together in the poem 'Am Ende', 99/95). In the end, of course, this goal-fixation recoils upon its own carriers: 'der Mann ist am Ende. . . . Die Männersache erledigt sich selbst' (459/453).

If men are 'am Ende', what *should* follow, and what is *likely* to follow? The retreat from further elaboration of the 'third way' means that only the second of these questions receives a concrete answer in *Der Butt*: the future, it seems, has nothing to offer except a reversal of the power relations between the sexes, with no room for a third possibility. The 'Machtwechsel der Geschlechter' (42/39) is exemplified in both historical and fictitious figures. Contemporary female political figures are cited as examples of the adoption of 'masculine' behaviour in the exercise of power by women: the novel refers to Golda Meir and Indira Gandhi, though had it been written a few years later no doubt Margaret Thatcher would have provided an even more exemplary *locus classicus* of the phenomenon that 'wo es Frauen gelang, politisch Einfluß zu gewinnen, haben sie . . . Politik immer nur im logischen Streckbett des männlichen Geschichtsverständnisses betrieben' (531–2/522–3). The problem, it is bleakly implied, is by no means confined only to our culture, as the narrator's discovery in India of the goddess Kali illustrates, who 'gilt als weiblicher Aspekt des Gottes Shiva. Ihre Kraft zerstört. . . . Wir leben in ihrem Zeitalter' (179/175). Within the fiction of the novel's own protagonists, the 'Vatertag' chapter follows through the dead-end logic of the 'role-change' hypothesis to its grotesquely brutal conclusion, rendering ridiculous along the way a would-be glimpse of androgyny in the sexual antics of the 'liberated' women: 'wir kommen ohne Gehänge aus, wir hängen nicht vom Gehänge ab, wir sind frei, das neue Geschlecht' (466/459).

There are also in *Der Butt* references to the other side of this coin—to a 'feminization' of history, but they are, significantly, much less concrete, as, for instance, in the flounder's statement that 'die Geschichte will weiblich geprägt werden' (530/521), or his call to give 'unserer armen, weil aller Hoffnung entfallenen Welt, dem Spielball nur noch ohnmächtiger Männlichkeit einen neuen, sagen wir ruhig femininen Sinn' (42/39). His closing address to the feminist tribunal (527–32/518–23) elaborates these notions at some length, echoing socialist invocations of the historical role of the working class in his call for women to take over the reins of history: 'es sei denn [dieser Teufelskreis] wird von denen aufgebrochen, die bisher keine Geschichte gemacht haben ... denen Geschichte immer nur Leid gebracht hat, die den kriegerischen Prozeß speisen und dessen Verschleiß an Menschenmaterial ausgleichen muß-ten: die Frauen als Mütter. Sie werden nicht mehr wortlos am Rande stehen müssen' (530/521). In a kindred passage, the narrator addresses Ilsebill on the potential of feminist nunneries (226–7/221–2). Here, the emphasis is very much on *male* characteristics that would *not* obtain any more: the one 'female' characteristic that *would* flourish is tenderness ('es nähme nur noch Zärtlichkeit zu', 227/222).

The novel's failure to be more precise about the process of 'feminiza-tion' is as striking as this determinedly male perspective from which it is tackled and the concomitant tangibility, on the other hand, of its opposite: the cynically depicted 'masculinization' of women. The 'Machtwechsel der Geschlechter', in other words, is no solution either, and where it cannot be undercut by grotesquery, it is demolished just as effectively by mocking hyperbole: 'Schon sehe ich die neue Zärtlichkeit aufkommen,' the flounder tells the Feminal in the fourth Month. 'Jeder und jede berührt sich und andere. Liebesglanz wird alles schönen. Millionen wunschlose Ilsebills. Beschämt von soviel Sanftmut werden die Männer ihrer Macht und Herrlichkeit entsagen. Nur noch Liebe wird sein und überall werden ...' (274/268).

There is, it seems, not only no 'third way', there is not even a tenable 'second way'. Or at least not at the thematic level. Perhaps what is discernible in *Der Butt*, though, is a kind of narratorial 'third-wayism' that, in its play with the whole gamut of attitudes from cynical disgust and scorn to visionary Utopianism, is closely tied to the failure to locate that 'Drittes' so tantalizingly posited in the opening pages.

In *Der Butt* Grass plays with both male and female attitudes to male and female attitudes. For all the near-lyricism of the 'womanly times' visions, much of the novel contains acerbic portrayals of womanhood that are also exemplifications—given the maleness of the narrator—of male attitudes. The dishwasher syndrome, with its echoes of the fairy-tale Ilsebill's insatiability, is a leitmotiv in point. The dishwasher is one among many of the treats that the wife (her voice mediated exclusively through the husband) keeps pushing for: 'Geschirrspülmaschine ... Antillen ... flattrige Kleidchen, Knautschware, schockige Hosen, knappe Pullis. Kriegst du alles' (96/92). Yet the dishwasher is not an arbitrarily chosen gadget: apart from its obvious associations here with all the paraphernalia of food and eating, it is well known to white-goods manufacturers as the classic item of household equipment in whose acquisition husbands are especially instrumental, as it not only is portrayable as 'a present for the wife' (and hence a bribe to purchase indulgence and an assuager of any pangs of conscience) but also alleviates the drudgery of the one function in which husbands have traditionally participated in the kitchen. The novel appears to ignore this in suggesting that washing-up was historically initially done by men, but then taken over by women; but the truth seems to slip out in the phrase 'deine Geschirrspülmaschine, die wir Männer erfunden haben, die du dir gewünscht hast' (142/139).

The narrative is shot through with ostensibly stereotypical 'male' allusions to ostensibly stereotypical 'female' characteristics. Thus we are shown women as inconsequential natterers about husbands and households:

Nachdem ich wie in Abwesenheit verhandelt war, sprachen die beiden Frauen gleichzeitig über Kindererziehung und über die mangelnde Qualität ihrer Geschirrspülmaschinen. Ilsebill nannte ihren einen Fehlkauf. Griselde sagte, sie stelle grundsätzlich jede Erziehung infrage (393/386).

Or we are presented with examples of women's inveterate indecisiveness:

Wie meine Ilsebill immer beides zugleich wünscht, indem sie freiberuflich und beamtet sein will, ländlich wohnen und großstädtisch in Szene sein möchte, einerseits das einfache Leben (selber Brot backen) anstrebt, andererseits nicht auf gewissen Komfort (neuerdings eine vollautomatische Wäscheschleuder) verzichten kann (532/523).

The implication that women can afford to be indecisive as they do not have to run the world and make the 'real' decisions exemplifies the indulgent patronizing smugness that peeps forth in remarks such as 'Ulla Witzlaff strickte glattkraus an einem Herrenpullover. (Die Mädchen sind ja gutmütiger, als sie tun)' (345/338). In the recurrent mockery of the Feminal and its members it masquerades as a would-be wickedly perceptive critique of a particular aspect of contemporary mores that is in reality snidely facile at best. It can also become more vulgarly assertive, as in the narrator's boorish sexual boasting as he enumerates his 'conquests':

Dabei hätte ich es mit jeder von ihnen gekonnt. Und mit Sibylle habe ich im großen und ganzen prima geschlafen. Und die kühle Siggi habe ich ganz normal durchgezogen, ohne daß sie geklagt hätte hinterher. Und auch das Mäxchen wurde von mir, als es mit Billy ihren Schleckleck anfing, wie nebenbei vernascht. Nur Fränki, dieses Fuhrmannsgemüt, lag mir nie (462–3/456).

The most scornful assessment of 'female' ways is put into the mouths of women—the protagonists of the 'Vatertag' chapter, who go over the ground already covered by the narrator, but now from a position not of condescending indulgence but of uncompromising contempt: 'die zickigen Weiber mit ihrer Tages- und Nachtcreme, ihren Dauerwellen und vierzehn Paar Schühchen, mit ihren Preßtränen Schondeckchen Sammeltassen, mit ihrem Krimskram im Handtäschchen und ihrer Bimmelbammelangst vor dem Dickwerden' (464/458). The cruellest playground taunts are now brought to bear: 'Oder willste ne Trine bleiben, Heulsuse, Pinkelemma, Lutschliese, Tittenmutti, Sparbüchse' (480/473). And here too, now more vulgarly formulated than ever, the sexual 'explanation' is adduced: 'Nur nicht alt werden! Nicht mehr begehrt, befummelt, begrapscht und in allen Löchern bewohnt sein von einem Stück Mann, spargellang; denn nur um das dreht es sich—um dieses ausgelatschte Stück Fummelfleisch, das ein Loch bildet, extra groß für den strammen Max' (465/458).

Critics of *Der Butt* have been much divided over the proper interpretation of the misogynistic attitudes that it so often and so aggressively parades. The bewildering interlayering of narrative voices does not allow of any easy verdicts. On the one hand, it permits one to give Grass the benefit of the doubt by inserting a redeeming distance between 'author' and 'narrator' and by reading the archetypal male chauvinist remarks and sensibilities as being deliberately placed there for our observation. On the other hand, there are, equally, readers who have not been willing to play the game of relativizing *Der Butt*'s attacks on feminism 'within the context of the work as a whole'.[2]

Critics of *Der Butt* who have looked at its presentation of women have not infrequently reacted with indignation and irritation. Thus Ruth K. Angress, in her 'Feminist Perspective' on the novel, points to its resolutely male viewpoint in both its broader outlines (the sweep of history mediated through male characters with women as separate, isolated individuals) and its detail (the failure in the first chapter to elaborate any relationship between the 'Auas' and their female offspring). 'The value of women', she points out, 'is measured in terms of what they are worth to men, but the male characters are not treated in an analogous manner, because they have many functions' (Angress 1982, 49). She criticizes the absence in the book of any treatment of the real aims of the women's movement—its failure 'to take into account that live feminists see the success of their movement linked to a greater democratisation of society and not to a continuation of patriarchal patterns in reverse' (ibid.,

---

[2] Peter Russell, for instance, in his examination of the jumble of attitudes towards women in *Der Butt*, evinces a symptomatic scepticism about claims 'that the meaning of *Der Butt* resides in those ultimate ambiguities so often said to be the property of great works of art!' (Russell 1980, 253).

47). Women as achievers and/or intellectuals are, Angress contends, the particular butts of the work's scorn—a point also made by G. P. Butler, who points out that although the members of the 'Feminal' are shown as having 'challenging jobs, occupations which involve training, talent, intelligence, responsibility', they receive no respect and are granted no dignity as human beings, being presented instead as 'a lot of silly-billies . . . with their futile "Feminal" . . . their fruitless squabbles . . . and their groundless pique' (Butler 1979, 28–9).

Angress finds *Der Butt* 'dominated by images that undermine the ostensible sympathy which the narrator occasionally shows towards the women's movement' (Angress 1982, 49). Similar contradictions have been picked up by other critics. Thus, in his article pointedly entitled 'Floundering in Feminism', Peter Russell talks of 'a contradiction in *Der Butt* between the proffered message and the concrete evidence'; many reviewers of the novel, he states,

found themselves troubled . . . by the confusion of its central theme, a confusion which has resulted in much confusion of response. Thus the message of the novel has been variously guessed at as an act of homage to women and cooks, as a serious contribution to the Women's Movement, as an attempt to 'épater les femmes', and as a scornful send-up of the Women's Movement (Russell 1980, 252–3).

Others have taken the bull by the horns and, rather than lamenting the novel's misogyny, have actually seen in it a key to the work's strength. Such an approach is exemplified by Erhard Friedrichsmeyer, who talks of 'the narrator's male chauvinist imagination as a *sine qua non* in the narrative texture of *The Flounder*' (Friedrichsmeyer 1983, 156). 'The narrator's male chauvinist imagination', Friedrichsmeyer contends, 'energizes some of the best scenes and episodes. To deny its artistic function and value would be, in a doubly figurative sense, to emasculate Grass's novel' (ibid.). Here, male chauvinism is presented as a token above all of the honesty of an author who 'does not . . . suppress elements of fiction springing from a male chauvinist imagination if he deems the dynamics of the scene demand their inclusion' (ibid., 157).[3]

For many critics of *Der Butt*, psychology—both 'male' psychology in general and the psychology of Günter Grass in particular—has a lot to answer for in explaining the narrative's misogynistic twists and turns. 'The novel', Peter Russell observes,

---

[3] Angress sees this male chauvinism in more sinister terms as a symptom of attitudes current at the time: '*Der Butt* may well be indicative of a backlash against women observed in many areas. . . . It tells us that the forces opposing organized women are incomprehension masked by irony, contempt born of condescension and verbal animosity only one step removed from open violence' (Angress 1982, 49).

was written during a period of crisis in Grass's own marriage. . . . But even the reader with no knowledge of these facts cannot help but sense that Grass is using the novel to explore his own experience of marriage, and work out in fictional form some of the problems besetting his own sexual and emotional relationships (Russell 1980, 245).

'I would suggest', Russell declares, 'that we are dealing here not with ambiguities, but with confusions: further that these confusions derive from confusions of feeling in Grass himself' (ibid., 253), explaining later:

Intellectually, Grass seems to have decided, in tune with the *Zeitgeist*, that male power must yield now to female . . . but his emotional being—powerfully and irrationally compounded of need, hostility and fear—continually belies and works against the simple, preconceived intention (ibid., 254).

On a similar note, Angress refers to the 'numerous passages which project castration fear . . . counterbalanced by scenes of sexual prowess' (Angress 1982, 47) and suggests a psychological motivation for the novel's characteristic tone: 'women are deeply suspect and have to be conquered through irony, violence or subliminal hostility' (ibid., 49).

Psychology can certainly go some way towards elucidating the novel's ostensible hostility towards women and the constant switches in its narrative strategy that make that hostility so difficult to pin down for any length of time. But these peculiarities of *Der Butt*, and the links between them, seem also to be part of the broader non-development of the notion of a 'third way' as something that might go beyond the problematic encounter of traditionally conceived 'masculinity' and 'femininity'. In an interview conducted in 1978 Grass conceded that for him 'l'alternative n'est pas évidente', and that 'je ne sais pas quel aspect pourrait avoir cette contre-image' (Casanova 1979[1], 178). It is symptomatic of the elusiveness of the 'third way' even after the appearance of *Der Butt* that the 'contre-image' in question is earlier in this interview defined as a 'contre-image féminine', whilst even more revealing are the thoughts with which Grass precedes his reference to the non-evident 'alternative':

Y a-t-il—et cela, je crois, constitue le point central du problème de l'émancipa-tion et la question fondamentale à poser—, y a-t-il une solution féminine à l'emploi masculin de la force? Le mouvement féministe le nie. Il voudrait seulement que les femmes participent—à droits égaux, disent-elles—à l'intelli-gence masculine du pouvoir et de la morale (ibid.).

Here, Grass, still working at the level simply of female involvement in specifically 'masculine' affairs, seems as far removed from concrete visions of 'was Drittes' as was the narrator at the beginning of *Der Butt*.

To talk so categorically, as Grass does here, of 'le mouvement féministe', as if there were a single and straightforward orthodoxy of feminism that was reducible to a demand for female participation 'à l'intelligence masculine du pouvoir et de la morale', is—to say the least— intriguing for someone who has just produced a lengthy novel on that very topic. But it also indicates a nodding, albeit partial, acquaintance with certain key notions of the feminist debate in the 1970s.

Der Butt was, in fact, being written at exactly the time when the West German women's movement was establishing itself as a focal point for a new kind of radical politics. Most observers are agreed that its origins lie in the breakup of the male-dominated student movement of the late sixties: indeed, the moment of its birth is conventionally located with great precision as September 1968, on the memorable occasion of the delegate conference of the Sozialistischer Deutscher Studentenbund at which the Berlin delegate Sigrid Damm-Rüger rounded, both verbally and with the aid of some well-aimed tomatoes, on the youthful patriarchs of the SDS's leadership.[4] This new-found feminist self-assertiveness was to lead very quickly to the establishment up and down the country of women's groups that, not without a certain confident irony, called themselves 'Weiberräte'. Although some issues—in particular in the early seventies the question of abortion-law reform—provided a common rallying-point for the women's movement, fissiparous tendencies were apparent from the outset, with a particularly marked division between the more traditional Marxists, who blamed capitalism for the oppression of women, and the 'Feministinnen' in the narrower sense, who perceived patriarchy as the product of a more deep-rooted sexual politics. By the mid-seventies the women's movement entered a new phase of self-analysis, characterized by a proliferation of encounter groups that was, in its turn, to be followed around 1977 by a more separatist self-assertiveness founded on notions of a feminist counter-culture.[5]

It is clear enough that the outward manifestations of these developments provide much of the raw material for the portrayals of 'feminism' that one finds in *Der Butt*. But it is also striking that the feminist debate was engaging, at the same time as Grass was working on his novel, with notions of the 'third way'—a way not just between but *beyond* 'masculine'

---

[4] For an account of this incident and Damm-Rüger's own assessment of its significance twenty years on see *die tageszeitung*, 13 Sept. 1988, 12.

[5] K.-W. Brand, D. Büsser, and D. Rucht, *Aufbruch in eine andere Gesellschaft. Neue soziale Bewegungen in der Bundesrepublik* (Frankfurt, 1983), characterize these two phases as 'Rückzug nach innen' and 'Ansätze zu einer feministischen Gegenkultur' respectively (131 and 134). Their section 'Die neue Frauenbewegung' (118–54) provides a useful overview, as do the articles by Frigga Haug, 'The Women's Movement in West Germany', *New Left Review*, 155 (1986), 50–74, and Renate Becker and Rob Burns, 'The Women's Movement in the Federal Republic of Germany', *Contemporary German Studies*, 3 (1987), 5–22, which lists in its notes the main books on the subject.

and 'feminine' principles. 'One suggestion', according to Hester Eisenstein in a recent survey of feminist thought,

much debated among feminists, feminist-influenced academics, and popularizers of feminism in the early 1970s was a return to the ancient concept of androgyny. ... Popularized versions of the androgyny model received widespread attention and a good deal of apparent acceptance.[6]

But the fascination with androgyny was to be a passing phase in feminism, coming as it did between earlier demands for equal 'participation' by women in the running of a male-dominated world and the later reassertion and celebration of specifically 'female' qualities in women.[7] Certainly by the 1980s at the latest androgyny was to be 'regarded ... as much more of a cul-de-sac in feminist circles than was the case a few years ago'.[8]

The impasse of androgyny has distinct echoes in *Der Butt*—not only in its failure to elaborate and concretize its early references to the 'third way' but also in the narrative's hostility towards those female characters who trespass upon male preserves, be they of personality traits or of social or political competence. Even more striking is the book's total failure to engage at all with *male* approaches to androgyny: even in *Der Butt*'s biologistic terms, there are no male counterparts to the flamboyant lesbians of the 'Vatertag' chapter, beyond such self-consciously coy asides as the narrator's reference to his 'gebrochene Männlichkeit' (77/74) or the vision through which the 'Feministische Initiativgruppe 7. August ... machte sich mit einer Vision lächerlich, nach der durch genetische Eingriffe menstruierende, empfangende, austragende, gebärende, säugende Männer möglich sein sollten' (51/47–8).[9] *Der Butt*'s contribution to the androgyny debate manifests itself, in other words, in an uneasy mixture of a telling silence, vaguely expressed presentiments of

---

[6] Hester Eisenstein, *Contemporary Feminist Thought* (London and Sydney, 1984), 60–1. Later, Eisenstein defines androgyny as 'the amalgamation of "male" and "female" traits into a new, monogendered personality' (140). Toril Moi, on the other hand, rejects the 'concept of androgyny as the *union* of masculinity and feminity' in favour of Julia Kristeva's notion of 'the deconstruction of the duality' (*Sexual/Textual Politics: Feminist Literary Theory*, London and New York, 1985, 14).

[7] Eisenstein, op. cit. 140–1.

[8] K. K. Ruthven, *Feminist Literary Studies: An Introduction* (Cambridge, 1984), 106.

[9] Brand/Büsser/Rucht (op. cit.) note the emergence in the 1970s of the 'Softi' as a type to be found among 'jüngere Männer aus der Alternativszene' who 'bereits einen neuen androgynen Persönlichkeitstypus jenseits des geschlechtsspezifischen Rollendualismus zu verkörpern scheinen' (150). The 'Softi', familiar enough to even the most casual observer of the West German 'Alternativszene', is notably absent from the pages of *Der Butt*, which is concerned solely with the threat of *female* incursions across the gender line.

lack, and shrill parodies whose effect is to render the very notion ridiculous and any serious discussion otiose.

The feminist debate about androgyny was by no means without its broader context in the radical discourses of the 1970s. Feminists—and others—were increasingly drawing attention to the associations of 'masculinity' with the instrumental rationality of modern technological civilization: 'That the scientific world view had its dangers was not a new idea. But what a feminist perspective contributed was the realization this stance was linked to male psychology and male dominance.'[10] In West Germany in particular such thinking was becoming part and parcel of the growing Green movement. To portray, as *Der Butt* does, the specific problems of war, poverty, and sexual aggression as subsets of an endemic exploitative attitude to the natural environment ('Die Natur wurde euch anvertraut,' says the flounder to the male sex in general, 'worauf ihr sie ausgelaugt, verschmutzt, unkenntlich gemacht und zerstört habt', 459/453), to see this as having reached a pitch at which the choice is between a terminal catastrophe and a radical change of course, and to portray that change of course in the form of an assertion of 'feminine' principles of tenderness, gentleness, and harmony is archetypally Green.[11]

Or at least that is how its seems today. At the time *Der Butt* was being written there was no Green Party in West Germany, either at the local or at the federal level. But 'Green' ideas were very much 'in the air' in the early and mid-seventies, and it is worth noting that in West Germany at least they were, in the first place, treated with considerable suspicion by traditional Social Democrats, and, in the second place, not infrequently explicitly or implicity associated with variously conceived notions of a 'third way'.

SPD and trade-union wariness of Green thinking stems in particular from the orthodox Left's traditional espousal of industrial growth and economic expansion—in other words, from precisely those 'masculine' exploitative attitudes to nature that *Der Butt* perceives to be paradigmatic of the current world crisis. In some respects, then, *Der Butt* can be read

[10] Eisenstein, op. cit. 101.

[11] There are even intriguing parallels between the whimsical vision of the feminist nunneries as 'Gegengewichte zu den allerorts herrschenden Männerbünden' (225/220), from which the New World will arise, and Rudolf Bahro's call in the early eighties for a 'Benedictine revival' in which Green communes would function as exemplary 'zones of liberation' with a similar goal in view. (These views are elaborated in, for instance, 'Dare to Form Communes' and 'Why Communes?' in Rudolf Bahro, *Building the Green Movement* (London, 1986), 86–91 and 92–8). On women and the Greens see Carol Schmid, 'Ecology and Feminism: How Feminist is the West German Green Party?', *ASGP Journal* (Association for the Study of German Politics), 15 (1988), 56–75. See also the chapter 'Grüne Frauenphilosophie', in Manon Maren-Grisebach, *Philosophie der Grünen* (Munich, 1982, 91–106), which looks at the idea of androgyny (103–4).

as something of a 'Green' text, its publication anticipating by some three years the actual foundation of 'Die Grünen' and the subsequent widening of the ecological debate. Yet at the same time the narrator of the novel is explicitly identified as a Social Democrat—and that, moreover, in passages where Grass's own autobiography is most transparently associated with the attitudes and activities of the narrator.[12] As the SPD was in the 1970s still a long way from the rapprochement with Green thinking to which all parties found themselves constrained in the 1980s, one can surmise that there is an unspoken tension at work in *Der Butt* between the traditional loyalties of the narrator (and of the author) and the ideas the novel formulates on the relationship between man and nature.

In fact, that tension may also be another part of the explanation for the way the novel jibs at coming to terms with notions of a 'third way'. Green politics in West Germany has involved 'third-way' thinking in many guises, and the pronouncement at the beginning of the party's 'Bundesprogramm' 'Wir sind die Alternative zu den herkömmlichen Parteien' is as much an expression of this as is their frequently cited slogan 'nicht rechts, nicht links, sondern vorne'. Certainly, in the seventies the Greens in their initial incarnations were able to tap an alternative 'third-wayist' undercurrent that had been present in German political culture for a long time, and the fact that this undercurrent had had—though by no means exclusively—uneasy right-wing associations must have made the espousal of Green ideas even more problematic, to say the least, for a self-confessed supporter of the SPD.[13]

The ambivalent attitude to the third way that *Der Butt* displays need not be seen simply as a function of the narrator's or author's personal psychology, or of the political constellation against which the book was written. It also seems to be part of a much longer-term pattern that runs through all of Grass's works, and one that has become especially clear in the more recent ones. Although the 'third way' posited in *Der Butt* must be primarily envisaged in terms of gender characteristics, the key reference near the beginning of the book does after all talk of 'Was Drittes. *Auch sonst, auch politisch*' (10/7, italics added). Many analysts of

---

[12] 'Schließlich sind Sie Sozialdemokrat', the flounder says to him very near the beginning of the book (21/18). Later the idea is taken up in particular in the sections 'Wie der große Schwung zur chinesischen Weltverköstigung führen soll' in the fifth Month, and 'Bebel zu Gast' and 'Die Reise nach Zürich' in the seventh.

[13] On the notion of the 'third way' in German politics see Helmut L. Müller, 'Der "dritte Weg" als deutsche Gesellschaftsidee', *Aus Politik und Zeitgeschichte. Beilage zur Wochenzeitung Das Parlament*, 27 (7 July 1984), 27–38. In the 1980s the idea could be found, in particular, in Green debates about the 'German Question', which served to remind the Social Democrats of their own flirtations with 'third-wayism' in earlier decades—on this see my article 'Alternative Approaches to the German Question', *German Life and Letters*, 38 (1985), 427–41.

Grass's work have noted the anti-utopianism of their political implications—a wariness of the radical and the visionary that became explicit in
örtlich betäubt and provided the central image of snail-like gradualism
in *Aus dem Tagebuch einer Schnecke*. Both of these books posited—
tentatively— a way ahead in Social Democracy. But by the time *Der Butt*
is written the Social Democratic programme seems to have worn thin: a
new, for want of a better name, 'Green' third way seems to beckon, but
falls victim again to Grass's old scepticism of all that smacks of utopia.

It is striking that in the novel that followed *Der Butt*—*Die Rättin*
(1986)—the 'third way' at last becomes concretized in the form of the
half-rat, half-human creatures called 'Watsoncricks', which seem to offer
hope that a decent and rational civilization will be built upon the ruins of
an earth where human beings have extinguished themselves in the
terminal folly of a nuclear war. *Die Rättin* picks up threads from many of
Grass's previous works—in particular from *Die Blechtrommel* (Oskar
Matzerath and his family play a major role), but especially from *Der Butt*.
Not only is the flounder himself again present but so is the *Märchen*
motif, and the 'Watsoncricks' are unwittingly unleashed upon a post-
atomic world by feminists from the boat *Die neue Ilsebill*, who have
stopped off at the Swedish port of Visby, where they take part in an
animal-rights demonstration outside a genetic research institute. The
'Watsoncricks'—named after 'jene zwei hochgeehrten Herren, die während der ausgehenden Humanzeit die DNS-Struktur aufgedeckt, den
Zellkern gespalten, Genketten lesbar gemacht hatten und Watson und
Crick hießen' (*Die Rättin*, 419)—escape and find their way on to the *Neue
Ilsebill*; the boat's journey in search of the gynocratic 'Feminal-City',
Vineta, that lies beneath the Baltic is cut short by the 'großer Knall',
which in a flash destroys the crew of women along with the rest of the
human race.

The 'Watsoncricks' drift into the port of Gdańsk, where they soon
establish control over the rats that inhabit the still-intact city—spared
destruction by a superpower agreement that designated it, because of
its artistic worth, a target for neutron bombs only. The rule of the
'Watsoncricks' ushers in an age of gentle order: 'Sie verkörpern Macht,
doch keine blindwütige Gewalttätigkeit. Lässige Disziplin ist ihnen
eingeboren' (ibid., 425–6); 'die Herrschaft der neuschwedischen Watsoncricks im Raum Danzig-Gdańsk erweist sich als milde und kommt ohne
Härte aus' (ibid., 477). It is an order marked by sexual equality:
'Offenbar ist zu guter Letzt die geschlechtliche Gleichberechtigung
doch noch gelungen. Was zu Humanzeiten nicht möglich war ... lebt
sich nun aus' (ibid., 427–8). Not for nothing are the 'Watsoncricks'
apostrophized as 'Neuschweden': their new world epitomizes an ideal
Social Democracy: 'Und in der Tat: man kann den Watsoncricks zur Zeit

ihrer Anlandung und Besiedlung der Speicherinsel ein gemäßigt ausgleichendes, nennen wir es, sozialdemokratisches Verhalten nicht absprechen' (*Die Rättin*, 495).

Social Democracy, then, seems vindicated after all, its salvation in a post-human world arriving at last via a concretization, of a kind very typical of Grass, of a 'third way'. But the 'Watsoncricks' are not androgyns—on the contrary, they live in pairs in happy families (ibid., 427–8). The third way that they epitomize is not the path between male and female that *Der Butt* had toyed with but rather one between humans and rats:

Indem wir den Anteil Ratte in uns bejahen, werden wir wahrhaft human. Und weil wir unseres menschlichen Anteils bewußt sind, ist uns das Rattige wesentlich geworden. Ursprünglich Menschenwerk zwar, weisen wir über unsere Schöpfer hinaus, denen rückblickend unser Mitgefühl gilt. Sie scheiterten an sich, während wir, dank des Rattigen in uns, zukünftig sind (ibid., 480).

Yet the 'Zukunft' so sanguinely asserted here turns out to be all too short-lived: some seventy-five years after the end of the human race the 'Watsoncricks' begin to develop bad habits. Not only do they take to drink but, faced with a population explosion among the ordinary rats, they take steps to control their numbers—steps that include eating plumper members of the subject species. As in *Der Butt*, the discovery of fire, and hence cooking, is at least partly to blame. But so too is the balance in their make-up between rat and human—there is, it transpires, too much of the latter and too little of the former: 'Es ist zuviel Mensch in ihnen' (ibid., 496). Once again, the third way has failed to live up to its promise: like the Indira Gandhis, the Madame de Pompadours, and the Golda Meirs of *Der Butt*, the 'Watsoncricks' of *Die Rättin* succumb to the corruption of power as the old Adam of their former masters asserts its dominance.

As with the Maria sequence at the end of *Der Butt*, so *Die Rättin* concludes on a Polish note. The parallels are again striking: the rats of Gdańsk rebel against the masters whose utopian promise has so dismally evaporated. They rally beneath an old cast-iron emblem they have found, left in the city by its former inhabitants—the emblem of Solidarność: the 'Watsoncricks'

begehen ... nun einen Fehler, indem sie, ihrer Macht allzu sicher, der schmiedeeisernen Schrift Aussage und bis in die Humanzeit zurückreichende Bedeutung unterschätzen. Jedenfalls bricht, kaum ist das eiserne Wort entführt und seitdem im Untergrund wirksam, nach und nach alles zusammen, was die Watsoncricks zur Sicherung ihres Systems aufgebaut hatten (ibid., 498).

Of Solidarność the 'Rättin' had already earlier proclaimed 'Dieser Gedanke war uns in Praxis schon immer eigen' (ibid., 214); now again she asserts: 'Was jene Schrift aus Eisen sagt, haben wir geübt, nicht der Mensch. Nichts zeugt von ihm, das fortleben könnte' (ibid., 504). Her bleak conclusion provides the novel's closing lines, as she responds to the desperate interrogation of the narrator, condemned to observe an earth devoid of humans from his little space capsule:

Nur angenommen, es gäbe uns Menschen noch ... Gut, nehmen wir an.
... doch diesmal wollen wir füreinander und außerdem friedfertig, hörst du, in Liebe und sanft, wie wir geschaffen sind von Natur ...
Ein schöner Traum, sagte die Rättin, bevor sie verging (ibid., 505).

Die Rättin is a more cosmically pessimistic novel than *Der Butt*. The crisis of human civilization is no longer located primarily in society's gender arrangements but manifests itself more directly in the twin issues of 'Waldsterben' (and hence the death of the Märchen for which the forests were the German setting—'Ohne Märchen werden die Menschen verarmen', remarks Rapunzel at one point (ibid., 433)) and nuclear war. Earnest narratorial concern at both is transparent throughout. These issues are, of course, again matters that have most exercized the Greens in West Germany; they also pick up important themes from *Der Butt* (though the specific problem of 'Waldsterben' as a manifestation of human depredations of nature was then unrecognized as a political issue). The 'third way out' now finds a concrete form: but it seems it can only be conceived of when it is too late—for humans at least. Here, though, for all its bizarreness it is not mocked or rendered grotesque. On the contrary, the narrator wonders at the beauty of the sleek 'aufrecht stehenden Neuschweden' (ibid., 478), with one of whom he even falls in love.

As far as the human race is concerned, the 'third way' of the 'Watsoncricks' is clearly no answer: not only is it too late but, for good measure, it goes sour. The resurrection of the ideals—and the emblem too—of Solidarność recalls an old motif in Grass: of the Poles as dreamers of dreams of a freedom that can never be had in this world. As the Rättin says: 'Wir erhoffen uns was. Unsere Gebete sind mit Sehnsüchten überladen. Etwas Höheres, das nicht, noch nicht zu haben ist—die Polen haben es dazumal Freiheit genannt—, schwebt uns wie greifbar vor ...'.[14]

---

[14] Grass's admiration for Solidarność is unambiguously reflected in his 1982 account ('Im Hinterhof') of a journey to Nicaragua, in which he notes distinct parallels between the situation of the Sandinistas and that of Solidarność: both, in fact, represent a kind of 'third way' between the superpowers and are thus equally unacceptable to their respective big neighbours. The account concludes: 'Das altmodische, wie man meinen möchte, im neunzehnten Jahrhundert begrabene Wort Solidarität tritt auf wie auferstanden. Ich bin ihm in Polen und Nicaragua begegnet. Im Vorfeld, im Hinterhof der Großmächte lebt es auf. Es sollte auch bei uns wieder heimisch werden' (*Widerstand lernen*, 50–1).

The phrasing is reminiscent too of that desperately absent 'griffige Utopie' of the *Butt* poem 'Was uns fehlt'. The utopia is perhaps glimpsed in the final scene as Maria, the sad, wise, and now—for once—laughing, Lenin Shipyard widow, talks with the flounder: 'Maria lachte. . . . Die sonst nie lachte, lachte knietief in der See' (556/547). The utopia was to be glimpsed again—if we are to believe *Die Rättin*—in the subsequent Solidarność of that same Lenin Shipyard. And at the end of *Die Rättin* that dream too, having faded once, is resurrected again. The outcome of its encounter with 'reality' is not difficult to predict. The 'griffige Utopie', 'Was Drittes', is not to be had—'Auch sonst, auch politisch, als Möglichkeit.'

IO

Implications of the Narrative Technique in *Der Butt*

MICHAEL MINDEN

Ich sei nicht nur als Autor, sondern auch als Mann betroffen. Und
zwar irgendwie schuldhaft.   (150/147)

I. Günter Grass

The assumption made by this essay is that the 'I' of *Der Butt* is not only a
narrative device but also a gesture of commitment. On the one hand,
there is the powerful sense that artistic endeavour secures access to the
ultimate questions of human experience by way of aesthetic achievement.
On the other, there is the certainty that the human subject is embattled
and limited by sexuality, history, politics. Grass the author stands next to
Grass the man, and there is no easy role or single identity into which both
vanish. After a brief survey of Grass's own comments, and of those of
some critics, on his narrative technique in *Der Butt*, this essay will
consider the aesthetic implications of Grass's act of narrative commitment.

In at least three interviews (Raddatz 1977[1], Arnold 1978, Casanova
1979[1]), Grass has explained how the decisive innovation in his narrative
position came with *Aus dem Tagebuch einer Schnecke*. 'Mit diesem Buch
habe ich mir durch die Einsetzung des Ich, des handelnden, politisch
handelnden Ich des Erzählers neue Prosaformen erarbeitet und neben
der politischen Erfahrung Schreib-Erfahrung gesammelt, ohne die der
"Butt" nicht möglich gewesen wäre' (Raddatz 1977[1], 29). In this work
the author enters his fiction in his own persona, but then also assumes
fictional form in the figure of Hermann Ott, in which the author-persona
reflects himself (Casanova 1979[1], 98). In *Der Butt* the same technique is
carried to much greater lengths. With the key phrase 'Ich, das bin ich
jederzeit', a pronominal mobility is initiated which introduces the
author's persona into the fiction at all levels, but with the prior
knowledge that this persona will, as it were, be fictionalized by the

demands of what Grass calls his 'epischer Stoff' (Raddatz 1977[1], 30). In another formulation (Arnold 1978, 28), Grass places more emphasis upon his active transformation of the 'Autoren-Ich' into a 'fiktives Ich', which is nevertheless always held in some relation to ('in Korrespondenz zu') the author-persona. At the end of the novel the narrator and the author do 'coalesce' (Durrani 1980, 815), but this identity is the sign of limitation: Grass's various emanations and reflections 'haben den Informationsvorsprung der Männer verloren' (Arnold 1978, 28), and the end must therefore be open: 'le livre devrait continuer, mais écrit par une femme', as Grass himself put it (Casanova 1979[1], 179).

In these formulations concerning Grass's introduction of an autobiographical 'I' into his fiction we recognize both Grasses, the empirical Grass and the author Grass, as it were, jostling for position. While announcing this abdication of anonymous authorial authority, Grass is at pains to reassert artistic power and control. There is the Grass who transforms, fictionalizes, and laboriously works out new prose forms, but there is also the one who recognizes that his discourse is not his alone, not only the finished work of the author, but that it could—indeed, that it needs to be—continued by another.

Critics too have devoted much attention to Grass's narrative technique in *Der Butt*. Osman Durrani distinguishes between the historical 'I's, the married 'I' who inhabits the present, the lyric poet, and the traveller 'I', retracing Grass's empirical steps (Durrani 1980, 813). Gertrud Bauer Pickar coins the term 'prismatic narrator' and speaks of a 'fracturing of the narrative consciousness and its identification with the novel's protagonist-narrator' who has 'projected historical identities' which are to be distinguished from 'the personalized authorial voice' that occasionally intrudes (Pickar 1983, 60). Helmut Koopmann differentiates crisply between 'the *narrated* "I"' and the '*narrating* "I"' (Koopmann 1983, 82). Patrick O'Neill discerns five narrative agencies: the flounder itself; the narrator telling tales to his wife; the narrator telling tales to the reader; the 'semi-fictionalised Günter Grass'; and the lyric poet (O'Neill 1982, 11). Guy Stern glosses the situation by suggesting that the 'I' is 'perhaps the embodiment of the spirit of narration', which 'can at any one time take multiple forms, who can often live in uneasy alliance or open conflict' (Stern 1982, 52).

If I have a quarrel with all these analyses, it is that they seem intent upon keeping the 'real' Günter Grass out of his own fiction, and that they thus reconstruct the omniscient narrative intelligence, 'spiritus rector' (Casanova 1979[1], 98), which was, I believe, precisely what Grass intended to avoid in developing this technique. To quote a few more examples in support of this accusation: Manfred Jurgensen concedes the

'Wandelbarkeit' of the novel's 'I' but grounds it reassuringly in 'eine grundsätzlich gleichbleibende persönliche Identität—die des Autors Günter Grass' (Jurgensen 1980, 129–30), without pausing to consider whether it is permissible to speak of identity as 'grundsätzlich gleichbleibend'. Koopmann speaks of the 'narrating "I"' as 'omniscient' and says that it 'disposes, narrating and reflecting, of everything' (Koopmann 1983, 82). Guy Stern explicitly states the opposite view ('It might reasonably be assumed that the narrator . . . would be omniscient in the conventional sense. Grass, however, casts many of his narrative strands in doubt' (Stern 1982, 53)), but invents instead an omniscient Günter Grass who has written a book warning us that 'neither side [i.e. neither men nor women] has a monopoly on either virtue or venality' (Stern 1982, 54). Noel Thomas has invented a similarly omniscient, detached sage when he tells us that '*Der Butt* contains a twofold warning: on the one hand Grass condemns men's relationship to power . . . on the other he warns against the possibility of women following in the footsteps of men' (Thomas 1980, 84). And it is all very well for Osman Durrani to say that Grass shows how 'neither sex can claim inherent superiority over the other' (Durrani 1980, 822), but this hardly takes into account—as Grass himself most certainly does (Hunt 1980, 90–1, Raddatz 1977[1], 30)—that one sex claims, and always has claimed, such superiority and that Grass happens to be a member of it.

Ann L. Mason puts the point well when she says of *Aus dem Tagebuch einer Schnecke*: 'the book seems to me to intentionally prohibit a decision between these alternatives', where the alternative is between reading the book *either* as fiction *or* as reportage; as written *either* by a literary persona *or* by the historical personality of Günter Grass (Mason 1976, 120).

While not wishing for a moment to detract from Grass's artistic achievement, to which the many analyses of his narrative procedures bear ample witness, it seems to me very important not to lose sight of that other Grass who has made a moral commitment, by speaking in his own voice and by attempting to dispel the aura of the artist. There are certainly critics who recognize that with his book Grass is not only creating a work of art but also entering a debate. Such a one is Ruth Angress, who condemns the book for its male chauvinism and concludes that women should read it because 'it tells us that the forces opposing organised women are incomprehension masked by irony, contempt born of condescension and verbal animosity only one step removed from open violence' (Angress 1982, 49). Similarly, Erhard Friedrichsmeyer acknowledges Grass's moral responsibility for the attitudes deployed in *Der Butt*, seeing the narrator's bias against women as a result of Grass's 'proclivity for the truth, however troublesome.' 'The narrator's male chauvinist imagination', he argues, 'is a *sine qua non* in the narrative texture of the *Flounder*'; for 'no man or woman can escape living his or her life without being trapped by the patterns a world of male dominance has wrought over the ages.' If Grass wishes to write seriously about the relationship between the sexes, it *has* to be in this voice, for 'the alternative, a narrative voice equivocating from a neutral androgynous zone, would be a presumptuous form of charlatanism' (Friedrichsmeyer 1983, 154–6).

Heinz Ludwig Arnold's comment about Grass's explanation of his new narrative technique puts the sense of moral commitment implied in Grass's narrative device as clearly as one could wish:

Für mich liegt in dem, was Sie eben skizziert haben, auch eine Art von Ehrlichkeit des Erzählers, nämlich die Ehrlichkeit des auktorialen Erzählers, der seine allwissende Position offen preisgibt, im Gegensatz zu jenem sich verbergenden Erzähler, der seine Figuren an seinen Fäden tanzen läßt, aber die Fäden nicht zeigt (Arnold 1978, 28–9).

In what follows I wish therefore to consider some aesthetic implications of this honesty, in particular the limitations placed upon the act of narration by subjectivity, gender, and violence.

II. 'Ich, das bin ich jederzeit'

'I, down through the ages, have been I.' Ralph Manheim's translation of this important phrase is a little misleading, but in what is an instructive way in our present context. Although the verb is in the perfect tense, the period of time referred to might seem to the reader to be the period about to be covered by the book, so that the words would effectively mean: 'the "I" you will be encountering in the course of the next six hundred pages odd is always me, so don't get confused.'

The original German does not *solve* the problem of who 'I' is. Rather, it initiates the problem which is inseparable from every act of saying 'I': 'to say "I" is an act which is always new', as Roland Barthes put it.[1] In Barthes's terms, Manheim, but not Grass, would be guilty of the 'general "bad faith" of discourse which would make literary form simply the expression of an interiority constituted previous to and outside of language'.[2] Those critics who concentrate on the artist Grass and his narrative techniques, while neglecting the other Grass who commits

---

[1] 'To Write: An Intransitive Verb?', in *The Languages of Criticism and the Sciences of Man*, ed. Richard Macksey and Eugenio Donato (Baltimore and London, 1970), 134–45 (141).
[2] Ibid., 141.

himself with his 'I', would, in my view, be guilty of something similar. To say 'I' is to enter the strenuous activity known as 'unsere Geschichte' (7/4). Like so much else in *Der Butt*, and indeed in Grass's work generally, it is, and always must be, a liberation and a limitation at the same time. 'On (at?) every occasion I am I': protean, but always, again, I; free to invent myself constantly but bound to declare myself with each invention and thus open myself to appropriation by others, becoming like the insect preserved in amber ('Ich bin der Einschluß', (512/503)). This particular image occurs in a passage in the ninth Month which also begins with an assertion of 'I': 'Und Ich? Ich bin nicht Jan. Ich bin Marias Halbcousin', and ends, significantly, with the words, 'Jan, das bin ich, Maria, nach deinem Rezept.'

The second paragraph of the novel, which begins with the apparently bold and untroubled assertion we have just been discussing, then goes on to exploit the extraordinary freedom which saying 'I' confers. The 'I' now itself appropriates another, including it in its fiction ('Auch Ilsebill war von Anfang an da', 7/4), and bounds on unconstrained for the next dozen or so lines with characteristic virtuosity. At length it reaches a point at which it seems to have achieved the freedom to rename itself ('auch ich hieß anders', 7/4), suggesting that perhaps the 'I' *can* escape itself, as the magic mushroom had encouraged Arnim and Bettina to fantasize that it could (359/352). But the transport of this 'I' must inevitably come up against other subjects saying 'I' and *resisting* appropriation: 'Doch Ilsebill will nicht Aua gewesen sein' (7/4).

Der Butt is made up of an 'I' telling stories, and this story-telling activity is to be understood in the context of the limitations which attend all such activity. It is always subject to reality, which is the same as saying subject to curtailment, reversal, dispersal. The proliferation of stories in the novel is emphatically represented as existing under the constant threat of interruption of one sort or another. There is a recurrent motif of dismissal: 'Sie hörte wohl nicht mehr zu' (150/147); 'Das erzähl sonstwem, nicht mir!' (296/290—in which there is a felicitous play on the meaning of 'erzählen'). Aua can be as recalcitrant as Ilsebill: 'Aber Aua wollte nicht. Sie hatte keine Lust, Mythen zu bilden' (101/97). The phantasmagoria of women dinner-guests behaves no differently: 'Die viel zu vielen Frauen am Tisch hörten wohl nicht' (397/390). Reality crowds in, and its representative is Ilsebill: 'Immer kommt Ilsebill und bringt sich mit' (523/514). That, presumably, is also the weight of the words 'Ilsebill kam' at the end of the book; all stories end and this the storyteller can only register passively ('Ich lief ihr nach'), for it is a reality which awaits invariably wherever his control ends.

The novel is rich in ways of indicating 'shadows' which it cannot dispel, truths before which it must be silent. First among these is world hunger. Ilsebill too, appropriately, is without wishes in the face of that reality (182/179). The situation in which any 'I' is spoken is not of Grass's devising, and it is an important virtue of the novel's narrative technique, of the 'I' of *Der Butt*, that it knows this and takes account of it.

III. 'Was immer ich vorgekocht habe, die Köchin in mir salzt nach'

Another of the conditions underlying the activity of story-telling in *Der Butt* is that the author is a man. In the early interview with Raddatz in *Die Zeit* Grass explained:

Der "Butt" handelt von den Geschlechtern und von ihrem Verhältnis zueinander. Ich zeichne die Männer in ihrem Machtgebrauch, in ihrem Machtwahn und in ihrem Hang zur Abstraktion, zur Verflüchtigung in ihre Systeme. Und immer innerhalb dieser Systeme taucht dann auch die Entdeckung auf, wie bodenlos, wie verloren sie sind innerhalb dieser Systeme, und sofort beginnt die Fluchtbewegung zurück zur weiblichen Position—oder zu dem, was man sich als Mann, wenn man die Machtposition so absolut besetzt hält, innerhalb dieses Systems als Frau vorstellt: als Ruhepunkt. Die Furcht der Männer, es könnte einmal diese letzte Zuflucht—und sei es als Wunschvorstellung—auch noch in Frage gestellt sein, ist existentiell geworden, sie prägt unsere Zeit (Raddatz 1977[1], 30).

This masculine predicament (although now appropriately topicalized) has been a theme in Grass's work since the first chapter of *Die Blechtrommel*. The narrative technique of *Der Butt* comes closer than do the earlier novels to tackling the unnerving truth that Grass's concept of the artist, although he significantly omits to say so in the passage we have just quoted, involves a very considerable 'Machtposition' (the 'Ich' with the detachment and power enabling him to 'draw' men), and the construction of (albeit aesthetic) 'Systeme'. In *Der Butt*, Grass not only stands by his 'I', he also stands by his gender.

The story-telling pursuits of the 'I' and its various projections in *Der Butt* are necessarily vitiated by male sexuality and its attendant attitudes. 'Dicke Gret' can be seen as a creation of the narrator's projected oedipal wishes and castration anxieties, and indeed much of the narrator's activity can be interpreted as compensatory aggression towards Ilsebill for his own male inability to bear children. These attitudes are neatly summed up in Ruth Simoneit's barbed remark: 'Ihr Männer seid immer nur brutal oder wehleidig' (345/338).

For Grass, story-telling is related to satisfaction, which, and not just for Grass, is related to the oral phase: 'The experience of satisfaction . . .

is an oral experience; one may therefore advance the hypothesis that desire and satisfaction are forever marked by this first experience.'[3] Where there is satisfaction, there are no stories, whether in prehistoric times when the story-telling mouth is always stopped by the third breast, or in the Poland of the seventies, where milk still plays its part: 'Jan und ich wollten. Maria brachte und ging. Auch frische Buttermilch glumste in Gläsern. Aber es fiel uns nichts mehr zu Swantopolk und Fortinbras ein' (551/542). Male story-telling and the 'zappeln' of the thirsty infant are cognate activities (for 'zappeln' see 14/11, 152/148, 417/410). In Grass's view, men are always psychologically subservient to women; to be understood *in relation* to women as they speak, in their doomed attempts to construct their systems and their identity as men. The whole novel might be headed 'Ilsebill zugeschrieben', and it is not a coincidence that all the dismissers and interruptors adduced in the previous section are women too.

Story-telling (and the exercise of the masculine version of 'creativity'—the discipline of the artist), at some level, is thus either a substitute for satisfaction or else a product of dissatisfaction.

As a *substitute* for satisfaction, story-telling is narcissistic and self-indulgent. It is 'wehleidig', a thumb in the mouth, an escape from reality. From a hostile perspective, the whole *Butt*-system can be dismissed as Gunzelin Schmidt Noerr dismissed it: 'so versucht das verwesende Patriarchat, in Selbstkritik noch ein wenig zu überdauern' (Noerr 1978, 93). However aesthetically or intellectually brilliant the construct may be, it can do nothing to alter the adversity of its objective situation.

But the implications are darker where story-telling becomes the *product* of dissatisfaction. The male story-tellers of *Der Butt* invent stories in a bid to secure ascendancy over women (the book ironically subscribes to the theory that men invented history itself to emancipate themselves from matriarchy), and they are humiliated when they fail; they then reinvent private wish-fulfilment fantasies, which simply perpetuate the shame of failure, as the motor of an endless succession of more stories. At the end of the first Month the 'I' invents a story which puts Aua exactly where he wants her: 'Dabei hat sich Aua später (was der Butt nicht weiß) von einem Elchbullen bespringen lassen' (103/99). There follows a configuration which seems the archetype of the relationship which exists for Grass between the masculine artist, women, and associated guilt:

Ich sah das, zwischen Weiden versteckt. Hörte Aua Laut geben, wie ich sie nie gehört hatte. Wollte mir auch ein Bild machen, wie ihre Brüste in die Moosbeeren hingen. Vergaß aber, kehrte Gedächtnisschutt (andere Geschichten) darüber und wollte mich nicht erinnern ... (103/99).

---

[3] J. Laplanche and J.-B. Pontalis, *The Language of Psycho-Analysis* (London, 1980), 288.

The whole section in which this passage occurs, 'Woran ich mich nicht erinnern will', makes the link between story-telling and guilt with which we are familiar from other of Grass's fictions. It ends the first Month and thus assumes the sort of structural and thematic weight enjoyed by the magnificent 'Glaube Hoffnung Liebe' section in *Die Blechtrommel*, which ends the first Book and makes the same sort of dark connection.

The guilt is bound up with the 'brutality' (to use Ruth Simoneit's word again) with which men avenge themselves for their dissatisfaction. Aua is subjected to a—beautifully imagined—abject humiliation. It is this image that the prehistoric artist 'I' desires to fix ('wollte mir auch ein Bild machen'), and it is with this desire that guilt is associated.

Grass, both as man and artist, is involved too. 'Ich sei nicht nur als Autor, sondern auch als Mann betroffen. Und zwar irgendwie schuld-haft' (150/147), the 'I' obsequiously tells Sieglinde Huntscha at one point. Friedrichsmeyer puts it well: 'Grass signals a self-indictment that encompasses not only social, but artistic attitudes as well' (Friedrichs-meyer 1983, 157). *Der Butt* too is characterized by brutality in its artistic structure. Three rapes mark out the architectonic shape of the book: that perpetrated by the Goth in 'Woran ich mich nicht erinnern will', that committed by Axel on Agnes in the fourth Month, and the multiple rape suffered by Sibylle in the eighth. And it is impossible to ignore the fact that this most intensely and consistently imagined story ('Ein Mann mit seiner gelebten Geschichte. Es war einmal . . .', 460/453), the artistic linchpin 'Vatertag', holding the whole *Butt*-system in place (the *Kunst-fick!*), is a paradigm of brutality inflicted upon women. Ultimately, of course, it is Grass, the abject, dependent, vengeful male, who is the author of the violence suffered by Sibylle.

This is not to say that 'Vatertag' is a disguised wish-fulfilment on the part of Grass. It is to pose a question about the nature of the (masculine?) imagination and its relation to art. In a sense, the rape and murder of Sibylle is associated with the darkest totalizing urges of the imagination, which, in the absence of any socializing corrective, sets itself up as absolute and liquidates others (for failing to satisfy its never-ending impossible demands). What the prehistoric Edek did to Aua, Grass does to Ilsebill. He systematically fashions an image of her most abject humiliation (there is an insistent similarity between the names Ilsebill, a name, of course, which is an anti-female insult in itself, and Sibylle), and then hedges it around with dozens of stories. This question about the source-contamination of the artistic impulse itself is not far away from the issues raised in Thomas Mann's *Doktor Faustus*.

The picture, however, is not nihilistic. What Grass's 'I' enables him to convey is that although his profoundest concerns are always also masculine, and thus tainted, they are not thereby invalidated.

If we consider first the question of story-telling—the masculine gender of the protean 'I' does not just subject it to women, it also binds it to them as part of the same logic. Therefore it provides an example of how *all* subjects, male or female, are locked into the world. Inevitably (and prominently in the age of feminism), the other subjects who will inspire, inform, and also block this specific male subject's stories will more often than not be women. It is also therefore appropriate that Ilsebill should be that representative other subject which resists appropriation.

But this makes of story-telling the space not only of narcissistic thumb-sucking and vicious compensation for dissatisfaction but also of human interaction. This interaction is a process of struggle between subjects which is metonymically represented in the power struggle between men and women. The situation is disharmonious, its representation necessarily asymmetrical, but it is reciprocal:

Die Köchin in mir und ich, wir schenken einander nichts. Zum Beispiel hat Ilsebill einen Koch in sich—der werde wohl ich sein—den sie bekämpft. Unser Streit von Anbeginn, wer als Komplex drall oder mager in wem hockt, fördert neue Gerichte oder alte, die wieder beliebt sind, seitdem wir historisch bewußt kochen (346/339).

The stories themselves bear the mark of this social involvement. First, as we said, in that they are always subject to dismissal, but also in their strategies, in their plots and characters. The male story-teller invents cooks, female entities within the male subject, straining to get out, who are themselves poets, myth-makers, story-tellers, authors of political cookbooks. Indeed, as Timothy McFarland points out, narrative is in some senses envisaged in the novel as a female property, proper, that is, to Aua's 'side', as against the Edeks' aspirations to master the world 'with mathematics and money' (p. 70–1). This is reciprocity, as imagined by a man.

In and through the power struggle between men and women we glimpse that shared space beyond the gender-specific. This is a common enmeshment in the strenuous activity ('doppelt waren wir tüchtig') of 'unsere Geschichte', so different, in its subtle indirection and in its always oblique and complex relation with the body, from the deep thud of the body itself, in all its brute detachment from the complications of saying 'I': 'den großen, eindeutigen, jede Nebenhandlung auslöschenden, nur aus sich bestehenden Zeugungstraum ... der tiefer wummert als je gedacht und dessen urdumme Kraft sich auch dort steilt, wo die Natur nichts geplant hat' (494/486). The life of the body is defined here as that which is distinct from the many meanings and proliferating plots of conscious human life.

In an interesting piece about the positive aspects of the inevitability of subjective distortion in every act of interpretation, Norman H. Holland explains how 'we are all caught up in the general principle that identity creates and recreates itself as each of us discovers and achieves the world in his own mind'.[4] Grass and *Der Butt* are also caught up in this principle. The psychological categories which Holland sees as generating continuity in the incessantly shifting life of experience are: 'defense, fantasy and ego style'.[5] All Günter Grass's work bears the stamp of a powerful and characteristic style. The invention of the eleven cooks is the key operation of fantasy in the book. The defensive operation is to invent each woman again, this time as members of the Feminal.

The historical projections are self-indulgent escapes, yet in the expansive space of self-indulgence the masculine 'I' visualizes women of substance and power, although it must pay for this inventive licence, this mobility and freedom, by being reduced itself to positions of relative weakness. Hence the projections of the 'I' around the historical cooks tend to be abject, subordinate, or despicable, or otherwise limited in some way. The women invented in the present, however, are defensively imagined. The 'I' in the present is forced into positions which deny its protean adaptability, and therefore reinvents the women so as to reduce them (by seducing them) as a compensatory gesture. The same dual attitude can be discerned in the novel's implied poet (the voice of the lyric poems), between a 'feather-blowing' marginal persona, and an assertive, concerned, aggressive one.

Reality, as its spokesperson Ilsebill is not slow to insist (108/104), demands assertion and a stable identity, and so the 'I' reinvents itself as a single inexhaustible seducer ('eine einzige hat mich nie halten können', 387/380) rather than a various array of backstabbing *Pantoffelhelden*. Indeed, in its retrospective, imaginative mode, the 'I' perceives clearly enough the emptiness of such behaviour ('das in wechselnde Betten verschleppte Unvermögen', 417/410), and the act of assertion in the present, predictably, has the most drastic effects upon the well-being of the imagination, as 'Wir aßen zu dritt' amply demonstrates.

Story-telling is thus both male escapism and the key to human interaction. It is what Sandford refers to as 'narratorial "third-wayism"' (p. 169). It has, as it were, both a sexed and a universal significance. Although it is impossible to separate these two, they are not identical.

[4] 'Unity Identity Text Self', *PMLA*, 90 (1975), 813–22 (820).
[5] Ibid., 820–1.

The same can be said of the book's implied vision of art and the imagination (i.e. of its own constitution), which is necessarily an extrapolation from the theme of masculine story-telling within it.

Grass himself perhaps feels that art has the great virtue of providing an alternative to the constrictions of everyday life—not a substitute but a zone of *Narrenfreiheit* with its own sort of value. These two uses of the verb 'nageln' make the point:

Vielleicht könnte meine gegenwärtige Ilsebill mich wieder nageln, auf den Punkt bringen, eindeutig machen. Sie sagt: 'Es wird bei der Stange geblieben. Das Kind soll wissen, wer sein Vater ist. . . . Mach keine Ausflüchte, bitte!' (108/104).

Strya und ich können das. Wir sind immer nur zeitweilig gegenwärtig. Uns nagelt kein Datum. Wir sind nicht von heute. Auf unserem Papier findet das meiste gleichzeitig statt (126–7/123).

In a way, the juxtaposition of these two passages brings out the inherent sexism of Grass's conception of himself-as-artist. We have on the one hand the woman narrowly representing practical reality, and on the other the smug camaraderie of the artists, who are above such things. But there is also the point that Ilsebill, in speaking for everyday reality, is espousing the cause of patriarchalism ('das Kind soll wissen, wer sein Vater ist'), while the artists are standing against any sort of one-dimensional system or understanding of reality, whoever may be proposing it.

What further distinguishes the artistic 'system' of *Der Butt* from the masculine systems Grass analyses in the quotation with which this section began is that, as an artistic construct, it engages with the resistance of reality, it knows its limits, it speaks its 'I' and, therefore, entails a 'you'. It is never *only* a vanishing act or an act of brutality. What it says, it says in terms of these necessary attitudes, but also in spite of them.

If there is something in the idea that the book is constructed around three cases of rape, then it nevertheless needs to be borne in mind that these rapes are not all committed by men upon women. The first is committed by a man upon another man, the last involves women assaulting another woman. Only the rape of Agnes by Axel is a straightforward case, conforming to the sort of male prejudice which suspects that women really like the violent and dominant sexual attentions of men ('einzig der ist ihr eindringlich geblieben', 262/257), and this case of rape appears to correspond, in the thematic economy of the whole book, to that period of sexual consciousness which the book projects as now approaching its end (just as Agnes herself is the nearest thing in the book to 'the ideal woman' of male projection).

Hence it is not rape as the figure of male violence to women around which *Der Butt* is artistically constructed, but rape as the ultimate figure of masculine-imagined violence. In German, of course, 'Gewalt' is included in 'Vergewaltigung'.

And if it is true, as we asserted above, that, in the climactic act of rape and murder, art and the imagination are inextricably bound up with this violence, then this startling and terrible identity, as well as indicting the masculine imagination, also moves us into realms of experience and its representation which lie beyond words. In this climax, as in the mysterious imagery of the mushroom, the creative and the destructive fuse. It is appropriate that, as L. W. Forster has shown, Grass has chosen to fashion the aesthetic climax of his book in an allusion to Euripides' *Bacchae*, for Greek tragedy appositely recalls an art which confronted the unsayable (Forster 1980, 67).

All this is to put forward the view that the limitations Grass imposes upon himself by entering into his fiction in his own persona, though considerable, do not invalidate what it can still say, nor negate its artistic seriousness. Or at least, that is the risk or project of *Der Butt* and the ethical will that informs it: 'Ich weiß nichts Besseres, als diese Angst oder Hoffnung auszuhalten und—während die Tür noch hält—meine Striche und Punkte zu setzen. Hier bin ich zu haben, wenn auch nie ganz' (284/ 278).

IV. 'Mitten im Satz war er tot'

The narrative technique of *Der Butt* facilitates a fluid relationship between the subject of the narrative and the narratives themselves. The moral of the book is: whenever the living subject interacts with story-telling, some good may still come of it. It is when they are separated that things go most seriously wrong.

This central point is made in the novel by reference to the fate of the original, orally transmitted, double fairy-tale about the talking fish. The simultaneous existence of the two stories is a model of positive tolerance. Both stories are about exaggerated desires, which receive their due rebuke from reality. Together, they are the model of the ebb and flow which takes place between different people as desiring subjects, animating and obstructing the spaces of real human interaction.

Both men and women can know the true nature and virtue of story-telling. The 'I' writes to Herr Dr Stachnik (who may well not agree with him!): 'Aber Sie und ich wissen, daß die Geschichten nicht aufhören können, immer wieder anders und anders wirklich zu verlaufen' (172/ 168), and later we read: 'Denn Amanda wußte, daß die Geschichten nicht enden können . . . daß jede Geschichte erzählt werden will, solange Kartoffeln genug im Korb sind' (297/291).

Such stories are carried by individual bodies and minds, it is their movement that counts: 'dieses Vermögen des Veränderns und des Wahrnehmens von Veränderungen, dieses Stück Gottähnlichkeit im Menschen, obgleich es Gott gar nicht gibt, nur das . . . halte ich für lebenswert' (Casanova 1979[2], 223). This is all testimony to human desire and the network of control and release it demands. In the same interview as the one from which the previous quotation is taken Grass also said: 'die Hemmung ist des Menschen vornehmstes Abzeichen' (223).

The single fairy-tale, however, seeks to impose a single truth and thus loses the dynamic complexity of the double model. It is a familiar political move. The alternative version is burnt, reminding us, as Siegfried Mews observed, of the Nazis' book burning (Mews 1983[1], 171–2) and of Grass's own identification of destructive flames with male history: 'das zeichnet den Mann aus . . . seinen Weg zeichnen Brand-spuren. So markierten Männer Geschichte' (468/461). As Grass explained in an interview with Siegfried Lenz:

Die Reduzierung der Wirklichkeit . . . Das hat politische Folgen, das prägt Verhaltensweisen, führt zu verstörtem Verhalten bei jungen Menschen, bei denen alles schon auf einen Wirklichkeitsbegriff reduziert ist, der keinerlei Bewegungen mehr oder nur noch wenig Bewegung erlaubt (Lenz 1982, 73).

It is, once again, a question of violence. One story, 'Eindeutigkeit', should not be violently imposed on the never-ending movement of stories which are 'immer wieder anders und anders wirklich', or, like Amanda's potato peelings, 'immer anders sinnfällig [fallend]' (296/290–1). The rigidity of the single meaning is surely akin to the act of rape, the disgusting violence of sexual dominance, enforced with dildo or by a gang of inhumanly erect bikers, as against the play of the first page of the novel: 'Also legten wir uns, wie wir uns jederzeit umarmt umbeint haben. Mal ich mal sie oben' (7/4). It is the single, dreadful narrative of 'Vatertag' (the only single-stranded Month in the book), as against the discursive play of *Der Butt* as a whole, which is *not* ultimately reducible to definite patterns, aesthetic or otherwise.

Grass's narrative of the composition of his own novel is revealing in this context. He said that 'Vatertag' had been in his mind from the beginning (Raddatz 1977[1], 30) but that otherwise he had attempted to keep an open mind on the question of the developing book's overall structure: 'Eine starre Position, die sich vielleicht für eine Novelle eignet oder für eine Erzählung, die kurz angebunden ist, würde für den Autor zur Fessel werden und den Stoff vergewaltigen' (Arnold 1978, 32). This is a fascinating glimpse of that 'jostling for position' between the two Grasses we mentioned at the beginning, in operation in the composition of the novel; on the one hand the artistic fixed point of 'Vatertag', but as against that, the play or openness of the other eight Months, moving to prevent any violation (and one can hardly fail to be sensitive to the word 'vergewaltigen' in this context) of the material, a violation, of course, that is fixed in its very heart, around which the play moves.

The vocabulary of binding and enchaining Grass uses in these words is also significant, for it underlines how the tyrannical single story imprisons its subject as well as abusing its object. These are the terms, of course, in which Grass sees the historical position of men. It is made clear in the poem 'Mannomann' (547–8/538–9) that the patriarchal story has been thoroughly appropriated into an alienated reality: 'Deine Träume, die typisch männlich waren, sind alle gefilmt.' Men are about to be released from their own story/history (the word-play is, of course, easier in German): 'Du bist . . . entlassen aus deiner Geschichte', and a question about the story the female voice will tell is raised in the play between the banal and the imponderable of the last line of lyric poetry in the novel: 'Was, Mannomann, wird deine Frau dazu sagen?'

As for his own contribution in *Der Butt*, I have tried to argue throughout that Grass is striving to reconnect stories to their subjects, and his own stories to his own subjectivity in the process. Richard Harvey Brown, elaborating a theme taken up before him by Walter Benjamin, has recently written of the division between narrative and the self in contemporary society, arguing that the functions of traditional narrative have been taken over by information, entertainment, social service, and ideology.[6] Grass's implication that the alienation of the story from the teller is effected by the transition of words from the voice into print surely belongs to the same cultural shift: 'Jenes Märchen aber . . . war als letzte Fassung druckfertig gemacht worden, während das ungedruckte Erzählen immer die nächste, die ganz anders verlaufende, die allerneueste Geschichte meint' (300/294).

The tyranny and alienating force of technology is clearly expressed in *Der Butt*, from the eye of the X-ray camera, which appropriates even the foetus—and, significantly, before its gender can be discerned (544/535)—to the overpowering 'In diesem Film gab es kein Entrinnen. Das Ende war vorgeschrieben' (501/492) of 'Vatertag'.

Yet Grass is too much of a realist (in the non-literary-historical sense) to indulge in pointless nostalgia for the oral transmission of narrative.

---

[6] Richard Harvey Brown, 'Narrative, Literary Theory, and the Self in Contemporary Society', *Poetics Today*, 6 (1985), 573–90 (575).

Indeed, as he said in an interview (Arnold 1978, 31), the arrival of Gutenberg increased perspectives rather than reduced them, for it opened up possibilities beyond the rigid perceptions of Church and State. Grass is as aware as anyone else that the technological media are now largely constitutive of reality and can only be dismissed at the risk of rendering oneself irrelevant. Grass, in recognition of this, features himself in his novel as a public figure, prominently involved, for instance, with the making of a television programme, and it is reasonable to assume that, on some level, he welcomes the challenge thrown out by the resistance of the media to all meanings but their own.

If *Der Butt* is often self-consciously *about* storytelling, it is not pretending to *be* the sort of counsel embedded in narrative of which Benjamin speaks in his famous essay,[7] and which nobody would claim is now possible. By stressing the subjective component in every thinkable narrative, including that sociologically complex commodity *Der Butt*, Grass is not invoking an early modernist sense of isolated fragmenting individualism. 'Die Geburtskammer des Romans', wrote Benjamin, 'ist das Individuum in seiner Einsamkeit, das sich über seine wichtigsten Anliegen nicht mehr exemplarisch auszusprechen vermag.'[8] If the assumption with which this essay starts is correct, then Grass writes to deconstruct the literary realism which was predicated upon the authority of the author; an authority which merely masked profound spiritual uncertainty: 'Mitten in der Fülle des Lebens und durch die Darstellung dieser Fülle bekundet der Roman die tiefe Ratlosigkeit des Lebenden.'[9]

No doubt Grass knows that the novel form and its development is inseparable from the technology of printing and *its* development, and the irony of a *novel*istic treatment of the flounder *Märchen* may well not have escaped him. Nevertheless, he accepts and affirms the complications of his own relationship with media technology (note how both *Die Zeit* and *Der Spiegel* found the 'am liebsten lüge ich gedruckt' headline irresistible, thus supporting a sophisticated irony which Grass must certainly have welcomed), for by so doing he does what he can to promote the 'sense of lived connection between personal character and public conduct' which Brown says once characterized societies that *were* still able to support narrative wisdom.[10]

For it *is* a question of wisdom, even if there cannot really be talk of Günter Grass as a distant sage talking in platitudes about men and

---

[7] Walter Benjamin, 'Der Erzähler. Betrachtungen zum Werk Nikolai Lesskows', in *Illuminationen: Ausgewählte Schriften* (Frankfurt, 1977), 385–410 (389).

[8] Ibid., 389.

[9] Ibid., 389.

[10] Brown, op. cit., 574.

women, or indeed about any of the other real topics which animate or escape the pages of *Der Butt*. What wisdom there is in *Der Butt* resides in its strategies for resisting the single truth for the many; for reconnecting words with their speaker (Grass, for better or for worse), and for encouraging the reader to feel at home with a multiple focus. 'Ach Butt! Dein Märchen geht böse aus' (552/543) must be read alongside 'Die Märchen hören nur zeitweilig auf, oder beginnen nach Schluß aufs neue. Das ist die Wahrheit, jedesmal anders erzählt' (555/545).

This wisdom springs from a knowledge of the limitations which surround it. The very principle of authority, the traditional source of wise counsel itself, is on trial in a disused cinema (for the institutions of the media can be put to many uses), and we have seen what restrictions are imposed upon the author's voice by the resistance of others and by his own sexuality. But there is another limitation which we have not yet mentioned, of which the book contrives to bear the traces, and that is the limitation imposed by death.

Narratives, in the end, cannot choose their own ends (although the flounder would like to think they could, 460/453). Just as the act of saying 'I' involves the subject in the certainty that it will be appropriated by others, so the apparent freedom of 'es war einmal' leads directly to the death of Sibylle. 'Vatertag' is *the* structural interruption in *Der Butt*, the fixed point which has to be read as a 'Gegenthema' or 'Störelement' (Raddatz 1977[1], 30) against the play of the rest of the text, and basically it means death, just as all the other Months are under the sign of birth. Every birth initiates a story which will be arbitrarily curtailed. Death is not a respecter of words, as Jan's death reminds us: 'Mitten im Satz war er tot' (516/508).

In reconnecting his text with death, including the shadow of his own, always unsayable, but always implied, Grass is doing what specifically *he* can to restore legitimate authority to the voice of the individual imagination as it once existed, so we are told, in the great story-tellers of the past: 'Der Tod ist die Sanktion von allem, was der Erzähler berichten kann.'[11]

---

[11] Benjamin, op. cit., 396.

'Aus einer Kürbishütte gesehen': The Poems

PHILIP BRADY

It is possible, as innumerable critics have shown, to note that *Der Butt* contains many poems and then to proceed as if they were not there.[1] The prose has indeed a kind of autonomy, it does not directly generate the poetry, nor are the poems essential links in the progress of the narrative. The poems too have their own autonomy—they allude to the prose on countless occasions but are never themselves alluded to. Readers of Grass are, in fact, used to keeping the novelist apart from the poet—there are, for instance, no poems in *Die Blechtrommel* or *Hundejahre*. Moreover, Grass the poet, elliptical, enigmatic, offers his readers very little chance of seeking the novelist within the poetry. Nevertheless, *Der Butt* is not Grass's first attempt at bringing what look like two distinct identities closer together. *Aus dem Tagebuch einer Schnecke*, which immediately preceded *Der Butt*, is, as Grass observed in an interview, the 'wichtigste Vorbereitung und Stufe' for the later novel, not least in the interaction of poetry and prose (Arnold 1978, 28). Its novelty lay, he suggested in the same interview, in the contiguity of autobiography and fiction, achieved through the introduction of 'das Autoren-Ich als Erzähler-Ich', and the poems, rooted in the non-fictional, in the factuality of Grass's own world, are important vehicles for that 'Autoren-Ich'. The poems in *Aus dem Tagebuch einer Schnecke* differ, however, in certain obvious ways from the poems in *Der Butt*: they are untitled, they lack the visible presence of the *Butt* poems, merging in some cases with the prose. Moreover, to hazard a more general comparison, they seem to have no structuring, no cumulative effect; that is, they do not create an entire dimension of central importance in the novel. The aim of this essay is to suggest that in *Der Butt*, on the other hand, the poems do create such a dimension.

[1] Thus Pickar, proposing to discuss the 'diversity of perspective' in the novel, does so without discussing the poems (Pickar 1983, 55). Adolph's account of irony likewise ignores the poems (1983). In the same volume Mayer (1983, 187–8) notes the repeated failure of critics to examine this aspect of *Der Butt*.

It is not easy to define the role of the poems, and it is important not to be too specific at the outset. Grass's own comments are helpful. He has emphasized the integration of the poems within the novel and their equal status with the prose:

Die Gedichte, die während des Schreibprozesses am *Butt* entstanden sind, stehen gleichrangig, nicht durch leere Seiten abgehoben, nicht durch eine andere Schrifttype betont, zwischen den Prosakapiteln innerhalb des Buches eingebettet (Raddatz 1977[1], 30).

The poems were not, in other words, inserted later into an existing prose draft. Grass seems indeed to have been working in not two, but three modes—prose, verse, and drawing:

Da standen zuerst einmal die Zeichnungen und Gedichte wie Vermessungs-pfähle, die das ganze epische Gelände absteckten ... Beim *Butt* ist es ein paralleler Prozeß des Schreibens und Zeichnens gewesen, bei dem manche Textseiten mit Zeichnungen beginnen, in Schrift übergehen, auch umgedreht (Müller, H.-J. 1985, 49).

Clearly the possibilities of interaction between three modes of expression are inexhaustible, and the separate publication of the *Butt* poems along with the drawings (in *Ach Butt*) suggests that the interaction between poems and drawings is important.[2] It can, however, only be touched on here. If we confine our enquiry, initially at least, to the two literary modes of verse and prose, we are in effect asking two allied questions: how the poems relate—individually or in groups or cumulatively—to their prose context and how they relate to each other.

It is worth beginning with obvious contexts and with obvious relationships. 'Wortwechsel' (542–3/533–4) is the penultimate poem. It follows the telegram from Ilsebill, 'Kommen erforderlich. Geburt steht bevor. Keine Ausrede bitte', and it is immediately followed by the birth of a daughter. It is a past-tense review over nine months, charting not so much the pregnancy as the adult relationship, with its alienating loss of words. Obviously the poem fits here and nowhere else, not simply because the pregnancy ends here but because with the birth fictional time catches up with private time and history runs out. History, the world of the cooks, has indeed no place in this poem, nor has the 'wir', emphatically the voice from the opening 'wußten wir nicht genau' to the

---

[2] *Ach Butt* also contains fourteen further poems not in *Der Butt*, several with corresponding etchings, which suggests that the enterprise was yet more extensive. For further graphic work—and therefore still further ramifications—see Mayer (1982). The interaction between verbal and graphic, already evident in Grass's first book (*Die Vorzüge der Windhühner*), seems to have continued into *Die Rättin*, there being, amongst the material for that novel, 'ein merkwürdiger Folioband voller Skizzen, Gedichtentwürfe, Zeichnungen' (Raddatz 1985, 49).

closing 'hatten wir keine Wörter mehr', any of the generality familiar from earlier poems, where it can often denote the entire male sex. 'Wir' is here surely two and no more. But the poem is in no sense simply keeping pace with the prose narrative. The poet, as it were, stands aside from the momentum created by the novelist and undermines a potential climax not simply by coming between a wife's telegram and the birth of a daughter but by doing so in a poem whose dead-pan enumeration avoids excitement:

> Im ersten Monat wußten wir nicht genau . . .
> Im zweiten Monat stritten wir ab . . .
> Im dritten Monat veränderte sich der faßbare Leib . . .

The relationship of 'Wortwechsel' to its immediate prose context is as precise as it is crucial. Its relationship to other poems in the novel is altogether more uncertain because, whatever links there may be between the *Butt* poems, they are bound to lack the irresistible logic of links in a prose narrative.[3] At one level, for instance, 'Wortwechsel' is the last in a broken line of poems—'Streit' (131/127-8) and 'Alle beide' (348/341) are two others—which variously focus on the domestic alienation between husband and wife. At another level it seems like a distant, ironic rejoinder to the first poem in the novel, 'Worüber ich schreibe' (11–13/8–9): the loss of 'Wörter' experienced at the birth is in marked contrast to the voluminous promises of words at the conception, promises underpinned by a rhetoric not unlike that of 'Wortwechsel':

> Über das Essen . . .
> Über den Wunsch . . .
> Ich schreibe über den Überfluß.

We may, however, perhaps read 'Wortwechsel' against the final poem, 'Mannomann' (547-8/538-9). The two poems, separated by only a few pages of prose, invite comparison not because they are the last two but because by this point in the novel the poet has almost ceased to be heard (there is only one other poem in the last two Months). 'Mannomann' generalizes where 'Wortwechsel' is specific. A line such as 'Du bist doch fertig, Mann' takes up once more the theme of the dethroned male, and

---

[3] Grass himself has proposed a certain coherence: 'c'est dans les poèmes que je suis le plus déchiffrable. Entièrement dévêtu de la fiction narrative, c'est là que l'auteur est le plus facilement reconnaissable. Les poèmes, dans *Le Turbot*, pris comme une ligne continue, forment un élément très personnel qui ensuite se vêt ou se déguise dans les chapitres narratifs en prose' (Casanova, 1979[1], 99). On the other hand, Raddatz's search for coherence had narrowed the range of the poems: 'stellte man sie [die Gedichte] zu einem eigenen Band zusammen, dann erhielte man die Legende einer gescheiterten Liebesbeziehung' (Raddatz 1977[2], 899).

there is in the poem a final, dismissive aggressiveness wholly unheard in 'Wortwechsel':

> Sag nochmal ich.
> Denk nochmal scharf.
> Blick nochmal durch.
> Hab nochmal recht.

The dual focus on private and public, on husband/Ilsebill and man/ woman, is, of course, central to the novel, but it is significant that the poet, by now a rare presence, emerges so close to the end in order to round off the one, private theme with the controlled monotone of 'Wortwechsel' and to bring the other, public confrontation into ominous view in the sustained hectoring of 'Mannomann'. The long sequence of poems has ended, in other words, not simply with two contrasting themes but also with two contrasting voices.

The last two poems are a convenient starting-point, but one that is perhaps misleadingly neat. The poems in *Der Butt* do not usually engage in such tidy pairs with the key themes of the novel. Nor, on the other hand, are they isolated from each other, changing only as the novel changes and ultimately, therefore, subordinate to the prose. They frequently are linked, however tenuously, and it is, in fact, possible to discern sequences of poems which, although only loosely—even ambiguously—coherent, signal changes of emphasis and direction. It is worth trying to trace some of these sequences.

The poems of the first two Months—to begin at the beginning—seem to change direction with the unexpected domesticity of 'Streit' (131/ 127–8):

> Weil der Hund, nein, die Katze
> oder die Kinder . . .
> weil Besuch zu früh ging . . .

Earlier poems have hinted at private troubles, but with 'Streit' and the poems that follow ('Helene Migräne', 'Manzi Manzi', 'Wie im Kino', 'Ilsebill zugeschrieben') the Ich–Ilsebill crisis is in the foreground. The poems before 'Streit', on the other hand, take a broader view, a view of historic changes and crises. At this early stage of the novel the distance between the time of the narrative and the time of the narrator is at its greatest, and the poems hint darkly at aeons of decline between then and now. The contrast between the elaborations of the novelist and the crisp understatements of the poet—one of the contrasts central to the mixture of prose and poetry in *Der Butt*—is perhaps nowhere more apparent than in the poet's capacity to encapsulate an entire downward progress in few words:

Über uns alle am leergegessenen Tisch
werde ich schreiben;
> ('Worüber ich schreibe', 13/9)
Schonkost seitdem, Rationen.
> ('Aua', 23/20)

The poet's hindsight spans history ('seitdem'), locating the point where
it 'begann (als Ahnung)' (55/52) or where he himself began:

> Irgendwann, lange vor Karl dem Großen,
> wurde ich mir bewußt,
> während du dich nur fortgesetzt hast.
> > ('Arbeit geteilt', 37/34)

Moreover, as that last line suggests, the poet's broad view embraces the
history of the Ich–Ilsebill tension. And the course of that history is
implied in the wry closing line of this same poem:

> Darf ich dir immer noch Feuer geben?

   The poet's hindsights yield more, however, than those dark hints.
'Was uns fehlt' (57–8/54–5) juxtaposes from line to line so many layers of
history that a panorama of historic delusions emerges:

> Wallenstein stellt Regimenter auf. . . .
> Die ihre Zukunft als späte Marxisten gesucht hatten,
> wollen nun frühe Christen sein oder Griechen

Over all this non-progress the poet has a kind of sovereign overview:

> Angekommen sind wir steinzeitlich blank.
> Doch habe ich meine Schreibmaschine dabei . . .
> Auf Lauchblätter tippe ich: Die Steinzeit ist schön.[4]

Incongruities and anachronisms of this kind tend to be submerged in the
particularities of the prose, even though this free play with the logic of
time is at the heart of Grass's narrative technique. In other words, it is
the poem which can give prominence to the following two lines, parallel
in form, but not adjacent in the poem:

> Heute—aber das gibt es nicht: heute:—. . .
> Jetzt—aber das gibt es nicht: jetzt—

The poet is ambiguously located in time, and the closing lines of the
poem appear not to take his *alter ego*, the amateur with the wide-angle
camera, too seriously, but there is a certainty of judgement that still
makes him a privileged onlooker. 'Vorgeträumt' (45/41–2) offers a

---

[4] *Ach Butt* (26) illustrates this motif—words are depicted printed along leek leaves.

similarly confident overview of self-deluding humanity, whose graffiti proclaim 'Glaubt mir glaubt!' and who can read a decline as a portent of upward progress—'Es geht wieder aufwärts.' Indeed, few poems in *Der Butt* open with such assurance:

> Vorsicht! sage ich, Vorsicht.
> Mit dem Wetter schlägt auch das bißchen Vernunft um.
> Schon ist Gefühl zu haben, das irgendwie ist:
> irgendwie komisch, unheimlich irgendwie.

The poet who appears, at least temporarily, to be above the fumbling vagueness of that repeated 'irgendwie' is at other times a prey to present insecurities. Grass seems, in fact, to play certainty off against uncertainty, to claim insights for a poet who is at the same time one of an endangered species. The irony is particularly clear in 'Am Ende' (99/95–6), a poem of almost classic formality, in which a rhetoric of repeated formulations ('Männer . . . Männer . . . Männer . . .') culminates—the poem is plainly structured towards a climax—in a bald question:

> Männer mit steiler Idee, der Taten platt folgten,
> sind endlich—fragen wir uns—am Ende?

It is only in the 'fragen wir uns' of the last line that the poet explicitly joins the 'Männer' whom he has hitherto been arraigning. The poet with his ironic insights is, finally, one of the doomed.

It is significant that 'Am Ende', a poem which suggests security and insecurity, comes immediately after a chapter concerned with a poet who devised a secure vantage-point from which to survey a perilous time. Simon Dach's arbour, his 'Kürbishütte', was a trivial thing in itself, offering scant protection, and it was artificial. Yet it is this creation of an artificial, seemingly fragile distance from events that enables the poet to keep those events in sight:

Denn im Grunde hat, aus einer Kürbishütte gesehen, der Dreißigjährige Krieg nie aufgehört, weil solch eine Kürbishütte . . . dennoch der geeignete Ort bleibt, die Welt ganz und ihre wechselnden Schrecken alle zu sehen (97/93).

Grass envies Dach his arbour, not simply for the vantage-point but because he too could then, like Dach, carve his beloved's name in the fruit. With Ilsebill for company the arbour could become a haven. Not, however, for Ilsebill, for whom it is a repugnant 'Scheißidylle'.

Placed at this point in the novel, the episode seems to throw light on the poems which surround it and on many that follow. Poetry does indeed provide within the first Month a vantage-point on the incomplete events of the narrative, the poet is indeed capable of the generalizing, wide-ranging view (there is truth as well as self-irony in that amateur with the wide-angle camera), but at the same time the overview is threatened, the poet's frailty and impotence impinge on his vision. 'Wie ich mich sehe' (95–6/91–2), the poem which immediately precedes the discussion of Dach and his 'Kürbishütte', observes that frailty at an unexpectedly singular, physical level. The poet's arbour is, in short, sandwiched between poems of utterly different character linked, however, by the theme of frailty and decline. 'Wie ich mich sehe' is a rare example of the kind of self-scrutiny more frequently practised by the graphic artist. Motifs within the poem occur, equally starkly juxtaposed, within the graphic work: the tired face, the eyes, the glasses laid to one side, the feather-blowing, expressive of nugatory effort.[5] And, if we accept the possibility that poems in *Der Butt* may work cumulatively, complementing or contradicting each other, then 'Wie ich mich sehe' gains an added, ironic power because it qualifies our view of the poet who, for all his hindsights and insights, is in a sense sighted in only one eye:

> Schon überlappen die oberen Lider.
> Das eine Auge hängt müde, verschlagen das andere wach.
> Soviel Einsicht und Innerei,
> nachdem ich laut wiederholt
> die Macht und ihren Besitz verbellt habe.
> (Wir werden! Es wird! Das muß!)

This is, of course, more than self-scrutiny, more than Grass the artist scrutinizing the poet in the mirror, and the poet recording the encounter. 'Wir werden!' echoes earlier, discredited slogans—the 'Glaubt mir glaubt!' and 'Aufwärts!' of 'Vorgeträumt', the 'ich werde' of 'Arbeit geteilt'—and through the proximity of those other poems this physical decay seems symptomatic of the endangered male, the male 'am Ende'.

Set in the context of other poems of the first Month, 'Wie ich mich sehe' suggests that the range and the standpoints of those poems are by no means fixed and predictable. 'Streit' (131/127–8), in the second Month, does, however, seem to mark a more signal change of focus in the poems. The novel itself makes one of its more obvious changes of direction at the beginning of the second Month—the lengthy documentary-historical episode at that point is centred in the television-filming in Gdańsk. In that distinctly less fictionalized setting the beginning of the chapter 'Ein Abwasch' (131/128) pursues non-fiction into a less public, domestic area:

---

[5] A face and blown feathers are depicted together, as are also a face and glasses (*Ach Butt*, 43 and 69). Glasses laid aside are a repeated motif (e.g. *Ach Butt*, 26, 69, 99). On the link between 'Wie ich mich sehe' and a further related drawing, see Mayer (1982, 19), who sees this poem as 'dieser Text, der sofort den Graphiker verrät'.

Vor Ilsebill fürchten sich meine Gläser. Als sie wegen nichts oder weil das Wetter umschlug oder weil ich ihr Essiggurkenwasser, das sie wie süchtig soff, ins Klo geschüttet hatte, als meine Ilsebill plötzlich, weil ihr der Faden riß, in kalte gelierte Wut geriet . . .

There is crisis in the domestic world, and 'Streit' and the poems that follow it approach that crisis from several angles. 'Streit' itself makes the crisis immediate, so to speak, and, in so doing, illustrates with exceptional clarity several of the sources of Grass's strength as a poet. The first stanza has a rhetorical underpinning close to that of the above-quoted prose passage, a rhetoric of 'weil . . . oder . . . weil . . . oder . . .'. But now the rhetoric is more sharply defined and it is holding together a disparate mixture of incongruous and trivial reasons for dispute, shaped to a climax on the humdrum raisins. Within that rhetoric the marital argument— 'nein, die Katze'—and the parental past—'die Kinder (deine und meine)'—are all the more loaded for being understated:

> Weil der Hund, nein, die Katze
> oder die Kinder (deine und meine)
> nicht stubenrein sind und herhalten müssen,
> weil Besuch zu früh ging
> oder Frieden zu lange schon
> und alle Rosinen gewöhnlich.

The second stanza contrasts markedly with this, shifting from a kind of record into elaborate metaphor, a shift common in the poems and a source both of their vividness and their complexity: words here jam drawers and are hook and eye—a beautifully concentrated mixture of the domestic and the aggressive. With the third stanza—to follow the poem one stage further—the chronicle returns with 'Jetzt geh ich', vividly coupling two very different levels of observation in the lines

> Rindfleisch fasert zwischen den Zähnen.
> Himmel Nacht Luft.

There is a lethal mixture in the marriage dispute, a mixture of tiredness, frustration, and open aggression, and Grass's varying angles on that mixture in 'Streit', 'Helene Migräne', 'Manzi Manzi', 'Wie im Kino', and 'Ilsebill zugeschrieben' create a highly individual group of poems. It is impossible to do justice to the achievement in a short space, but it has surely something to do with the way in which selective close-ups on a present crisis—the whole of 'Wie im Kino', the explosion into abuse in 'Manzi Manzi'—convey the tensions—of Ilsebill 'Zu mager vom vielen Joghurtessen' (155/151) or of migraine—without emotionalizing the issues or rendering them entirely private. 'Helene Migräne' and

'Manzi Manzi', for instance, have sharp but different focuses. The first homes in on the minute particulars of an atmosphere:

> Schon wieder droht,
> stößt Tasse auf Teller zu laut,
> stirbt eine Fliege,
> stehen frierend die Gläser zu eng,
> schrillt der paradiesische Vogel.
>
> (143/140)

'Manzi Manzi', on the other hand, records speech:

> Ausreden! Laß mich ausreden.
> Du hast nichts mehr zu sagen.
> Du hast Jahrhunderte lang.
> Dir schalten wir einfach den Ton ab.
>
> (144/140)

Both poems, however, are rooted in the general perspective of the novel at a point where the flounder admits

daß sein Rat von dazumal, den hochgotischen Frauen die Migräne als weibliches Vorrecht einzureden, zwar deren Schönheit gesteigert, doch der Männersache wohl kaum gedient habe (137/133–4).

Taken together—they are in fact printed together—the two poems seem to put a particularizing gloss on that sweeping summary.

The more global pessimism of the opening poems has yielded to close-ups of the Ich–Ilsebill relationship. It is a temporary change of emphasis—the 'gescheiterte Liebesbeziehung' that Raddatz detected is evident hereabouts, but it does not remain in focus. The poet, first articulating the male 'am Ende' and now the husband, is followed by the poet as poet, self-doubting, impotent before the world's problems. 'Mehrwert' (172/168), concluding the second Month, seems at a point of change. The domestic tension is still there, the Bohemian glasses were at an earlier stage in the novel emblematic of the relationship—'Barock-gläser ... die zueinander wie du und ich stehen' (133/130). But the last line of the poem, as indeed the title itself, opens out from the 'local' conflict, hinting at quite other matters:

> die Glasbläser, liest man, wurden nicht alt.

That suggestion of other fates becomes a dominant theme in the poems of the third Month and beyond, whilst that rather inactive 'liest man' is to return in many forms as the poet diagnoses his own passivity.

Vasco, well-fed traveller across a starving world, ineffectual and self-contradictory, haunts the poems of the third Month: 'Wohlgenährt leidet

Vasco am Welthungerproblem. Wieder- und wiedergeboren ist Vasco
jetzt Schriftsteller' (179/175). The argument reaches a general conclusion
in 'Geteert und gefedert' (207–8/203), in which blown feathers have
become synonymous with futile 'Möwenkonflikte', with the unproductive act of writing 'gegen die Zeit' and with—this is a poem built through
allusion rather than connection—a naïvely ineffectual 'Glaube'. Earlier
poems have discredited acts of faith, now faith is itself destructive,
scorning doubt and leaving it 'geteert und gefedert'. It is no accident that
in a poem so rich in images of futility—'ich blies, hielt in Schwebe',
'schlief daunenweich die verordnete Macht'—what has been lost is the
very activity, 'Zweifel', that for Brecht was the precondition of effective
change.[6] Unlike Brecht, Grass sees no alternative to the self-serving
purveyors of lies, of whom the poet is simply the latest variant:

> Neulich habe ich Federn,
> wie sie sich finden,
> mir zugeschnitten.
> Erst Mönche, Stadtschreiber später,
> Schriftführer heute halten die Lüge in Fluß.

'Geteert und gefedert' is a generalizing poem. There is, however,
another mode—poems facing, so to speak, the physical exuberance of
Grass's fictional creation, Gret, who, when she feeds an abbot to death—
'Wer alles hungern mußte, damit es ihm satt aufstieß' (215/211)—
confronts her creator with the world's hunger. What in the prose has
been an expression of outright disgust at Calcutta, and a lurid, half-
joyous celebration of Gret, becomes in the poems a structured discussion
about the impotence of the writer, assailed by problems. For the only
time in the novel, Grass groups three poems together, thus emphasizing
and consolidating the presence of the poet. The first of the three, 'Drei
Fragen' (192–3/188–9), once more a poem supported by a symmetry of
questions ('Wie kann ich ...? Wie sollte ich ...? Wie will ich ...?'),
faces the problem simply. Grass is asking questions and pin-pointing
contradictions in an unabstract way not unrelated to that of Brecht, but
where Brecht sees through the paradoxes to a kind of action, Grass is
stuck with the paradoxes, not so much questioning society as displaying
his own contradictoriness:

> Wie will ich,
> wo die Hand auf dem Foto
> bis zum Schluß ohne Reis bliebt,
> über die Köchin schreiben:
> wie sie Mastgänse füllt?

---

[6] See, for example, the poem 'Lob des Zweifels' (*Gesammelte Werke* (Frankfurt, 1967),
ix, 626–8).

Where 'Drei Fragen' is spare, 'Zuviel', which follows it, is elaborate—
George Orwell, a book of statistics, along with other problems which
'nicht aufhören wollen, privat zu kichern', combine to besiege the poet.
The question has shifted from failing to resolve a contradiction ('Drei
Fragen') to failing to cope with a host of crises. At one level the
problems, whether public or private, have equal status, but at another
level they have not—there is surely an element of self-irony in the anticlimax which ends the final list of choices:

> Indien
> oder der Oligarchische Kollektivismus
> oder die familiäre Weihnacht.

And there is a further, more ingenious irony in the striking change of
style from a bald enumeration of the distant problems to an unfactual,
metaphorical summary of the domestic problems—only the world
problems are, it appears, capable of inhibiting metaphorical flourishes:

> Jetzt lese ich über Verhörmethoden in naher Zukunft.
> Jetzt will ich mir Zahlen merken:
> gegenwärtige Mortalitätsmuster
> der Kindersterblichkeit in Südasien.
> Jetzt zerfaser ich von den Rändern her,
> weil vor den Feiertagen das nachgelassene Gezänk
> in Päckchen verschnürt wurde: Ilsebills Wünsche...

With 'Esau', the third poem of the group, the domestic strife is out of
sight, world hunger has been traced back to Esau, an early exemplar of
the price of hunger, his birthright sold for a mess of pottage. The need
for food has created its own limited morality ('Ausgezahlt lebe ich
linsengerecht') and has restored the brass tacks to a religious miracle:

> Und als er auferstanden am dritten Tag,
> war sein Verlangen nach Linsen groß.

Food and, inescapably, hunger have become a central theme, as the
first poem in the novel had indeed promised, and that theme is perhaps in
sharper, more singular focus in the poems than in the prose. Moreover,
Grass's self-doubting poet, retreating before so many problems, is a part
of that theme, gaining perhaps sharper definition when he then comes to
confront a version of himself in Martin Opitz. Opitz has to face the
charge that prosody and metrics have obscured his vision: 'er, der
regelkundige Opitz, habe der Hebungen und Senkungen wegen des
Menschen ganze Erbärmlichkeit mit Wortplünder verhängt' (248/243).
Opitz no longer writes those honest poems which look straight 'ins
Jammertal'. He is empty and sick, he has become the poet who 'keine
Worte fand' (255/249).

The problems which had already threatened to overwhelm the poet are now excreted. As 'Leer und alleine' (245/239–40) puts it:

> So viel Leere
> ist schon Vergnügen: allein auf dem Klo
> mit dem mir eigenen Arsch.
> Gott Staat Gesellschaft Familie Partei . . .
> Raus, alles raus.

The identity with Opitz at this point is close—both are infected, and Opitz with his 'schwarze Pest' leads directly from the prose into the poem in which the *Butt* poet and his time have 'Dünnpfiff':

> Angst, weil die Zeit—die Uhr meine ich—
> chronischen Dünnpfiff hat.

Poetry, excrement and diarrhoea have become inseparable—a grotesque twist to every *fin-de-siècle* association of poetry with sickness and to every modernist demythologizing of the poet. 'Kot gereimt' (286/280)—the very title couples the two disparate worlds—puts matters plainly. Excrement offers self-knowledge:

> Wir staunen uns an.
> Wir haben uns was zu sagen.
> Mein Abfall, mir näher als Gott oder du oder du.

And it is Opitz who, in the last stanza of this same poem, makes the final connection between poetry and excrement, in lines whose mixture of close-up observation and metaphorical argument is, however startling in this instance, by now a familiar feature of Grass's technique as a poet:

> Alle Gedichte, die wahrsagen und den Tod reimen,
> sind Kot, der aus hartem Leib fiel,
> in dem Blut rinnselt, Gewürm überlebt;
> so sah Opitz, der Dichter,
> den sich die Pest als Allegorie verschrieb,
> seinen letzten Dünnpfiff.

Deprived of the cushioning effect which a complex prose-narrative can have, the plain speaking of a poem such as 'Kot gereimt' may well read like gratuitous extremism. This, however, is again one of those points in the novel where it is difficult to read one poem in isolation from others. Opitz himself and 'Kot gereimt' in particular are, in fact, one aspect of a varied if bleak account which is emerging at this stage and which has the *Butt* poet at its centre. Thus, although Opitz figures, inextricably overlapping with the present, at the end of 'Spät' (264/258–9), the emphasis lies elsewhere. It lies in that present, with the poet who, for all the overlapping, is viewing Opitz from a distance. There is in 'Spät' an unexpectedly reflective quality—'Natur', 'Glück', 'Schönheit', 'Sinn' have not been key words hitherto. If it is a surprise to discover where the beauty is being found, in what 'Natur' therefore consists, then this itself suggests that the poem has seemed to be distanced from the physical, distanced through Grass's delaying tactics and through the emphasis on neutral absolutes—'nie' and 'ganz':

> Ich kenne nur,
> soweit sie sich zeigt,
> die Natur.
>
> Mit tastendem Griff
> sehe ich sie in Stücken,
> nie
> oder nur, wenn das Glück mich schlägt,
> ganz.
>
> Was soviel Schönheit,
> die sich am Morgen schon
> in meinem Kot beweist,
> soll oder zweckt,
> weiß ich nicht.

The situation is extreme, but the language, pared down and undemonstrative, does not match it. Sickness and 'Angst' and 'Dünnpfiff'—the Opitz-associations, as it were—are less in focus than the poet in the here-and-now, imperfect in his grasp, lacking understanding.

The poet, already 'leer und alleine', takes his withdrawal one stage further in the poem which concludes the fourth Month, 'Unsterblich' (292/286). Now the 'Raus, alles raus' of 'Leer und alleine', the first poem of the fourth Month, is taken to a point where self-scrutiny has no value, since the poet is 'abgelebt' and, in an updated version of the pathetic fallacy, expects to see nothing because he feels nothing. In fact, the world outside is still there, clearly delineated:

> Stare auch in den Birnen,
> Schulkinder, die der Bus gebracht hatte,
> den Sparkassenneubau . . .

That world is, however, impermanent. Ilsebill too is still there, but there is no conflict, she merely 'kommt überladen'. The poet himself, it might be said, is no longer even blowing feathers. Besieged by the problems, defeated by those three earlier questions, he has withdrawn, existing to others but not to himself:

> Schon grüßen die alten Nachbarn.
> Sie wollen aus allen Fenstern
> mich wirklich gesehen haben.

The separate voice of the poet is perhaps nowhere more apparent than at this point. His is a kind of extreme withdrawal and a concentrated self-absorption which has no real equivalent in the prose and which would, indeed, almost seem to undercut the narrative energies of the novelist. There is an air of all-passion-spent finality about 'Unsterblich', which, if the course of the poems were straight and straightforward, would sound like a conclusion. But the empty, 'abgelebt' poet is simply one version of the changing distances between the poet and the events of the novel.

Those events and, with them, the theme of hunger, re-enter the poetry with Amanda Woyke, replacing the withdrawn poet. Three of Amanda's children die of starvation, and her 'Klage und Gebet' (307–9/301–3), apart from being the longest poem in the book, is also more clearly rooted in the narrative than any. In ballad-fashion the poem relates her disasters, elaborating the details of the prose. The poet, in other words, is back out of limbo, back with the theme of hunger. And again poetry is achieving its own effects of rhetoric, of contrast. Towards the end there is a brisk account of an unconcerned summer:

> Als sei nichts, schlug der Holunder aus.
> Buchweizen, Hafer blieben nicht taub.
> Pflaumen zum Trocknen genug.

But the poem has opened with a stanza of markedly different rhetorical character, a stanza which gradually unwinds, letting the particulars delay the calamity:

> Als ihr die Würmchen,
> hießen Stine Trude Lovise,
> weil der Halm faulgeregnet, vom Hagel erschlagen,
> von Dürre und Mäusen gebissen war,
> daß gedroschen kein Rest blieb,
> Hirse nicht körnte, Grütze nicht pappte,
> kein Haferschleim süß und Fladenbrot sauer wurde,
> weghungerten alle drei . . .

The realities and the metaphors of hunger and satiety, the source of so much cross-reference and allusion between prose and verse, have been taken up again in Amanda's 'Klage', but now in the form of a sustained narrative, made more immediate by the direct and indirect speech of the victim. The contrast between Amanda and, at the end of the previous poem, Ilsebill—returning 'überladen'—is striking. Amanda has a grain of hope about the after-life, and Grass shapes the end of the poem to make all the more pointed the hopelessness of life on earth:

> und Hoffnung körnchengroß,
> daß Stine Trude Lovise nun Engel seien
> und satt.

Ilsebill, on the other hand, had been loaded with shopping for the weekend. And there is an equally sharp contrast between the uninvolved, self-aware poet of 'Unsterblich' and the involved, self-unaware poet who narrates Amanda's misfortunes. Grass is again contrasting different degrees of involvement, different distances between the poet and events. Moreover, those distances continue to change with the two poems that follow—'Übers Wetter geredet' (317–8/311) and 'Am Hungertuch nagen' (335–6/329). 'Übers Wetter geredet' has non-involvement as its subject, but it is not the total withdrawal of 'Unsterblich', it is rather the shoulder-shrugging unconcern of society, its callous 'beiläufig' wrapped up in complex syntax:

> Ob jene Zahlreichen,
> die weit entfernt hungern,
> doch sonst kaum auffallen,
> daran gehindert werden dürfen,
> ist eine Frage, die beiläufig
> immer wieder gestellt wird.

The poet himself, far from withdrawing, is both a part of that society and also its critic. His criticism now remains general—that is, whereas earlier poems such as 'Drei Fragen' or 'Zuviel' recorded a highly individual confrontation with world hunger, in which Gret figured and Ilsebill, 'Übers Wetter geredet' is consistently satiric:

> Sachlich sein.
> Bei uns bleibt genug zu tun.
> Die vielen kaputten Ehen.
> Methoden, nach denen zwei mal zwei vier ist.
> Notfalls Beamtenrecht.
>
> Am Abend stellen wir zornig fest,
> daß auch das Wetter vorausgesagt falsch war.

Few poems in *Der Butt* make complete sense independently of their context. 'Übers Wetter geredet' is one of those few. 'Am Hungertuch nagen', on the other hand, is not, even though its satiric argument is very similar. The empty promise of 'Mehlschütte', with which the poem opens, derives from the heavenly 'Mehlschütte, die aber leer war', which Amanda experienced in the previous chapter, but the poem moves from this fictional past into a present whose arguments are grotesque:

> Gegen den Hunger ist viel geschrieben worden.
> Wie schön er macht.

and whose spokesmen are self-betraying:

> Es ist die Nachfrage, sagte Professor Bürlimann,
> die immer alles am Ende regelt—
> und lächelte liberal.

'Übers Wetter geredet' and 'Am Hungertuch nagen' are the last of the long sequence of poems arising, whether directly or obliquely, from hunger and associated matters, and the barbed economy of their closing lines expresses at least a part of what the poems contribute. Food is a central strand in *Der Butt*, but it is the poems which repeatedly bring into sharp relief the paradoxes and the evasions, and they do so in a variety of styles which has at one extreme the sort of plain speaking that crisply demolishes Professor Bürlimann and at the other the long unravelling stanzas of Amanda's 'Klage'.

By singling out themes rather than styles and by simplifying what is never in fact a tidy progression, we can perhaps speak of three clusters of poems around, very roughly, the history of male decline, the domestic antagonisms, global disaster. There is one further stage, still associated with food, but more tenuously, which produces poems of a particularly enigmatic character—the mushroom poems. Here, the interaction between poems, prose, and graphic work seems particularly intricate, and it is impossible to divorce the poems from either their prose context or their graphic equivalents. It is, first of all, worth briefly enumerating certain obvious varieties of prose meaning associated with the 'Pilze'.

For Amanda, with whom the subject first, very briefly, arises, mushrooms mean food, food which came too late for her three dead children:

> Pflaumen zum Trocknen genug.
> Es lohnte, in die Pilze zu gehen.
> (308/302)

Sophie, on the other hand, is one who 'wenn sie in die Pilze ging, neben eßbaren Sorten nun auch solche in Betracht zog, die politisch wirksam sein können' (372/366)—that is to say, she seeks mushrooms which can kill. With Sophie, however, mushrooms also acquire their other, phallic meaning: she, the eternal virgin, is applauded by the tribunal and depicted in a poster in a phallic version of 'La Liberté guidant le Peuple':

Die torfbraunen Haare mit Tricoloreband hochgebunden. Das Mündchen geschwungen offen, als singe sie Revolutionäres. Und vor der Barrikade entwurzelte Pilze, eindeutig anspielend, als habe ein entmannendes Massaker stattgefunden (406-7/400).

And the mushroom has more abstract connotations: 'in die Pilze gehen', an idea constantly linked with Sophie, can mean seeking a love that is lost—'Oder wir gehen mal wieder, wie ich mit Sophie ging, tief in die Pilze, um sie [die Liebe] zu suchen' (371/364). Mushrooms have in fact a quintessential ambiguity, they connote poison, food and phallus, hate and love:

Wenn sich alles und auch der Widerspruch all essen auf einen einzigen Punkt verengt. Wenn wir—wieder einmal in die Wälder gegangen—nicht mehr die unvergleichbar schöne Idee, sondern ihr Gegenteil meinen, das auch seine Schönheit hat: verkleidet als Pilz steht der Haß auf Moosgrund und unter Eichen, eigentlich nicht zu verwechseln (373/367).

With the Romantics yet further meanings are accreted. The Grimm Brothers and company, failing to agree on which version of the flounder tale to choose, go mushroom-picking in an act of entrusting themselves to nature. As Bettina puts it, 'Wir sollten uns der Natur anvertrauen und in Körbe einsammeln, was sie uns bietet' (358/351). And with the Romantics, Arnim and Bettina in particular, mushrooms acquire their psychedelic associations, and it is Bettina who pin-points their liberating properties:

Von denen gehe Zauber aus. Sie wisse, daß der Fliegenpilz, selbst wenn man nur wenig von ihm speise, Träume mache, die Zeit aufhebe, das Ich erlöse und alles, so grob es gegeneinander stehe, miteinander versöhne (359/352).

The graphic art, moreover, in which the mushroom image is prominent,[7] offers a variation on the theme of the creative mushroom: two of the earlier *Butt* poems, each concerned with the endangered male, are drawn tumbling in some confusion out of upturned funnel-shaped mushrooms (Mayer 1982, Figs. 6, 7).

'Pilze bedeuten', states the poem 'Sophie'—and the intransitive speaks volumes (351/345). The poems which pursue some of these meanings ('Sophie', 'Hinter den Bergen', 'Auf der Suche nach ähnlichen Pilzen', 'Zum Fürchten', 'Fortgezeugt') are more enigmatic than most because more than most they exploit the multiple associations of one element within the prose. And it is not least the ambiguity of those associations that seems to engage the poet.

It is, however, the same poet. Indeed, one of the fascinating aspects of the mushroom poems is the extent to which they recapitulate. 'Hinter den Bergen' (361–2/355), for example, uses the poet's distance to disillusioning effect, undermining obliquely the mushroom-induced escapes of the Romantics. The subject is now different, but in other, earlier poems the poet had destroyed dreams ('Am Ende', 'Gestillt'). Now a solipsistic idyll is being demolished, an idyll already expressed in that one single, singly placed 'zufrieden':

Was wäre ich ohne Ilsebill!
rief der Fischer
zufrieden.

[7] 'Man sieht, daß das Pilzmotiv, das im Roman nur den sechsten Monat beherrscht, im graphisch-lyrischen Bereich eine umfassende Wirkung entfaltet hat' (Mayer 1982, 20).

It is an escapist, self-deluding, anti-realist contentment, full of Romantic echoes and at the same time taking up, if in a different setting, the smug, contented, 'liberal' smile of Professor Bürlimann. It is, indeed, another form of withdrawal:

> Außer uns alles erfunden.
> Nur das Märchen ist wirklich.

Once again Grass shapes and points the anticlimax, deflating and ironic—Bettina in her euphoria has supplied the language, she has spoken of the mushroom which 'die Zeit aufhebe, das Ich erlöse', she and Arnim have made words which find in water their own 'Spiegelbild', and now the poem, in elaborating the dream, exposes it:

> Höher, tiefer, güldener, doppelt so viel.
> Schöner noch als gedacht.
> Gespiegelt bis ins Unendliche.
> Und weil kein Tod, kein Leben mehr als Begriff.
> Jetzt das Rad noch einmal erfinden dürfen.

Feeling, we recall from the first Month ('Vorgeträumt'), can soon swamp 'das bißchen Vernunft', and it can be at once vaguely 'komisch', vaguely 'unheimlich'. The poet who in that early poem had counselled 'Vorsicht' introduces a not dissimilar note of sobriety in 'Hinter den Bergen' with the last stanza. He too has been dreaming, not via mushrooms and not of things grown higher and deeper and more golden, but of 'Brot, Käse, Nüsse und Wein'. But not even this is a dream of fulfilment. The dream is nullified because the poet, recalling his emptied, absent, 'abgelebt' counterpart in 'Unsterblich', is missing: 'nur fehlte ich, mich zu freuen.' Neither the Romantic dreamings of Bettina nor this less-than-Romantic dreaming of bread and cheese is accepted. 'Ich will wach bleiben'—thus the poet in 'Spät', threatened by the spurious 'Sinn' that comes from dreams. 'Hinter den Bergen' seems to be echoing that earlier declaration.

'Spät', which speaks also of confusion and imperfect, fragmented grasp ('Mit tastendem Griff | sehe ich sie in Stücken'), seems in fact to anticipate a theme which returns with the mushrooms. They are inherently confusing not simply because they are often difficult to identify but also because they can be both creative and fatally destructive. 'Sophie' (351-2/344-5), the first of the mushroom poems, expresses that uncertainty. Moreover, it expresses it at a point where, in the previous chapter ('Indische Kleider'), the narrative has come very close to the certainties of autobiography: the narrator and Ilsebill, she in her 'fliegenpilzrot' dress, go shopping in Hamburg. There is, in marked contrast to the precisely observed close of that chapter, extreme uncertainty in the opening of 'Sophie'. The verbs lack objects, 'anders' is nowhere and is repeated:

> Wir suchen
> und meinen zu finden;
> aber anders heißt er
> und ist auch anders verwandt.

The uncertainty is sustained—only the 'Pfifferlinge' of the third stanza begin to make the subject clear. The poem moves in fact between a generalizing non-narrative present and a more specific narrative past. Thus the second and third stanzas are narrative, some of their details anticipating details within the prose, but the fourth stanza returns to the present tense and to the generalizing mode, bringing sexual metaphor and the lethal possibilities of the mushroom close together in lines which, in linking sexuality, mushrooms, and the pursuit of metaphor, manage to read a dangerous ambivalence into all three:

> Pilze bedeuten.
> Nicht nur die eßbaren
> stehen auf einem Bein
> für Gleichnisse stramm.

It is worth remembering that 'Alle beide' (348/341), the poem which concludes the fifth Month and therefore immediately precedes 'Sophie', sees a lethal ambivalence enacted in marriage, where 'das gewohnte Küßchen danach' and the knots in the carpet vividly encapsulate love turned to hate, where open warfare is preferable, producing the paradox: 'Ein Segen, der Fluch'. To move from 'Alle beide' to 'Sophie' is not to move worlds, but it is to exchange one voice for another, the one insistent ('Angst ... Angst ... Angst ... Verängstigt ...'), particularizing ('Zwischen den Einbauschränken ...'), recording ('Er sagt nicht ... Aber, sagt er ... Aber, sagt sie ...'), the other selective, distanced, not so much recording conflict as emblematizing it in the mushroom.

No other group of *Butt* poems clusters so allusively round a single, central, ambivalent image: the seeking and finding of mushrooms. 'Zum Fürchten' (386–7/379–80), for example, retains the lethal associations, the loaded 'Nicht nur die eßbaren' of 'Sophie', but conflates them with fairy-tales, letting them infect the latter with menace:

> Die Pilze und Märchen
> holen uns ein.

Mushroom and Romantic creativity become one overlapping threat, and both produce a fear which invades the private realm. The 'natural' fear of

'Jede Knolle treibt jüngeren Schrecken', continued later in the ironic 'Viele Pilzkenner sterben früh', is interrupted by fear of a different order, when uncertainty assails a poet once more removed, 'abgelebt', within the domestic setting:

> Immer war schon wer da.
> Zerstörtes Bett—bin ich es gewesen?
> Nichts ließ mein Vorgänger stehn.

The mushroom is, it seems, a double threat. It threatens the life of the 'Pilzkenner' and, in its phallic symbolism, it threatens the sexual identity of the poet. Reality, so to speak, is dangerous, but there is, on the other hand, no security to be had in the realm of symbols. Moreover, the mushroom exposes the imperfect vision of the poet: where Sophie 'fand und fand', he found nothing—'ich verlor meine Brille'. Again the glasses suggest frailty.

It is the density of meaning which most impresses in these poems, the way in which, for example, the juxtaposition of Sophie, finding and finding, and the poet, losing his glasses, encompasses so much that is now familiar: the sexual conflict, the themes of decay, of frailty, of ineffectualness. Grass seems at this point not so much to be exploring multiple meanings in order to disentangle them as trying to retain the pregnant ambiguity of 'Pilze bedeuten'. Two poems in particular show the extreme stage of concentration that is reached—'Auf der Suche nach ähnlichen Pilzen' (374/367–8) and 'Fortgezeugt' (408/401). The two are, moreover, so close in form as to suggest that Grass has found something akin to an appropriate form for that concentration and ambiguity.

The similarities are obvious: both poems consist of five three-line stanzas, both centre in the third stanza in the concrete, 'seen' mushroom:

> Dieser Hut paßt
> einen Kopf kürzer
> auf Maß.
>   (374/367)
> Es steht der Pilz
> schirmlings
> und lüftet die Wurzel.
>   (408/401)

The differences are, however, considerable. 'Auf der Suche nach ähnlichen Pilzen' has a spareness and an economy rarely encountered in the *Butt* poems. In a sense it takes up the 'anders heißt er' of 'Sophie', but it now closes up on the single case, the single uncertainty. Within the economy of the poem single words stand out sharply—'daneben', 'verloren', each expressive of failure, each concluding a stanza on one word—as does the sole overt metaphor in the poem, which makes light itself a part of the deception:

> auch das Licht
> schummelt sich durch.

And the deadpan last stanza manages to make certainty unsettling by juxtaposing 'falsch' and 'genau'—the certainty is the certainty of having been mistaken:

> Zwar sind es Boviste,
> doch falsche,
> genau.

A few lines earlier there has been talk in the prose of a similar insight, a similar seeing-through, 'Wenn wir uns endlich durchlöchert und durchschaut haben', but the poem is, by comparison, drained, dispassionate, almost impersonal.

At certain points 'Fortgezeugt' contrasts with 'Auf der Suche nach ähnlichen Pilzen', less perhaps in manner than in range—that is, in its allusions to the complex contradictions of an uncertain future. The flounder has just anticipated a world where women will be 'verschlossen . . . endgültig zu' and where the race will die out—hence the summary opening:

> Ein Gedanke entvölkert.
> Rattenlos
> rollt ins Abseits.

The mushroom suggests, however, a more paradoxical prospect. Roots in the air, it presages not extinction but an ambiguous mixture—it is both inescapably male in its symbolism and also, because inverted, symbolic of the sexual revolution: 'Unten will oben.' Two quite separate meanings are being held against each other when male insecurity faces phallic pride:

> Wann kappt der endliche Schnitt?
> Doch staunend auch du
> und offen.

She, far from being 'verschlossen', is open, but the threat is no less—there is not even a hint of feeling in 'staunend'. The poem ends indeed on a suspended threat, a threat held in check by the element of unserious or half-serious play:

> Aber es bleibt nur
> drohend beim Spiel.

Compared with this, 'Auf der Suche nach ähnlichen Pilzen', with its sharper focus on a single mistaken identity, seems to move away from enigmas to close on an emblematic image of uncertainty.

There is perhaps in the contrast between these two poems something of that polarity which recurs in so many *Butt* poems and which is, as we noted, a central element in the novel as a whole, namely that polarity between a private, close-up focus and a broader view. It is, leaving aside every difference of tone and manner, a polarity which is to return in the last two poems, the poems with which we began—'Wortwechsel' and 'Mannomann'.

'Zeug fort—beiß ab', the injunction at the end of 'Fortgezeugt', is richly ambiguous—those who witness also procreate—and it is a reminder of the ambiguity at the heart of the feminist tribunal. Those who testify against the male must also, to create any future, procreate through the male. Whatever the outcome, that male is being emasculated,[8] although, if the mushroom associations still operate, and within this cluster of poems they surely do, then there are lethal and psychedelic risks in that 'beiß ab'. It is fitting to conclude at this point of ambiguity, where a nexus of meanings within the prose narrative is being concentrated in four words of poetry, words which gain indefinably through the control and the distance that the rest of the poem creates. It is, like so much in the *Butt* poems, an effect unobtainable in prose. This is not to say, however, that the strength of the *Butt* poems lies merely in the familiar strengths of poetry against prose. Grass's use of poetry is, in fact, highly original, so much so that it seems pointless to look for models. The originality lies in the relationship between poet and prose-narrator. The poet may come close to the narrator,[9] may take up the narrative fairly directly on occasion:

> Mitgekocht wurden:
> ein Händchenvoll Graupen, Kümmel, Majoran
> und wenig vom Bilsenkraut gegen die Pest.
> (254/249)

Or he may share the narrator's present:

> neben mir
> träumt sich Ilsebill weg.
> (422/416)

[8] The threat acquires graphic expression in a drawing (*Ach Butt*, 29), in which unambiguously phallic mushrooms are depicted alongside a kitchen knife. The picture faces 'Manzi Manzi', thus creating a different but obvious link.

[9] Closest proximity is achieved by those poems which occur in *Ach Butt* but have been absorbed into the prose of *Der Butt*: 'Federn blasen' (*Ach Butt*, 94) occurs word for word in prose in the novel (451/444); 'Schöne Aussicht' (*Ach Butt*, 89) occurs slightly altered (543/534).

Nevertheless, the poet's is a separate voice, variously linked to the prose, variously independent of it. The separateness is important—the poet is free of the overlapping histories of the narrator, his present tense is, so to speak, more present than that of the narrator. Hence the immediacy of an opening such as 'Er sagt nicht meine, die Frau sagt er' (348/341), hence too the sustained immediacy of poems such as 'Wie ich mich sehe', 'Am Ende', 'Wie im Kino', among others. Moreover, the poet within his present is distanced from the complex labours of the narrator and is, therefore, capable of ironies, overviews, and abbreviations denied to the latter. Thus the practice of poetry is being vindicated close to, but not wholly within, a prose narrative. The poet, distanced within his own 'Kürbishütte', has become part of the fabric of a novel.

List of Contributors

RONALD SPEIRS is Senior Lecturer in German at the University of Birmingham

JOYCE CRICK is Senior Lecturer in German at University College London

DAVID JENKINSON is Senior Lecturer in German at Goldsmiths' College, University of London

TIMOTHY MCFARLAND is Senior Lecturer in German at University College London

HANNE CASTEIN is Senior Lecturer in German at Goldsmiths' College, University of London

JOHN J. WHITE is Reader in German at King's College, London

ANTHONY PHELAN is Lecturer in German at the University of Warwick

PETER PROCHNIK is Lecturer in German at Royal Holloway and Bedford New College, University of London

JOHN SANDFORD is Professor of German at the University of Reading

MICHAEL MINDEN is Lecturer in German at Cambridge University and Fellow of Jesus College

PHILIP BRADY is Reader in German at Birkbeck College, University of London

Bibliography

This bibliography is selective, and lists the works by Günter Grass, interviews with him, and secondary literature on *Der Butt* and related topics cited in the essays in this volume. For a full bibliography on *Der Butt* up to 1982, see Siegfried Mews (ed.), *"The Fisherman and His Wife": Günter Grass's 'The Flounder' in Critical Perspective* (New York, 1983), 209–17.

All references to the text of *Der Butt* are in the form (112/109), the first numeral referring to the German paperback edition and the second to the English paperback edition, as follows:

Günter Grass, *Der Butt* (Fischer Taschenbuch Verlag; Frankfurt, 1979 and subsequent reprintings).

Günter Grass, *The Flounder*, translated from the German by Ralph Manheim (Penguin Books; Harmondsworth, Middlesex, 1979 and subsequent reprintings).

Other works by Günter Grass are all cited in the editions published by Luchterhand (Darmstadt and Neuwied, formerly Berlin and Neuwied) as follows:

Die Vorzüge der Windhühner (1956)
Die Blechtrommel (1959)
Katz und Maus (1961)
Hundejahre (1963)
örtlich betäubt (1969)
Aus dem Tagebuch einer Schnecke (1972)
Denkzettel: Politische Reden und Aufsätze (1978)
Das Treffen in Telgte (1979)
Kopfgeburten oder die Deutschen sterben aus (1980)
Ach Butt, Dein Märchen geht böse aus: Gedichte und Radierungen (1983)
Widerstand lernen: Politische Gegenreden 1980–1983 (1984)
Die Rättin (1986)
Zunge zeigen (1988)

Interviews with Günter Grass

Arnold, Heinz Ludwig, 1978. 'Gespräche mit Günter Grass', *Text + Kritik*, 1/1a, *Günter Grass*, 5th edn., 1–39.

Casanova, Nicole, 1979[1]. *Günter Grass: Atelier des métamorphoses: entretiens avec Nicole Casanova* (Paris).

—— 1979[2]. '"Am liebsten lüge ich gedruckt"', *Der Spiegel*, 2 Apr. 1979, 219–25 (selection from Casanova, 1979[1] in the original German).

Figes, Eva, 1978. 'Woman Talk', *Observer*, 15 Oct. 1978, 37.

Hunt, Irmgard Elsner, 1980. 'An Interview with Günter Grass', *Dimension*, 13, 84–91.

Lenz, Siegfried, 1982. *Über Phantasie: Gespräche mit Heinrich Böll, Günter Grass, Walter Kempowski, Pavel Kohout*, ed. Alfred Mensak (Hamburg).

Müller, Hans-Joachim, 1985. *Butzbacher Autoren-Interviews*, 3 (Darmstadt).

Raddatz, Fritz J., 1977[1]. '"Heute lüge ich lieber gedruckt": ZEIT-Gespräch mit Günter Grass', *Die Zeit*, 12 Aug. 1977, 29–30.

Smyth, Robin, 1978. 'Food for Thought', *Observer Magazine*, 1 Oct. 1978, 34–7.

Secondary Literature on *Der Butt* and Related Topics

Adolph, Winnifred R., 1983. 'The Truth Told Differently: Myth and Irony', in Mews 1983[2], 121–33.

Angress, Ruth K., 1982. '*Der Butt*: A Feminist Perspective', in Pickar 1982, 43–50.

Ascherson, Neal, 1978. 'A Fish out of Water', *Observer*, 8 Oct. 1978, 41.

Butler, G. P., 1979. 'Grass Skirts the Issue: A Reaction to *Der Butt*', *Quinquereme*, 2, 23–33.

Demetz, Peter, 1983. 'Günter Grass in Search of a Literary Theory', in Mews 1983[2], 19–24.

Diller, Edward, 1983. 'Raw and Cooked, Myth and *Märchen*', in Mews 1983[2], 91–105.

Durrani, Osman, 1980. '"Here Comes Everybody": An Appraisal of Narrative Technique in Günter Grass's *Der Butt*', *Modern Language Review*, 75, 810–22.

Durzak, Manfred, 1979. 'Ein märchenhafter Roman: Zum *Butt* von Günter Grass', *Basis*, 9, 71–90.

—— 1985. 'Der Butt im Karpfenteich: Günter Grass und die Literaturkritik', in Wolff 1985, 87–110.

Forster, Leonard, 1980. 'An Unsystematic Approach to *Der Butt*', in August Obermayer (ed.), *Festschrift for E. W. Herd* (Dunedin), 55–77.

Friedrichsmeyer, Erhard, 1983. 'The Swan Song of a Male Chauvinist', in Mews 1983[2], 151–61.

Hayman, Ronald, 1985. *Günter Grass* (London).

Hunt, Irmgard Elsner, 1983. *Mütter und Muttermythos in Günter Grass' Roman 'Der Butt'* (Europäische Hochschulschriften, 1st ser., 647; Berne).

Jurgensen, Manfred, 1980. *Erzählformen des fiktionalen Ich: Beiträge zum deutschen Gegenwartsroman* (Berne and Munich).

Karasek, Hellmuth, 1977. 'Nora—ein Suppenheim', *Der Spiegel*, 8 Aug. 1977, 103–4.

Koopmann, Helmut, 1983. 'Between Stone Age and Present, or the Simultaneity of the Nonsimultaneous: The Time Structure', in Mews 1983[2], 75–89.

Mason, Ann L., 1976. 'The Artist and Politics in Günter Grass' *Aus dem Tagebuch einer Schnecke*', *Germanic Review*, 51, 105–20.

Mayer, Sigrid, 1982. '*Der Butt*: Lyrische und graphische Quellen', in Pickar 1982, 16–23.

—— 1983. 'The Critical Reception of *The Flounder* in the United States: Epic and Graphic Aspects', in Mews 1983[2], 179–95.

Mews, Siegfried, 1983[1]. 'The "Professorial" Flounder: Reflections on Grass's Use of Literary History', in Mews 1983[2], 163–78.

——— (ed.), 1983[2]. *"The Fisherman and His Wife": Günter Grass's 'The Flounder' in Critical Perspective* (New York).

Müller, Ulrich, 1985. 'Frauen aus dem Mittelalter, Frauen im mittleren Alter: Günter Grass: *Der Butt*', in Wolff 1985, 111–35.

Neuhaus, Volker, 1979. *Günter Grass* (Sammlung Metzler; Stuttgart).

Noerr, Gunzelin Schmidt, 1978. 'Über den *Butt*', *Text + Kritik*, 1/1a, *Günter Grass*, 5th edn., 90–3.

O'Neill, Patrick, 1982. 'The Scheherazade Syndrome: Günter Grass's Meganovel *Der Butt*', in Pickar 1982, 1–15.

Pakendorf, Günter, 1980. 'Günter Grass: *Der Butt* oder das Märchen von der Emanzipation', *Acta Germanica*, 13, 175–87.

Perels, Christoph, 1978. 'Über den *Butt*', *Text + Kritik*, 1/1a, *Günter Grass*, 5th edn., 88–90.

Pickar, Gertrud Bauer (ed.), 1982. *Adventures of a Flounder: Critical Essays on Günter Grass' Der Butt* (Houston German Studies, 3; Munich).

——— 1983. 'The Prismatic Narrator: Postulate and Practice', in Mews 1983[2], 55–74.

Raddatz, Fritz J., 1977[2]. '"Wirklicher bin ich in meinen Geschichten": *Der Butt* des Günter Grass, eine erste Annäherung', *Merkur*, 31, 892–901.

——— 1985. 'In Zukunft nur Ratten noch', *Die Zeit*, 6 Dec. 1985, 17.

Reddick, John, 1983. 'Günter Grass's *Der Butt* and the "Vatertag" Chapter', *Oxford German Studies*, 14, 143–58.

Rollfinke, Dieter and Jacqueline, 1986. 'The Excremental Wheel of Fortune', in D. and J. Rollfinke, *The Call of Human Nature: The Role of Scatology in Modern German Literature* (Amherst), 160–90.

Russell, Peter, 1980, 'Floundering in Feminism: The Meaning of Günter Grass's *Der Butt*', *German Life and Letters*, 33, 245–56.

Stern, Guy, 1982. '*Der Butt* as an Experiment in the Structure of the Novel', in Pickar 1982, 51–5.

Thomas, Noel L., 1980. 'Günter Grass's *Der Butt*: History and Significance of the Eighth Chapter ("Vatertag")', *German Life and Letters*, 33, 75–86.

Tudor, J. M., 1988. 'Soups and Snails and Political Tales . . . : Günter Grass and the Revisionist Debate in "Was Erfurt außerdem bedeutet" and *Der Butt*', *Oxford German Studies*, 17, 132–50.

Vormweg, Heinrich, 1978. 'Eine phantastische Totale: Nachtrag zur "Butt"-Kritik', *Text + Kritik*, 1/1a, *Günter Grass*, 5th edn., 94–100.

Williams, Gerhild S., 1980. '"Es war einmal, ist und wird wieder sein": Geschichte und Geschichten in Günter Grass's *Der Butt*', in P. M. Lützeler and Egon Schwarz (eds.), *Deutsche Literatur in der Bundesrepublik seit 1965* (Königstein im Taunus), 182–94.

Willson, A. Leslie, 1982. 'The Numbers Game', in Pickar 1982, 56–62.

Wolff, Rudolf (ed.), 1985. *Günter Grass: Werk und Wirkung* (Sammlung Profile, 21; Bonn).

Index

DER BUTT

GENERAL